HELLEBORES

HELLEBORES

A COMPREHENSIVE GUIDE

C. Colston Burrell

C. COLSTON BURRELL
and
JUDITH KNOTT TYLER

Photography by
C. Colston Burrell and
Richard Tyler

Foreword by Daniel J. Hinkley

Timber Press

Frontispiece: An exceptional dark purple *Helleborus torquatus* grows in a rocky pasture in western Bosnia. (Judith Knott Tyler)

Photography by C. Colston Burrell and Richard Tyler unless otherwise indicated.

Published in 2006 by

Timber Press, Inc.
The Haseltine Building
133 S.W. Second Avenue, Suite 450
Portland, Oregon 97204-3527, U.S.A.
www.timberpress.com

For contact information regarding editorial, marketing, sales, and distribution in the United Kingdom, see www.timberpress.co.uk.

Reprinted 2007

Printed through Colorcraft Ltd., Hong Kong

Library of Congress Cataloging-in-Publication Data

Burrell, C. Colston.
Hellebores : a comprehensive guide / C. Colston Burrell and Judith Knott Tyler ; photography by C. Colston Burrell and Richard Tyler.
p. cm.
Includes bibliographical references and index.
ISBN-13: 978-0-88192-765-8
1. Hellebores. I. Tyler, Judith Knott. II. Title.
SB413.H443B87 2006
583'.34--dc22
2005022499

A catalog record for this book is also available from the British Library.

For Dick Tyler and Bruce Ellsworth

CONTENTS

FOREWORD

My first winter in Puget Sound was in 1983. In the midst of Seattle's Washington Park Arboretum, on a frigid February morning, I met my first hellebore. On a feral slope adjacent to an unkempt garden devoted to winter interest was a self-managed surprise of *Helleborus ×hybridus*, known then as *H. orientalis*. Somewhat deflated and whiskered with hoarfrost on this crisp morning, their colors and forms captivated me, but mostly I was roused by their audacious resolve to blossom at such an unreasonable time of the year.

Those plants I encountered on that day at the arboretum, even in retrospect more than two decades later, were some reasonably good plants—nicely shaped cups of almost yellows, almost reds, and almost whites. From an eye undefiled by knowledge of potential, these plants were all and more than I as a gardener would ever need.

During the past two decades, if only as a minor cheerleader from the sidelines, I have had the privilege of witnessing the embrace and evolution of a genus of plants for our collective enjoyment. Together with their European counterparts, the North American horticultural community has united to mold the direction of breeding—durability, shape of blossom, and intensity of hue—in the plants that we grow in the places we grow them.

It is precisely this awakening of a genus of plants—from their undiluted state in the wild to those in our gardens—that this book chronicles so thoroughly. In the text, the authors underscore the importance of understanding the hellebore's natural genesis while acknowledging the architects and engineers who have contributed to its ascension. Admirably, rising above the scholarly facts and figures is a discernible reverence for a singular genus of plants.

I continue to be beholden to those in our field who do permit themselves—if permission is even remotely an option—the luxury of obsession with one plant genus. They are the investigators and historians who allow the generalists—some would say unpolished dilettantes, like myself—to grasp so little about so many things. Occasionally there is published a work that seduces by content and by style to a degree that makes me second guess this sophomoric approach to the plant kingdom. Such it is with this book on a most remarkable genus of plants.

I am acquainted with the authors of this book and know that they are well-rounded horticulturists, far from the overtly obsessed galanthophile, hemerocallophile—you get the idea. Their gardens are chock-full of rarities—shrubs, vines, trees, perennials, grasses—all of which are appreciated for their abilities to create interest throughout the year and habitat for wildlings. During the season of hellebores, however, their passion for this genus swells to the enviable proportions that it deserves.

As I savor the first hellebore flowers of the year, I, too, find myself tempted to succumb completely to its charms, to bury myself in its taxonomy and commit myself to extracting the premium of its potential. When the days lengthen and my capriciousness is duly noted, I remember that the hellebores are only part of a greater whole that I will continue to appreciate. I lack the discipline to be consumed. But that does not prevent me, when I lift that first flower of such flawless element and marvel at its hues and speckles, character, and fortitude, to again return to the learned wealth from authors and gardeners who have provided me with such depth of understanding of the plants that we grow.

DANIEL J. HINKLEY
Windcliff
Indianaola, Washington

ACKNOWLEDGMENTS

WHY ANOTHER BOOK on a subject amply covered in extant literature? Well, first of all, no American book covers all the species and hybrids. More importantly, the latest advances in breeding are largely undocumented in the popular press. The seed strains currently available far surpass most named plants, so the simple goal of promoting seed strains seems reason enough for a new volume. Beyond that, many species grown from wild-collected seed have become available, and new hybrids have been developed that beg to be promoted.

This book is by no means meant to be a taxonomic revision of the genus. That task is left to minds more scientific and less schizoid than ours. We do, however, want to present the most up-to-date picture of the species possible. We stand on the shoulders of many giants to bring you this volume.

Gardeners and plant enthusiasts are generous people, and hellebore fanatics are no exception. Everywhere we went in Britain, Europe, and across America, people shared freely of their time, knowledge, and plants as we researched this book. A great many of them are featured in these pages. They are included in the chapters that deal with their particular interests, talents, or contributions. We would like to thank Veronica Adams Cross; Graham Birkin; Ian Collier; David Culp; Kelly Dodson; John Dudley of Elizabeth Town Hellebores; John Elsley of Song Sparrow Nursery; Ullrich Fischer; Jerry Flintoff; Russell Graham; Barry Glick of Sunshine Farm and Nursery; Nancy Goodwin of Montrose Gardens; Eric Hammond; Joseph Heuger and Peter Oenings of Heuger Nursery; Dan Hinkley of Heronswood Nursery; Sam and Carleen Jones of Piccadilly Farm; Hans Kramer of de Hessenhof; Peter Leigh of Post Office Farm Nursery; John Massey, Jill Pearce, and Kevin Belcher of Ashwood Nurseries; Brian Mathew; Tim and Susan Murphy; Ernie and Marietta O'Byrne of Northwest Garden Nursery; Elfi Rahr; Henry Ross of Gardenview Horticultural Park; Gisela Schmiemann; Elizabeth Strangman; Georg Uebelhart of Jelitto Seed Company; Bobby J. Ward and Roy Dicks; Robin and Sue White of Blackthorn Nursery; Emily Herring Wilson; Lindy Wilson; and Glenn Withey and Charles Price. Any omissions are accidental.

Special thanks are surely due to Will McLewin and Matthias Thomsen for reviewing the species descriptions. We have relied heavily on the writings of others for information on historical as well as medicinal uses and taxonomic information. These authors and their great works are listed in the bibliography at the end of the book. Dick Tyler reviewed the manuscript, offered encouragement, made helpful and smart-ass comments, and provided many of the gorgeous pictures that grace these pages. He also drove thousands of miles on our trips through Europe. Thanks, Dick! Bruce Ellsworth cooked dinner on nights when Cole was busy writing, and he held down the fort, watered plants, and pampered the birds while Cole was on the road gathering information and photos.

Denise Adams, the high priestess of heirloom plants, provided us with innumerable citations and opened her extensive library of historic nursery catalogs and books to us. Our "The American Story" section in Chapter 2 owes a great debt to her extensive research, invaluable assistance, and review. Others who helped in our research efforts include Peter Brandham of Kew Garden; Andrew Bunting of the Scott Arboreum; Robert Dirig of Bailey Hortorium Herbarium; Mike Garofalo; Nina Lambert of Ithaca, New York; Linda Eirhart of Winterthur, Delaware; Hans Hansen of Shady Oaks Nursery; Dan Heims of Terra Nova Nursery; Patricia Scolnick of Breeze Hill Laboratory; and Asa Swain, who reviewed all 100 years of *Horticulture* magazine.

Thanks to Marietta and Ernie O'Byrne, Lucy Hardiman, Helen Kraus, Doug Ruhren, and Jim Sherwood for reviewing the manuscript and suggesting much-needed improvements. Melissa Morrison and Nancy Goldman helped organize the appendices. Dr. Eastwell, Dr. du Toit, and Dr. Pike graciously provided a summary of their research into black death of hellebores, and Dr. Kraus and Dr. Warren provided their nutrient study. Dr. Fanelli and Dr. Dole allowed us to reprint their cut flower study.

We are grateful to our editor, Lisa Theobald, for her gentle editing, and Tom Fischer, Eve Goodman, Max Gibson, and the rest of the staff at Timber Press for all they did to make this volume a reality.

Dan Hinkley generously contributed the poetic foreword to this book, and we are humbly grateful.

Portions of this manuscript appeared in *American Gardener* and Brooklyn Botanic Garden All-Region Guides. Thanks to the American Horticultural Society and the Brooklyn Botanic Garden, respectively, for allowing us to adapt this material.

C. COLSTON BURRELL and
JUDITH KNOTT TYLER

PREFACE

THE FIRST HELLEBORE I encountered was the pristine white Christmas rose (*Helleborus niger*). The seductive plants grew in the garden of Mary T. Corley, my mentor and first employer when I was an aspiring gardener. Mary was an avid horticulturist. She had been growing plants, including hellebores, most of her 60 years when I first went to work for her at 8 years of age. She employed me to pull weeds for a penny a minute. I was the only kid in the neighborhood who actually got the roots out! My 60 cents per hour earnings weren't half as valuable as the lessons I learned working side by side with Mary. She recognized my potential and quickly set me to more challenging and rewarding gardening tasks. In addition, she started teaching me, in a gentle but persuasive way, everything she knew about plants and gardening. She also gave me a generous raise! I gardened with Mary for nearly 20 years, and I learned so many great plants from her. She grew things in the 1960s that today's gardeners think are new to horticulture.

The Christmas rose was always at the top of my list of favorites. Mary ignored the conventional wisdom that said Christmas roses did not grow well in the southern United States. As a result, her plants thrived and produced copious seedlings, some of which I took home to my own garden. I also carried home some of the free-seeding Lenten roses (*H.* ×*hybridus*) and stinking hellebores (*H. foetidus*) that graced her garden. Still, it was the Christmas rose that I liked best. The flowers were huge, and her plants were likely descended from 'Potter's Wheel', a large-flowered selection popular in England at that time.

Eventually, I went on to college, and not too many years later Mary went into a nursing home. Her son let the garden go to weeds, and ultimately all the hellebores disappeared from both our gardens. Though the original plants died away, my passion for hellebores did not.

I have grown many hellebores over the years since I first discovered this fantastic genus. I know without doubt that I will never get bored with them, though I've bored more than a few of my friends. Christopher Lloyd calls people like me "helle-BORES." His disdain for collectors of all ilks is legendary. I continue to collect and now grow most of the recognized species, as well as hundreds of hybrids and seed strains. My collection includes the best plants the world has to offer. There are new colors, shapes, and flower types being introduced all the time. New species are being named, and the taxonomic revision of the genus promises many surprises in the years to come. In addition, more wild forms are making their way into seed lists and nurseries, so there is always something new to try.

I depend on other great gardeners to produce most of the plants I grow. I have met many excellent breeders and nursery people who contributed knowledge, encouragement, and plants to my endeavors. Foremost among them is my co-author, Judith Knott Tyler, who with her husband, Dick, owns Pine Knot Farms. Hellebores are their specialty, and many of my best plants come from them. When Judith suggested the need for an American book about hellebores, I quickly jumped at the chance. I'm not sure she actually wanted me to co-write the book, but I made a leap of faith and offered. Being a well-bred Southern lady, she politely accepted, and here at last are the fruits of our labor.

Are hellebore people more sophisticated than average gardeners? I don't think so. Young or old, neophyte or veteran, most who see hellebores are sure to fall under their spell. We are certain that you will, too.

C. COLSTON BURRELL

*   *   *

FEBRUARY IS A DULL, GRAY MONTH when even winter grows tired of itself. Any plant that is brave enough to bloom during this fortuitously short month is greeted with pure joy. In our Southside Virginia garden, we are able to enjoy the blooms of most of the *Helleborus* species throughout this dreary month. They show us the promise of spring when viewed from our kitchen window and give us a reason to go outside into the garden on those days when winter's chill is held at bay by the sun's rays.

We purchased our very first hellebores in 1983 from Sam and Carleen Jones, who own and operate Piccadilly Farm, a nursery near Bishop, Georgia, that specializes in hellebores, hosta, and unusual shade plants. These two generous friends are in all likelihood responsible for most of the hellebores sold in the United States since the mid 1980s. The Joneses had the first contemporary nursery in the States to offer hellebores in large numbers, and countless plants have been shipped from Piccadilly over the years. Their lovely woodland garden features a hillside full of *H.* ×*hybridus*, which is an unforgettable sight when in bloom.

I began to breed *H.* ×*hybridus* because February was a slow month in the nursery business and because I wanted a plant with pure white flowers. When I first began to grow hellebores, the only flower colors we had in our garden and nursery were the colors found in wild forms of *H. orientalis*. Dusty rose-pink flowered plants descended from *H. orientalis* subsp. *abchasicus* and greenish-white flowers with spots from *H. orientalis* subsp. *guttatus* dominated the color palette. In the subspecies *guttatus*, the interior of the flower is freckled with spots the color of ripe raspberries—not an unattractive feature, but not the pure, gleaming white I dreamed of when I created plant combinations in my mind. My pure white hellebores were to be underplanted with white-flowered *Vinca minor* 'Miss Jekyll' along with the early white-flowering *Crocus chrysanthus* 'Ard Schenk'. I longed to create the illusion of a snow scene in our Virginia garden, which sees a significant snowfall only once every three or four years. With this pristine image firmly implanted in my mind, I gathered the plants that were closest to white and began what has turned into an obsession that occupies a large part of my life.

In the early years of my hellebore addiction, any new stock we managed to acquire came in the form of seedlings from growers in the U.K. and Europe. In 1992 we made our first trip to the U.K. and brought home a few *H. ×hybridus* plants and a plant of *H. ×sternii* 'Blackthorn Strain' from Washfield Nursery. I love campanulas, and we first went to find them at Washfield on the recommendation of David Culp, who at that time was a buyer for a garden center outside Philadelphia. David was already severely addicted to hellebores, and while I wouldn't go as far as to call him a pusher, he was definitely responsible for furthering our growing dependency. The garden David shares with Mike Alderfer in Pennsylvania is a premier example of a collector's garden, not only full of unusual and interesting plants, but also beautifully maintained and fascinating year-round. Mike and Dave generously shared seedlings from some of their English hellebores with us and traveled with us on our third trip to the U.K. We both brought home suitcases full of plants, one of which left a trail of water along the concourse at an international airport.

With the winter trips to the U.K., what had formerly been a minor dependency grew that third winter into a full-blown habit. Oh, the plants we found available there! The colors, form, and general bearing of these lovely English hybrids were of a class so far above what I had at home. I had not dreamed that such flowers were even possible, much less already available in the marketplace. When compared to our new English hybrids, the plants I was growing were so inferior we were forced to discard much of our stock and begin again. We kept only a few plants—a creamy white, some apple-blossom pinks, and a large red. Each visit stretched our credit card as far as the plastic allowed. It also swelled our garden beds as we brought back stock to brighten up our winter days.

At first, the imported plants grew slowly, and many died. Hellebores do not like to be bare-rooted and washed free of soil, as is required to pass U.S. Customs. There were years when we lost seedlings to damping-off, years when we lost transplants to mice, and years when we lost very expensive double-flowering plants because moles tunneled under their roots. We experienced the standard litany of trials and tribulations familiar to all gardeners. Eventually we began to see an improvement in our production methods and we most definitely saw improvements in the quality of our own crosses.

What of the white hellebore I yearned for, the one for which the quest began? The progeny of that first venture into the world of plant breeding is with us today in the bloodlines of the seedling strain that we call "Our Best Whites." Each year as the winter solstice approaches, we begin to see the first buds and blooms of 'O.B.W.' poking out of the foliage. The plants have large, creamy white flowers with ruffled edges and a boss of bright gold stamens. Although I have now grown many other white-flowering hellebores, plants with better form, plants with sepals displayed in the perfectly rounded shape that our customers have come to prefer, there will always be a spot in my garden for my first adventure into plant breeding: my first pure white-flowering hellebore.

JUDITH KNOTT TYLER

1

HELLEBORE MORPHOLOGY

Christmas rose and Lenten rose . . . are nature's gift to gardeners in the dismal months after Christmas, when the weather is cold and discouraging and spring seems a long way ahead. At a time when few other flowers brave the elements . . . only the snowdrops in their prim whiteness and fascinating variety of forms can compete with hellebores.

Elizabeth Strangman in *The Gardener's Guide to Growing Hellebores*
(Rice and Strangman 1993)

Garden hybrids have the form and flower carriage typical of acaulescent (stemless) hellebores.

WHO COULD FAIL TO BE SMITTEN WITH HELLEBORES? Anyone with an appreciation of beauty is quickly seduced. Hellebores seem to cast a spell from which you never awaken. Is it the flowers? They lack cloying fragrance to draw you in. Many are small and subtly colored. Even the most colorful fall short of riveting or festive. What can it be? Their precocious nature is part of their allure, but what makes them so much more than alluring? For many, hellebores are an obsession. What other flower, save for cousin *Adonis*, punches through the ground with flowers open while frost and snow surround them? Like most early bloomers, *Adonis* is fleeting. Not hellebores; they bloom for two months or more—longer where spring arrives slowly and nights stay cool. Their rich green foliage provides summer and winter structure. For us, they are the whole package—fantastic foliage, precocious bloom, and beautiful flowers. In short, elegant simplicity.

Most hellebores are native to mountainous regions of Europe, in open oak and beech woodlands, scrub, grassy meadows, and on rocky slopes. These areas are characterized by limestone bedrock and calcareous, humus-rich soils. Western Europe, including the British Isles, is home to three species. The odd plant out is *Helleborus thibetanus*, which is native to China, well outside of the epicenter of hellebore distribution. The rest of the species fall in between, with the bulk of them centered in the Balkan region of the former Yugoslavia. In all aspects, the plants are both charming and beautiful. In their native lands, few species but the Christmas rose (*H. niger*) are grown in gardens. This wildling is often found in churchyards due its association with the birth of Christ. Today, we value the wild species for their delicate beauty in woodland and informal settings. (Refer to Chapter 3 for more information on species and their distributions.) The hybrids are by far the most popular garden hellebores worldwide, cherished for their early bloom, showy flowers, and decorative evergreen foliage.

FLOWERS

Hellebore flowers lack conspicuous petals. Five petal-like sepals create the show, a characteristic shared by most members of the buttercup family (Ranunculaceae). Relatives such as buttercups (*Ranunculus*), windflowers (*Anemone*), and winter aconite (*Eranthis*) share the open, cup-shaped flower. Inside the five showy sepals hides a ring of up to 32 subtle petals, modified into tubular or funnel-form nectaries. The center of the flower sports two to ten pistils surrounded by multiple rings of up to 125 stamens. The ovaries, or carpels, of the flower are an essential characteristic for distinguishing certain species. Some carpels are fused at the base, while others are free. After pollination, the sepals of most species fade to rose or green and often persist in an attractive state until the seed is ripe.

Occasionally, double flowers occur in the wild as a result of spontaneous mutation. Doubling is known to occur in *H. dumetorum*, *H. niger*, *H. orientalis*, and *H. torquatus*. Doubling occurs when the nectaries, which are actually modified petals, become

The buttercup family (Ranunculaceae) contains many popular garden plants, including *Anemone*, *Hepatica*, *Actaea*, *Aquilegia*, and *Clematis*.

The hellebore flower consists of five petal-like sepals surrounding a ring of petals reduced to nectaries, a boss of stamens, and a central cluster of pistils.

petaloid, or petal-like. In the place of the tubular nectaries, flattened petals are produced inside the ring of five sepals. The effect can be quite attractive.

Sexually speaking, hellebore flowers are *protogynus*, which means the stigmas are receptive before the stamens in the same flower shed their pollen. This adaptation generally keeps a flower from fertilizing itself and encourages cross-fertilization. Honey bees (*Apis mellifera*), bumble bees (*Bombus* spp.), and other small bees are the primary pollinators of hellebores. They visit the flowers quite freely and move pollen throughout the garden. The flowers can be self-fertile, however, and the pollen from a single flower can fertilize the same flower if the stigma is still receptive. More commonly in nature, pollen from one flower fertilizes another flower on the same plant. This is, in fact, a common occurrence in our gardens, though cross-fertilization from one plant to the next also occurs freely.

Flowers are borne clustered at the tips of persistent, leafy aerial stems or on ephemeral flowering scapes with leaflike bracts. The flowers are carried singly (occasionally doubled), as is common in *H. niger*, or in clusters of three or more. The flowers emerge in winter or early spring, before the new leaves in most species. True leaves are borne on long petioles. After the seeds ripen, the flowering stems do not bloom again.

FRUITS AND SEEDS

The fruit of a hellebore consists of a cluster of dry follicles surrounded by persistent sepals. Follicles split along one inward-facing seam to release the dark brown or black seeds, which are ovoid and sometimes flattened on two sides so they stack neatly in their vessels. The seeds of some species possess fleshy arils called *elaiosomes*, which encourage ants to distribute them. This dispersal mechanism is called *myrmecochory*. Sex pheromone mimics are exuded by the eliasomes to lure ants to the ripe seeds. The plants win because the seeds are taken away from the parent, and with less competition they have a better chance of survival. The ant, for its part, gets some fats and starch from the elaiosome—not a bad deal for all involved.

Hellebore seeds experience a combination of *endogenous dormancies*. This means that when the seed is released from the follicles, the embryo must undergo morphological and physiological changes before it can germinate. The embryo within the seed is immature or not fully developed at the time of dispersal in early summer. The underdeveloped embryo matures as the seed ripens. A chemical inhibitor further suppresses germination. This kind of dormancy is called *physiological inhibition*. Once the embryo is fully developed and the hormones that inhibit germination are turned off by chilling, a process called *cold stratification*, the seed is ready to germinate. Most fresh hellebore seed germinates after a warm ripening period followed by modest chilling for 60 to 120 days.

First to emerge as the seed germinates is the radicle (seed root), which penetrates surprisingly deep in a short time. Two untoothed cotyledons (seed leaves) emerge next, and soon after them the first true leaf, which is divided in most species. Of

Hellebore follicles begin to swell soon after pollination, even though the sepals remain colorful. By the time seed is ready to disperse, the sepals have faded to green and the follicles are inflated.

Hellebore seeds are usually oval and dark brown when the follicles split to release them; mature seeds are shiny black.

course, there are exceptions. *Helleborus vesicarius* exhibits a more complex dormancy and forms only cotyledons the first season. After a second chilling, the shoot and first true leaves emerge. *Helleborus thibetanus* is also a maverick. The cotyledons never emerge from the seed. Instead, a single three-parted leaf emerges straight from the germinating seed. Most hellebores flower within two to four years of germination. (See Chapter 7 for more details.)

STEMS AND LEAVES

The prevailing convention is to divide hellebores into two groups based on whether or not the plants produce persistent aboveground stems. The terms used for describing the two different growth forms are *acaulescent*, or stemless, and *caulescent*, or stemmed. The majority of species are considered acaulescent, the stem being entirely underground and represented by a rhizome. Caulescent species bear persistent aboveground stems with distinct leaves borne up the stem. The flowers of caulescent species are borne at the apex of year-old stems. After flowering, the old stems die, and new stems emerge from the crown that bear flowers the following year. The succulent nature of the stems makes them susceptible to winter damage. As a result, they are far less hardy than their acaulescent relatives.

In reviewing the taxonomy and anatomy of the genus *Helleborus*, Will McLewin (of Phedar Research and Experimental Nursery, Stockport, U.K.) and Brian Mathew (who recently retired from Kew Gardens, Richmond, U.K.) propose additional classes of plants that are intermediate between the two conventional types. The main characteristic used to separate caulescent from acaulescent is the persistent, aerial stem. Though not aerial-stemmed, acaulescent species do indeed have short, usually subterranean stems with very short internodes. Though McLewin and Mathew currently maintain the status quo, *H. niger*, *H. vesicarius*, and *H. thibetanus* do not fit neatly into the traditional classification. These hellebores bear short stems that differ structurally from either established

A typical caulescent species such as *H. foetidus* has a persistent, leafy stem and a weakly developed root system.

Acaulescent hellebores like this garden hybrid have thick rootstocks with fleshy roots, ephemeral bloom scapes, and pedately divided basal leaves.

group as well as from each other. In time, the terms used to describe hellebore stems will undoubtedly change.

Hellebore foliage is beautiful and perplexing. It helps if you have a penchant for geometry and the ability to count above 20. Most hellebore leaves are variations on a theme. The thick petiole joins together three leaflets at the same point. The leaflets are generally oval to lance shaped and are often, though not always, toothed. Those with three undivided leaflets are deemed *ternately* divided. When the two outer leaflets are divided, the term applied is *palmate*. When the outer divisions are finely divided and seem to circle the petiole, the leaves are called *pedate*. The outer leaflets of most species are usually divided or lobed, and some species display leaves cut into as many as 100 pencil-thin segments.

Most species are deciduous in the wild, though in gardens the abundance of moisture and nutrition can keep them green and growing. Some, like *H. thibetanus*, are summer dormant, while others fall quiescent in autumn and winter. *Helleborus orientalis* and hybrids, as well as *H. niger*, are fully evergreen, as are all the caulescent species. *Helleborus vesicarius* is unique in displaying winter foliage after complete summer dormancy.

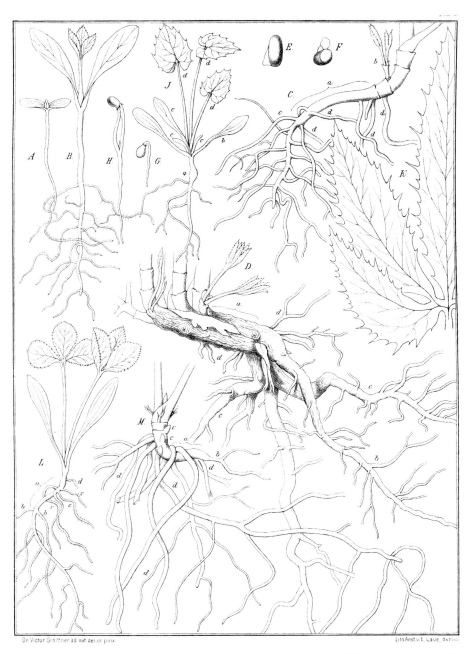

Victor Schiffner of Prague University wrote the first monograph of the genus *Helleborus* in 1890 (*Monographia Hellebororum*). His illustrations clearly show the distinctions between stems, rhizomes, and the fibrous roots.

Most hellebore leaves are pedately divided, with three main divisions and up to 100 different dissections. Variation is the rule, as evidenced by this group of *H. ×hybridus* leaves.

ROOTSTOCKS

Hellebores grow from thickened, slow-creeping rhizomes with thick, fleshy, sparsely branching roots. These thick rootstocks account for the longevity of acaulescent hellebores. The rhizomes grow horizontally and produce new buds at the bases of the current year's stems. Leaves and flowering scapes arise directly from the rhizome in most species. The ephemeral bloom stalks of stemless species leave behind rounded, flat scars.

Older rhizomes develop a spiraling or corrugation (ridging), with each band representing a node where a leaf was attached. In time, the multistemmed crowns become congested and woody, with dozens of eyes. Old roots seem to serve mostly for anchoring the plant, while new roots, which are produced in autumn and spring as the rhizome elongates, provide maximum water and nutrient uptake. Root growth appears to be temperature dependent, with cool soil promoting rapid growth and warm soil slowing or stopping root growth altogether. Older roots branch when damaged, but the bulk of activity is associated with fresh growth.

2
HELLEBORES
THROUGHOUT HISTORY

One of the delightful qualities of winter flowers is that they last so long. Hellebores flattened by the cold or rain come up again after the storm and appear fresh and delicate in the shelter of the dark, deeply cut leaves.

Elizabeth Lawrence in *A Southern Garden* (1942)

Alchemy is often regarded as the precursor of the modern science of chemistry prior to the formulation of the scientific method. One goal of the alchemist was to find a remedy that would cure all diseases and prolong life indefinitely. (From *Early American Gardens: For Meate or Medicine*, by Ann Leighton, 1986; originally published in George Baker's *Jewel of Health*, 1576)

THROUGHOUT HISTORY, hellebores and humans have been intertwined. The Christmas rose (*Helleborus niger*) has been celebrated in the stories and songs of advent since at least the 1500s. The legend of the Christmas rose was told many times. One version describes how a shepherd on his way to Bethlehem had no gift to take to the Christ child. He was penniless and could not even find flowers to gather as none bloomed in winter. Disappointed, he cried many bitter tears. His tears fell on the ground and in their place sprouted flowers as beautiful as roses. Feeling happier, the shepherd presented the Christmas roses to the baby Jesus.

Another version of the legend speaks of a young girl named Madelon, who wanted to worship the Christ child. Seeing the gold, frankincense, and myrrh brought by others who were drawn to the humble birthplace, she despaired that she had no gift to bring, for Madelon was poor. In vain, she searched for a flower to bring, but the winter had been cold and harsh, so there were no flowers. Saddened, she began to weep. A passing angel stopped to comfort her and "smote the ground" that was wet from her tears. There, a beautiful bush bloomed with white roses. "Nor myrrh, nor frankincense, nor gold," said the angel, "is offering more meet for the Christ Child than these pure Christmas Roses." And thus, young Madelon went her way and worshiped the Prince of Peace, bearing the gift of her heart and tears.

Finally, the story of the Oracle-flower goes like this. In the Middle Ages, the hellebore was also known as the Oracle-flower. Country people used to put 12 Christmas rose buds in water on Christmas night. Each bud symbolized a month, and the weather for the following year could be forecast according to the state of the buds. A closed bud meant bad weather, an open one good.

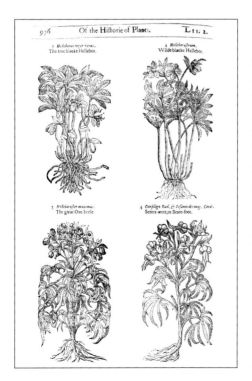

As fanciful as these stories are, the most common recorded uses for hellebores in early history were not concerned with religion, ritual, or aesthetics. In Europe and America, long before they were valued for their ornamental qualities, hellebores were in demand for their medicinal prowess (see Appendix A). The botanical name *Helleborus* may derive from the Greek roots *helein*, which means to kill, and *bora*, food. The literal translation is "food that kills."

The ancients knew the black hellebore, believed variously to be *H. niger*, *H. foetidus*, *H. cyclophyllus*, or perhaps *H. viridis* (now *H. occidentalis*).

Hellebores are featured in many herbals, including this reproduction from John Gerard's *The Herball* of 1633. Pictured from top left to bottom left are *H. niger*, *H. occidentalis*, and two forms of *H. foetidus*.

Under the feudal system, plants were grown as crops, not only for food, but also for medicines, materials for clothing, and for various other uses, with the majority of the rural population foraging to collect their potherbs and medicaments. Hellebores, as with other plants used for medicinal purposes, were wild crafted or kept in apothecary gardens. In *The Herball* (1633), John Gerard noted, "We have them all in our London gardens." Pleasure gardens were the provinces of the aristocracy—they were at least confined to the wealthiest homes, and even these concentrated on useful plants. Growing a plant for purely ornamental purposes might have been incomprehensible to the commoner. But in time, hellebores and other plants grew in aesthetic importance as people began to heal their souls as well as their bodies.

THE EUROPEAN STORY

By the mid-1600s, leisure time, although still primarily the province of the wealthier classes, was more common and public gardens and arboreta were established, where people could see unusual plants. Joseph de Tournefort was professor of botany at the *Jardin de Plantes* in Paris. He collected plants in Greece, Turkey, and surrounding areas from 1700 to 1702. His journal entries and letters were published after his death in a book entitled *Relation d'un voyage du Levant* in 1717. Specimens he collected near Uludag (ancient Mount Olympus) in present-day Turkey are likely the plant we know as *H. orientalis*.

The mid- to late 1700s is sometimes called "The Golden Age of Botany." During this time, hellebores were studied and written about by plantsmen from Carl Linnaeus to William Curtis. In 1753, Linnaeus described three hellebore species: *H. foetidus*, *H. niger*, and *H. viridis* (now likely *H. occidentalis*). From 1787 to 1800, Curtis published *The Botanical Magazine*, self-described as

> The Botanical Magazine; or Flower-Garden Displayed: in which the most Ornamental Foreign Plants, cultivated in Open Ground, the Green-House and the Stove, are accurately represented in their natural Colours. To which are added Their Names, Class, Order, Generic and Specific Characters, according to the celebrated Linnaeus; their Place of Growth and Times of Flowering: together with the most approved methods of culture. A work intended for the use of such Ladies, Gentlemen and Gardeners as wish to become scientifically acquainted with the Plants they cultivate.

The magazine's first issue, published in London, described and depicted *H. niger* and included perhaps the first published information on *H. lividus*. Under the listing for *H. lividus* is written, "It is not a little extraordinary that this plant which has for many years been cultivated in this country, should have escaped the notice of Linnaeus," and "it flowers as early as February; on which account, as well as that of its singularity, it is a very desirable plant in collections."

Hellebores in Germany

In the 1850s in Berlin, Alex Braun began collecting hellebores to study at the garden of the University of Berlin-Schöneberg. In his *Index Seminum*, he described two forms of the plant we know as *H. orientalis*, a purple-flowering plant he called *H. abchasicus*, and a white-flowering plant with spots that was named *H. guttatus*. It is interesting that some observers record the color of the flowers of *H. abchasicus* as purple and others pink, and some report spots while others do not, possibly an example of the variability typical of hellebores as well as the differing writing styles and the simple fact that color is viewed differently by individual people. This plant had been grown for several years as *H. abchasiae*, named for the region Abkhazia (a republic of Georgia on the Black Sea); its name was later changed to *H. abchasicus*.

A contemporary of Braun, Karl Koch, at one time the director of the Berlin Botanic Gardens, traced the early history of *H. abchasicus* and how it spread through the gardens of the day. The plant was purportedly sent to the Saint Petersburg Botanical Garden by the Imperial Gardener Rögner from Kutais, Georgia, a town in the Russian Caucasus, and distributed from there to other botanical gardens, first in Germany and appearing in France and Belgium by 1857. *Helleborus abchasicus* appears in the catalog of the English firm James Booth and Son in Hamburg around the same time.

From 1853 to 1880, German breeders created hybrids involving *H. kochii*, now known as *H. orientalis* subsp. *orientalis*, as well as *H. orientalis* subsp. *guttatus* and *H. orientalis* subsp. *abchasicus*. Max Leichtlin, a respected horticulturist from Baden-Baden, created many hybrids, especially dark-flowering forms, which were grown at the Berlin Botanic Gardens. Plants with names such as 'Abchasicus Albus', a white-tinged green; 'Frau Irene Heinemann', listed as purple with darker veins and spots; and 'Gretchen Heinemann', a rosy purple with spots, were available in Germany in the 1870s and 1880s from Carl Heinemann's nursery in Erfurt. The 1899 Otto Fröbel and Company catalog from Zurich, Switzerland, listed hellebores in many unusual colors. The plants were said to display "rounded overlapping petals" and were available in "dark violet, copper red, sulphur yellow, indigo blue black, dark brown red, pink, white and spotted forms."

Taxonomic work with hellebores was also being done at this time. In 1890, Victor Schiffner of Prague University published his monograph, *Monographia Hellebororum*, piquing interest throughout the horticultural community. Schiffner's work attempted to describe what he called the "Euhellebores," the green or green and purple hellebores that cross so easily with one another, both in nature and in a nursery. In 1908, Ernst Ulbrich became responsible for the botanical collections in Berlin. Ulbrich studied the taxonomic classification of the sections and wrote a monograph entitled *Die Arten der Gattung Helleborus* in 1938, which listed an index with descriptions of *Helleborus* species.

One particular early-flowering clone that made its appearance about this time and haunts hellebore annals to this day is a form now known as *H. orientalis* subsp. *abchasicus* 'Early Purple' or 'Early Purple' Group. Plants in this group came into commerce in the late 1800s, listed as 'Atro-roseus', 'Ruber', and 'Coccineus' as well

Schiffner's lithographs, rendered from pressed herbarium specimens, detail the morphology of eight species, including *H. vesicarius* with fanciful, inflated follicles. (From *Monographia Hellebororum*, 1890)

Schiffner's lithograph brings life to the delicate dove gray and celadon green *H. purpurascens*. (From *Monographia Hellebororum*, 1890)

as *H. abchasicus* and *H. colchicus*. For many years, plants listed as *H.* "atrorubens of gardens" and *H. abchasicus* were grown somewhat interchangeably; in one case, the Archer-Hind herbarium specimen was labeled "*H. atrorubens = A. abchasicus*." This plant was described as delightful and it circulated throughout the horticultural community. The interchangeable epithets were disseminated as well, causing much confusion. The plant grown as 'Early Purple' is nothing like the true species *H. atrorubens* but does resemble *H. orientalis* subsp. *abchasicus*. Given the similarity in color of the two different species, it is easy to understand how the confusion began.

HELLEBORES IN BRITAIN

Multicolored forms of *H. orientalis* were being introduced to English and Irish gardeners in the mid-1800s as well. Several people, including Sir Frederick Moore, who sent some of the first yellowish flowering plants to plantsman and author E. A. Bowles, grew hellebores at the National Botanic Gardens, Glasnevin, Ireland. Hellebores were also grown in the garden of the Reverend Canon H. N. Ellacombe, who followed his father H. T. Ellacombe as the vicar of Saint Mary's Church, Bitton, Gloucestershire.

The vicarage garden was called a "plantsman's delight." Canon Ellacombe was one of the first in Britain to receive the new hellebore hybrids produced in Germany, which he shared with others. In 1879, Thomas Moore wrote in the 5 April edition of the *Gardeners' Chronicle* about a box of flowers sent to the magazine by the younger Ellacombe, describing the range of colors and comparing them favorably with those of Barr and Son, the leading hellebore nursery of that time.

Thomas Archer-Hind of Coombe Fishacre in Devonshire was among those who grew selected color forms of hybrid hellebores, which he gathered from a number of sources. In *Hellebores* (1989), Brian Mathew reports that Archer-Hind's family called him "The Hellebore Man," indicating a more than passing interest in the genus. He is remembered for describing the new species *H. torquatus* in the 8 March 1884 edition of *The Garden*, the Royal Horticultural Society's (RHS) monthly magazine, and for his breeding work with the new hybrids. Archer-Hind also wrote in *The Garden* of a collection of hellebores that was "by far the most extensive in existence," owned by Peter Barr, one of the people with whom he exchanged plants. Plantsman E. B. Anderson acquired a group of hellebore plants from Archer-Hind, which, according to Mathew, included a range of colors from "pure white, through cream to pink and lilac and on to deep maroon and crimson. Some unspotted, some with large spots on a white or pink ground, others peppered with small dots. Most of them were cup shaped with overlapping tepals, others show the more pointed tepals of some of the species."

Barr, a partner in the nursery Barr and Sugden, later to become Barr and Sons of Covent Garden, was actively working with *H. ×hybridus* and *H. niger* at his nursery in Tooting, Surry. In the 1880s, the Barr catalogs listed as many as 50 selections, including nine different selections of *H. niger*. Hellebores with the appellations 'Abchasicus Ruber' (a deep purple), 'Afghan Prince' (a deep slaty purple), 'Arthur Collins' (profusely spotted reddish purple), on to 'Sulphureus' (yellow) and 'W. E. Gladstone' (a rosy pink with veins inside) are listed in the Barr catalogs between 1879 and 1893—a veritable smorgasbord of choices! The Barr nursery continued to breed and introduce hellebores well into the 20th century. In 1926 and 1927, two cultivars named 'Black Knight' and 'Prince Rupert' won a coveted Award of Merit from the RHS. *Helleborus niger* was also being grown; a nurseryman in Didsbury near Manchester, William Brockbank of Brockhurst, grew hundreds of plants and is said to have named at least one of their selections 'Brockhurst'.

Barr, Ellacombe, and Archer-Hind corresponded and exchanged seed and seedlings with Heinemann and Leichtlin in Germany and other discerning plantsmen of the day. By the advent of World War I (1914), hellebores had spread to become staples of winter gardens not only in England and Germany, but across Europe. Keen gardeners were experimenting with crosses, and in 1931, J. H. E. Stooke of Danesmere, Hereford, exhibited the first recorded intersectional cross of *H. niger* with *H. argutifolius*. The plant was later described under the name *H. ×nigercors* in the December 1934 (15th edition) of the *Gardeners' Chronicle*.

In much of England and Europe, two devastating wars and the periods of reconstruction that followed resulted in gardening for pleasure being replaced by gardening for sustenance. On some of the largest estates, the once-famous herbaceous borders were dug up and beds of turnips and potatoes were planted in their stead. By this time, many of the celebrated German and English hellebore clones were lost to commerce. *Helleborus niger* was not forgotten. Plants tucked back under shrubs or along the edges of walls continued to grow and produce their bright white flowers in wintertime. Once growers could concentrate on ornamentals again, *H. niger* returned as a holiday cut flower. Little new breeding was done with garden hybrids until the middle of the 20th century. In her notes, plantswoman Helen Ballard of Worcestershire wrote of having a plant that came from nurseryman Walter Ingwersen, who collected his form of *H. torquatus* in Serbia in 1929, which eventually provided breeding material for producing some of the dark hybrids.

EUROPE AFTER WORLD WAR II

After World War II, Eric Smith and Jim Archibald at the Plantsman Nursery were among the first to resume work with hellebores in the U.K. A lecture on hellebores by respected plantsman E. B. Anderson, published in the RHS journal in 1957, was very well received and rekindled interest in the plant. Hilda Davenport-Jones and later Elizabeth Strangman of Washfield Nursery in Kent sold and bred a number of interesting plants; several breakthroughs in hellebore breeding came from their work. Davenport-Jones introduced *H. niger* 'Potter's Wheel' and raised *H. ×nigercors* 'Alabaster'; Strangman bred the picotee strain of *H. ×hybridus*, a white flower with a narrow raspberry-pink edge. She also discovered two double-flowering *H. torquatus* on a collecting trip to the Balkans in 1971, which she named 'Dido' and 'Aeneas'. These two plants gave rise to the double hybrids known as the Montenegrin Doubles. Their genes are found in many of today's doubles, including Party Dress Hybrids.

Helen Ballard's incomparable work at Old Country, her garden and nursery in Worcestershire, set a standard of excellence perhaps still unmatched. She was so taken with hellebores that she purportedly taught herself German to understand material written about the genus in that language. Ballard began to experiment with crossing *H. orientalis* with several other species. As advancing age made it impossible for her to continue her work, she arranged for Gisela Schmiemann to take many of her plants to Cologne, Germany. Schmiemann has made additional crosses using both the famous Ballard plants and others of her own hybridizing. Since Schmiemann also sold hellebore seed for a number of years, many breeders in the United States, Australia, New Zealand, and Japan incorporated some Ballard blood into their stocks. Schmiemann also published Ballard's breeding notes in *Helen Ballard: The Hellebore Queen*, making Ballard's theories and methods available to a new generation of hellebore breeders.

Günther Jürgl and Heinz Klose followed in the footsteps of the early German pioneers in hellebore breeding. Jürgl lived and worked in Sürth near Cologne. One of today's top hellebore breeders, Hans Kramer, told us that Jürgl was a true gentleman, always willing to share his novelties with other people: "He was a kind and generous man, who without hesitation would dig up a plant" to share a division from his

Washfield Nursery distributed the exceptional *H. niger* known as 'Potter's Wheel' around the world. Don Jacobs of Eco Gardens (Decatur, Georgia) still distributes offspring of that plant under the name 'Eco Potter's Wheel'.

stock. Jürgl also sent hellebore seed to enthusiasts all over the world. Working with his own hand-pollinated plants, Jürgl produced a number of double-flowering plants in the mid- to late 1980s, long before the rest of the hellebore world began to grow doubles. Two plants from his stock were some of the first doubles in the U.K. One was pink, or appeared pink because of the number of spots on its white background, and the other was white with spots. Kramer noted that the plant named 'Günther Jürgl', of which he questions, "who named that so, I am sure he did not himself," was perhaps the best of the lot.

Jürgl worked with Heinz Klose, a friend and fellow hellebore breeder. At his nursery in Kassel-Lohfelden, Klose continued the breeding begun in Germany in the 1850s. This collection included all the hellebores he could gather together, both descendants of old German cultivars and more modern hybrids. Klose grew hybrid doubles as early as 1985. He increased the range of colors, trading plants and seeds with Jürgl and other fanciers. Some of his selections were 'Nachthimmel', a powder blue cultivar with blue-black spots, and 'Gewitternacht', a red-black. Klose produced and released thousands of hellebore seedlings before his death in 2001.

Professor Joseph Straub was another German enthusiast. He wanted a white-flowering hellebore that would bloom at Christmas time. *Helleborus niger* did not grow well in his area, so Straub concentrated on the hybrids derived from *H. orientalis* when working toward his white-flowering plant. All plants producing red or pink flowers were given away. Straub found a nearly pure white double, perhaps the first, at the

Helen Ballard, seen here in her nursery, set a new standard for the shape and color of hybrid garden hellebores. (Ullrich Fischer)

Max Planck Institute, mixed in among darker colors. After his death, another double-flowering white with spots, which was growing on Straub's grave, was given by Straub's widow to Schmiemann, who named the plant 'Professor Straub' in his honor.

Other people were working with hellebores; both professionals and keen amateurs sold or distributed fresh seeds, which made it possible for growers in other parts of the world to obtain new species and hybrids unavailable by other methods. One such amateur was Leon Doyen, a retired Belgian engineer. Doyen traveled over mountain passes and flatlands from the Adriatic to the Alps collecting seeds from some species seldom seen in cultivation, which he shared with other keen growers in the United States and Europe. Marlene Ahlburg, a retired biology teacher who enjoyed growing and breeding plants, wrote in her 1989 book *Hellebores: Christmas Rose, Lenten Rose* of the methods used to breed and cultivate hellebores. Ahlburg had a particularly nice strain of plum-red *H. ×hybridus*, an ancestor of some of today's strains.

Today, seed lists from Phedar Nursery and Jim and Jenny Archibald entice both keen amateurs and professional breeders alike. Stories of their collecting trips make delightful dinner conversation; their lists of fresh seeds are as tempting as any calorie-laden dessert.

BRIAN MATHEW

Brian Mathew (left) continues to expand our knowledge of hellebores in the wild, while seedsmiths Jim and Jenny Archibald make them available to gardeners worldwide.

One of the most respected mavens in the horticultural world is also one of the world's authorities on hellebores. Brian Mathew grew up in an idyllic situation for a budding naturalist—a small village surrounded by fields and woodlands. In this apparently enchanted environment, he encountered his first hellebore—a purple-flowering hybrid growing on a pile of garden refuse. The subsequent rescue and study of this plant became the kernel of an idea that grew into the 1989 book *Hellebores* and establish Mathew as one of the preeminent authorities on this genus.

A training course at the RHS Garden Wisley, on-the-job experience in the horticultural fields of the celebrated Ingwersen family, and a significant and lengthy career in botany with the Herbarium at the Royal Botanic Gardens, Kew,

Winter at RHS Garden Wisley in Woking, U.K., finds hellebores and spring bulbs blanketing a sunny bank.

have endowed Mathew with the ability to understand a plant in both its scientific categorization and as an actual entity growing in the garden. Such extensive preparation coupled with considerable fieldwork gave him a unique perspective when he wrote his monograph on the genus, only one of a number of scholarly, yet entertaining and educational, works. Representative of his generous spirit is the invariant custom of giving credit to those who work with him on the varied and far-reaching projects that fill the hours of his supposed retirement.

Working with Will McLewin on a series of articles on hellebores written for the RHS publication *The New Plantsman* (now *The Plantsman*) is just one of any number of literary undertakings currently underway. The pair compliment one another in perspective, temperament, and style. The result of their collaboration is a series that is insightful and interesting, not an easy achievement when dealing with a subject as complex and frustrating as species hellebores.

Mathew has received honors from horticultural societies throughout the world, and rarely is a recipient more deserving of accolade. Few people manage to produce the volume of work he has achieved, even fewer manage to make a taxonomic work interesting to those outside the scientific or horticultural community, and none instill the level of humor and humanity that is standard issue in anything written by him. Brian is truly a man for all horticultural seasons.

THE LEGACY

Hybridizers such as Helen Ballard and Elizabeth Strangman provided a wide, firm base upon which breeders such as Robin White of Blackthorn Nursery, Kevin Belcher of Ashwood, and Hans Kramer of de Hessenhof have built. Their plants set a new standard for *H.* ×*hybridus*.

Others excel in pursuits unrelated to breeding. On the other side of the world, Japanese botanist and plant collector Mikinori Ogisui is responsible for completing the availability of the known species by sending plants of *H. thibetanus* to the U.K. for study. This species, almost completely unknown before the early 1990s, is now grow worldwide and inspires breeders with its potential for more hybridizing and excited gardeners with its unique beauty.

The future of hellebore taxonomy is in the able hands of Brian Mathew, Will McLewin, and Matthias Thomsen. They are working tirelessly to elucidate the complex relationships between the wild species and to provide a taxonomic revision of the genus through their serial articles published in *The New Plantsman*. By providing seeds from the more unusual species, McLewin has also helped to spread hellebores throughout the world.

Several books released on hellebores generated additional interest in Europe as well as America, Australia, and New Zealand. A translated edition from the German of Ahlburg's *Hellebores: Christmas Rose, Lenten Rose*, Rice and Strangman's *The Gardener's Guide to Growing Hellebores* was published in 1993. Schmiemann's book, *Helen Ballard: The Hellebore Queen*, published in 1997, provides information to a cadre of enthusiasts hungry for information about this fascinating genus. It is fair to say that these books sparked a revolution in hellebore breeding worldwide.

Though most of the original hybridizing took place in Europe, many American breeders are producing exceptional plants. Many older selections were gleaned from gardens and saved from obscurity. Bloodlines from America have even made their way back to Europe and are featured in new hybrids. One version of Ashwood's 'Pink Ice' was created by crossing *H. thibetanus* with *H. niger* 'Nell Lewis', received from Pine Knot Farms in Virginia. The future is bound to hold a wealth of surprises.

THE AMERICAN STORY

The first arrival of hellebores in America is lost to the collective consciousness. Due to their close association with both religious holidays and medicine, hellebores likely arrived on North American shores early in the continent's colonial history. Few of America's famous colonial botanists or gardeners mention hellebores in their writings. This does not necessarily mean that the plants were not present in their gardens, however. Medicinal and veterinary derivatives of hellebore, chronicled in Appendix A, were routinely mentioned in the literature. The earliest cultivation of hellebores may have been for use as an insecticide to treat other plants rather than as ornamentals in their own right.

We propose two reasons for the paucity of hellebores in early America. Hellebores are succulent plants, prone to desiccation if stored too dry or rot if stored too moist. They are slow to recover from transplant shock. Imagine a bare-root plant wrapped in straw making an ocean voyage. You think today's travel delays are bad! It took months for a plant sent from England to arrive in the hands of some American gardener skilled enough to revive it. Hellebores are notoriously slow from division, too. Without a reliable source of plants, it seems likely that hellebores would languish in obscurity, much the way a coveted but slow-to-increase selection might today.

The fact that hellebore seeds, when stored for any period of time, enter a deep, complex dormancy likely contributed to their scarcity as well. Fully dried seeds need three different temperature regimes to germinate. All hellebore seeds need a typical warm-moist period and then cool-moist stratification. Old, dry seeds need an additional warm-moist period to develop. Depending on when seeds are sown, this additional requirement can add a full year to the germination period. Remember that no refrigerators were available in which to stratify and chill seeds. Even today, seed stored for long periods is devilishly difficult to germinate, and it takes a great deal of patience.

By the 16th century, English botanists and plantsmen were passionately combing the world for new plants, but their discoveries had to travel as seeds, corms, dry rhizomes, and roots. Failure was common. Many plants went down with ships; others rotted or dried out en route. Nathaniel Bagshaw Ward (1791–1868) of London was a physician with a passion for natural science and a particular love of ferns. Historians report that the ferns in his garden were being suffocated by London's poisonous atmosphere. In a bottle where Ward kept the cocoon of a moth, he discovered that fern spores were germinating and growing. On a hunch, he commissioned a closely fitted, glazed wooden case. In the protected environment, his ferns thrived. The Wardian case was born in 1829.

The new Wardian cases made it possible for tender young plants to sit on a ship's deck protected from salt spray yet exposed to light. In July 1833, Ward shipped two glazed cases filled with ferns and grasses to Sydney, Australia, a voyage of several months. To his delight, the protected plants arrived in good condition. Almost overnight, it became possible to send living plants overseas in the protected, even nurturing environment of the Wardian case. Exchange of plants around the world exploded. No doubt, hellebores were among plants shipped in these cases. In fact, Australian horticulturist Trevor Nottle postulates the role of the Wardian case in getting the first hellebores to Australia.

However they came, by seeds or as plants, in a Wardian case or wrapped in rags, hellebores did arrive in America. The early American references to hellebores we found were most often in the context of medicine or vermifuge rather than ornament. Perhaps medicinal plants were not documented as scrupulously as ornamentals, or perhaps those who grew hellebores were not record-keepers. We'll never know.

We saw few letters and personal documents while researching this book. Our primary reports come from nursery catalogs, period books, and magazine articles. Of particular interest are extant records of what people could buy and what they could read in the popular press. Using these resources, we attempt to tell the story of hellebores through the eyes of American gardeners. No doubt we have missed many important citations, and many manuscripts and letters have gone unread. We invite readers to share any information, especially anything prior to the mid-1800s, that you may have about the sale or use of hellebores in America.

THE EARLY YEARS

Early American garden literature featuring hellebores is scant. When the name *hellebore* does appear, it is often unclear which plant is actually intended. Some references to hellebore no doubt actually meant the plant *Veratrum*, which was alternately called hellebore, white hellebore, and false hellebore. The name *red hellebore*, also recorded in early literature, is believed to refer to the helleborine orchid, *Epipactis helleborine* [currently *Serapias helleborine*]. Confusion prevails.

Our first records lie in the letters of Pennsylvania botanist and nurseryman John Bartram (1699–1777). Bartram is often called the "father of American botany." He was a self-educated man and a voracious reader. He also studied Greek and Latin, and his observations of the natural world were astute. Bartram had an insatiable and highly intellectual curiosity about natural history, especially plants. He collected throughout many of the eastern colonies, later joined by his son William (1739–1823), also an avid botanist and naturalist.

In 1728, Bartram established the first botanical garden in America in Kingessing, Pennsylvania, on the Schuylkill River. There he raised both native and exotic plants.

He was not only a competent farmer, but he aided the sick with his knowledge of medicinal plants. Because he apparently preferred the journey of discovery to the job of recording, his journals paint only a partial picture of his accomplishments.

Bartram writes of hellebores several times in his early correspondence, but *Helleborus* is likely not the intended plant. In their 1992 book, *The Correspondence of John Bartram*, Edmund and Dorothy Berkeley note that Bartram sent a letter to Peter Collinson in 1735 in which he referred to "2 sorts [of] hellebores," which were likely *Veratrum* (and possibly *Coptis*, which was called *Helleborus trifolius*), since Bartram sent mainly native plants to Collinson.

Additionally, they note that Bartram wrote to a Dr. Colden on 16 January 1742–43 that "Our rivers have been open all along & we have had warm weather for ye season, & I now have in my Garden ye Meserion, Black helebore, groundsel, hen bit, Esula & Veronica in flower & many others is budding." This could refer to a true *Helleborus*, as *Veratrum* is much later to bloom and the timing of the other plants mentioned fits. Some believe that the name *black hellebore* refers to *H. niger*. This is indeed a direct translation of the botanical name, but Mathew postulates that it may indeed refer to *H. cyclophyllus*. The main difference between the two plants that bear the common name *hellebore* is that *Veratrum*, called white hellebore, has white roots; hence the name. All *Helleborus* species have dark roots, and when dried they appear black. Black hellebore may well refer to any true *Helleborus*, as distinguished from a light-rooted *Veratrum*.

Imagine our delight when one of the few early references to true hellebores came from our home state of Virginia. Lady Jean Skipwith held court at Prestwould, her impressive Southside Virginia plantation on the Roanoke River. Peggy Cornett, director for the Thomas Jefferson Center for Historic Plants at Monticello, wrote in the January 2000 *Twinleaf Journal* that

> The highly educated Jean Skipwith left remarkable lists of flowers that she grew in southern Virginia between 1785 and 1805. . . . Jean Skipwith was a skilled gardener and she possessed an astute knowledge of botanical Latin. The libraries at Monticello and Prestwould both contained copies of Philip Miller's eighth edition of the *Gardener's Dictionary*, 1768, [an English book that lists 12 species of hellebore] and Lady Skipwith often cited this botanical tome. Skipwith's floral documents, as described by Ann Leighton in *American Gardens in the Eighteenth Century: For Use or for Delight*, were either left on the backs of old bills or neatly recorded in lists with such titles as "bulbs to be got when I can" and "Wildflowers in the Garden."

The extensive gardens at Prestwould were counted among the best in colonial Virginia, and Skipwith's passion for plants was legendary. In her book, Leighton writes that Skipwith's garden journals from the 1790s list "stinking black Hellebore." Though virtually nothing remains of the garden, Skipwith's records indicate that she planted two islands in the Roanoke River, now submerged by the waters of the

John H. Kerr Reservoir. A third island was used for livestock. Skipwith wrote that the hellebore, which she called "Bears-foot" or "Scttcrwort" (*H. foetidus*), was one of several herbs that were ostensibly used for settering, or dressing wounds of livestock. Did she also enjoy their early green flowers and finely cut foliage? We believe that no gardener with a keen eye for beauty could help but admire their bravado in the face of winter's chill.

THE 19TH CENTURY

The earliest recorded commercial sale of hellebores that we found was *H. viridis* [currently *H. occidentalis*] by Prince Nursery, Flushing, New York, in 1822. This plant was commonly grown for use as an insecticide and vermifuge, so it is questionable whether plants sold here were for ornament. Interestingly, by 1834, the species was documented as naturalized on Long Island in New York. The 6th edition of *Gray's Manual of Botany*, published in 1889, expands the naturalized range to include Pennsylvania and West Virginia. New Jersey was added in the 7th edition, and today, *H. occidentalis* is found from New York and Michigan, south to North Carolina and Tennessee. Someone grew this plant.

Philadelphia nurseryman and author Bernard M'Mahon (1775–1816) published *The American Gardener's Calendar* in 1806. It was the most comprehensive gardening book published in the United States in the first half of the 19th century. As any author or reader knows, popularity is judged by staying power. Eleven editions of the book were printed between 1806 and 1857, so it was no doubt widely read. Modeled on a traditional English month-by-month formula popular at the time, it provided instructions on planting, pruning, and soil preparation. Ten species of hellebores were featured.

Peter Hatch, director of gardens and grounds at Monticello, wrote in the January 1993 issue of *Twinleaf Journal* that

> M'Mahon borrowed extensively from English works, especially those of Philip Miller and particularly from John Abercrombie, author of *Every Man His Own Gardener*, first published in York, England, in 1767 under the name of Thomas Mawe. M'Mahon's sixty-three page *General Catalogue* of recommended garden plants (3,700 species) was unrealistically biased in favor of traditional Old World species. It is doubtful whether a majority of them were then found in the United States.

With such bias to English books in mind, M'Mahon's recommendation of 10 different hellebores is likely just a dream of what might have been, rather than a record of what was actually grown or sold in America at that time. This seems particularly likely given that we found few other writers or authors that mention hellebores until after the mid-1800s. The 18th edition of Abercrombie's *Every Man His Own Gardener*, published in 1805, goes into some detail about hellebores, so no doubt M'Mahon was captivated. One of the most interesting passages is the description of propagation, which we believe holds the key to the successful establishment of hellebores on the American side of the Atlantic. Abercrombie writes of *H. niger* in the chapter "Notes for September" that "This is the time to slip and plant out many kinds of fibrous-rooted perennial plants, to increase them . . . part the roots of daisies, polyanthuses, and auriculas, gentianella, London-pride, Christmas-rose." If plants were produced only by division, it is no wonder so few were available. Division is a slow way to produce hellebores.

By the mid-1800s, a broad range of species was being sold by several popular nurseries. Also, propagation techniques had apparently improved. Many books published at this time, including Jane Loudon's 1843 *Gardening for Ladies*, provide details on propagation from seed and division. This book, published in England and later adapted for American readers, was among the first to provide detailed propagation information. Ellwanger and Barry, an influential nursery in Rochester, New York, offered nine species in 1860. Curiously, the offerings were among the same species that M'Mahon mentioned in *The American Gardener's Calendar*. No doubt enthusiastic patrons purchased plants. Ellwanger and Barry's list was surely the 19th century equivalent of today's lusty offering from Heronswood Nursery in Washington and Plant Delights Nursery in North Carolina.

Was George Ellwanger the tireless promoter that Tony Avent of Plant Delights Nursery is today? Ellwanger's 1889 book, *The Garden's Story*, dismisses the ornamental potential of hellebores by comparing them to crows in winter, tolerable for interest until the colorful songbirds return, as "a very good thing to have until there is something better to take its place." Odd for a book that had the opportunity to promote plants sold by his nursery, which still listed three hellebore species in 1882. Another early mention comes in Herman Bourne's *Flores Poetici: The Florist's Manual*, published 1833. He notes the poisonous nature of *Helleborus* and also describes the physical attributes of *H. atrorubens* (actually *H. orientalis* subsp. *abchasicus*).

At least Ellwanger and Bourne mentioned hellebores, however dismissively. Many writers of the day ignored them completely. We must remember that only educated people at this time were widely read. Educated gardeners purchased and devoured influential tomes such as Robert Buist's 1839 *The American Flower Garden Dictionary*, Thomas Bridgeman's 1840 *The Florist's Guide*, and Joseph Breck's 1851 *The Flower-Garden*. Unfortunately, all these popular books make no mention of our beloved genus. It is not surprising that hellebore popularity was slow to rise when so many books did not promote the plants.

Why weren't these authors writing about hellebores? They were the people in the know—the arbiters of taste. The obvious answer is that they neither knew of them nor grew them. But how could that be? Perhaps hellebores were popular among only the common man throughout this period. Maybe the plants were stigmatized because they were used to treat lice. Lice were not a malady of the learned classes, or at least not one they cared to acknowledge. Even a vermifuge with showy flowers would surely seduce anyone with an eye for beauty.

Could a stigma have dampened the public's enthusiasm for hellebores? Or was it simply a matter of taste? Tastes at this time were varied, but they ran toward the flamboyant. Some favored annuals and tropicals for bedding. Garden historian Denise Adams told us that the "Victorian penchant for the new and unusual motivated nurseries to offer extensive listings of roses and dahlias in addition to the usual selection of trees, shrubs and herbaceous plants for residential gardens. The fact that hellebores rarely appeared in books and catalogues at this time does not mean they did not grace gardens. It was indicative that they were not considered fashionable at this time."

Not all writers of the period ignored hellebores, however. Aspiring and accomplished gardeners turned to Peter Henderson's 1881 *Handbook of Plants and General Horticulture* for advice and inspiration. Henderson (1822–1890), a Scottish-American scientist, was known to some as the "father of American horticulture." He learned methods of gardening in the Old World and emigrated to the United States in 1843. Few men did more to simplify the handling of plants for commercial use. He opened his greenhouses as models for his many visitors and his growing methods were widely copied. Other influential books by Henderson include *Practical Floriculture* (1868) for professionals and *Gardening for Pleasure* (1875) for the amateur audience. Henderson's *Handbook* extols the early-flowering of *H. niger* and notes that it was introduced to horticulture from Austria in 1596.

In December 1883, *The Ladies Floral Cabinet*, a monthly circular published in New York from 1873 to 1895, featured a short but detailed piece on *Helleborus*. The main species featured was *H. niger*, which is covered in exciting detail. The article notes that *H. niger* is the most often cultivated, but that the "few" other species are "very ornamental." The inclusion of *H. lividus*, with details on cultivation, is noteworthy. Few publications mention this plant even today. The article further notes that it is seldom seen due to difficulty of propagation "since it has not the creeping underground stems of the other species, and the seeds do not ripen well." This piece is important not just for bringing a new species into print, but also for indicating the two common ways that hellebores were propagated at that time.

Another bright spot around the turn of the 19th century was the *Cyclopedia of American Horticulture*, first published by Liberty Hyde Bailey in 1891. The *Cyclopedia*, a standard reference for American gardening according to historian Adams, was full of information to titillate winter gardeners with a penchant for new plants. Bailey (1858–1954) is often credited with the development of agricultural education in the United States. He served as dean of the College of Agriculture at Cornell University from 1903 to 1913. Bailey worked to make botanical knowledge available to farmers and gardeners and to make botanists understand the practical problems of agriculture and horticulture.

Bailey clearly lauds the ornamental prowess of hellebores and even suggests ways to force them in a cool greenhouse. More importantly, he offers recommendations for propagation, noting that division is slow, and that "if seed matures they will germinate well if planted immediately in pans or in rich open ground." He also notes that *H. viridis* (now *H. occidentalis*) is "not so much used as the other species here given." It is immediately obvious that the plant once valued and grown widely for its medicinal prowess had taken a back seat to the showier species valued purely

AMERICAN NURSERY LISTINGS FROM 1800 TO 1950

The following listings are alphabetical by species name, as in the catalog. The currently accepted name follows the listed name, which appears in brackets.

[Helleborus atrorubens] *H. orientalis* subsp. *abchasicus*
Manning, Boston: 1887

[Helleborus Atro-Rubra] *H. orientalis* subsp. *abchasicus*
Behnke Nurseries, Beltsville, Maryland: 1949
Ellwanger & Barry, Rochester, New York: 1860, 1867, 1882

[Helleborus caucasus] *H. orientalis* subsp. *orientalis*
Ellwanger & Barry, Rochester, New York: 1860

Helleborus foetidus
Ellwanger & Barry, Rochester, New York: 1860, 1867

[Helleborus hybrida] *H. ×hybridus*
Park Seed Company, Greenwood, South Carolina: 1938

[Helleborus iberica] *H. orientalis* subsp. *orientalis*
Ellwanger & Barry, Rochester, New York: 1860, 1862

[Helleborus lividus trifolata] *H. lividus*
Ellwanger & Barry, Rochester, New York: 1860

Helleborus niger
Prince Nurseries, Flushing, New York: 1820, 1822, 1854 1857
Ellwanger & Barry, Rochester, New York: 1860, 1862, 1867, 1875, 1917
Hovey & Co., Boston: 1859
Manning Nurseries, Reading, Massachusetts: 1887, 1889

C. E. Allen, Brattleboro, Vermont: 1889
New England Nurseries, Bedford, Massachusetts: 1910
Joseph Breck & Sons, Boston: 1917
Joseph Harris, Coldwater, New York: 1934
Storrs & Harrison, Painesville, Ohio: 1937
Park Seed Co., Greenwood, South Carolina: 1938
Lamb Nurseries, Spokane, Washington: 1939
Behnke Nurseries, Beltsville, Maryland: 1949

Helleborus niger [latifolius] *H. niger*
Lamb Nurseries, Spokane, Washington: 1939

Helleborus orientalis
Ellwanger & Barry, Rochester, New York: 1862, 1867, 1875, 1882
Lamb Nurseries, Spokane, Washington: 1939

[Helleborus pallidus] *H. dumetorum*
Ellwanger & Barry, Rochester, New York: 1860

[Helleborus purpureus] likely *H. orientalis* or *H. ×hybridus*
Ellwanger & Barry, Rochester, New York: 1860

[Helleborus trifolius] *Coptis trifolia*, occasionally *H. lividus*
Bartram, Philadelphia: 1807
Landreth, Philadelphia: 1811, 1826, 1828

[Helleborus viridus] *H. occidentalis*
Prince Nurseries, Rochester, New York: 1822, 1844, 1854, 1857
Ellwanger & Barry, Rochester, New York: 1860, 1862, 1867, 1875

for ornament. Several subspecies and varieties appear here for the first time in print. Bailey's list contains two selections of *H. niger* and eight of *H. orientalis*. It is worth noting that the entries for *Helleborus* were written not by Bailey himself, but by K. C. Davis, a science teacher from Ithaca, New York. We were unable to track down information about Davis, so we do not know the extent of his interest in the genus, though it appears he was a specialist in the Ranunculaceae. The 1935 edition of the *Cyclopedia* adds three species: *H. foetidus*, *H. corsicus* [now *H. argutifolius*] and *H. lividus*.

Many herbarium specimens of hellebores reside in the L. H. Bailey Hortorium at Cornell University. The most notable is a specimen of *H. odorus* from 1877 from a plant cultivated on Long Island, New York. Other early collections include *H. niger* from 1916, *H. foetidus* from 1938, *H. orientalis* from 1940, *H. cyclophyllus* from 1944, and several *H. argutifolius* collections from the 1940s and 1950s. Multiple collections of *H. viridis* (now *H. occidentalis*) are not surprising, given its long history of medicinal use. The collection contains specimens from all over New York, including Canandaigua in 1913 and New York Botanical Garden in 1935. Of particular interest are specimens collected from a garden connected with the Ellwanger and Barry Nursery of Rochester, New York, in 1937 and Letterman Seed Company of Canton, Ohio, in 1933.

THE 20TH CENTURY

After the turn of the 19th century, the popularity of hellebores skyrocketed, and more references emerged in the popular press and in nursery lists. We believe, though it is only a guess, that a jump in popularity was due in part to the fact that by the late 1800s, several species were offered by nurseries. The 1906 edition of Bailey's *Cyclopedia* featured a full account and promotion of eight different species. The gardening press was more popular than ever and was reaching a wider, more diverse American audience of gardeners and nature lovers. Fresh seed produced on plants in the United States surely germinated more readily than seed shipped from abroad.

The Garden Magazine, published in Garden City, New York, from 1905 to 1924, was influential and widely read. Through its years of circulation, many articles on hellebores appeared. Harold Clark wrote in his 1906 piece, "Bulbs and Perennials for November Planting":

> The Christmas rose (*Helleborus niger*) blooms outdoors in winter, but north of New York it is safer to grow it in a cold frame. By this means you are reasonably sure of having flowers for cutting at Christmas. It has only a few leaves that are divided into six or seven lobes. They are dark green and rather uninteresting. The large white flowers, one and a half to two inches across, are very beautiful indeed. Just bring the potted plants indoors two weeks before you want the flowers, and as soon as the blossoms are cut out go the plants. Is there anything quicker?

JANUARY
1912
Vol. XIV. No. 6

Pruning Dormant Fruit Trees
Family of Boston Ferns   Collecting Stonecrops
Alkali Gardening   Keeping Poultry

15c.
$1.50 a Year

THE GARDEN
MAGAZINE

FARMING

COUNTRY LIFE   DOUBLEDAY, PAGE & CO.   THE WORLD'S
IN AMERICA   Chicago   GARDEN CITY, N. Y.   New York   WORK

The Garden Magazine was one of many popular periodicals to feature articles detailing the culture and ornamental merits of hellebores. *Helleborus niger* graces the January 1912 cover.

Neltje Blanchan's 1909 *The American Flower Garden* proclaimed *H. niger* a "perennial for a thought-out garden." Blanchan (1865–1918) notes evergreen foliage and flowers "even under the snow" as attributes. She advises planting near the house for easy winter viewing and notes that "cut flowers make excellent table decorations if taken young," warning they become speckled as they age.

Mabel Cabot Sedgwick's 1907 *The Garden Month By Month* mentions both the popular Christmas and Lenten roses but also reports on *H. viridis* var. *purpurascens*, which she described as having "drooping green flowers purple tinted, and grayish foliage. Needs slight protection in winter. Should not be disturbed. Plant in border or edge of shrubbery. Prop. by division. Any rich well-drained soil." This description actually sounds like the wild species *H. purpurascens*, an early date for the cultivation of this species.

Amateur botanist Harriet Keeler (1846–1921) achieved national recognition for her nature writing. As an amateur, she relied on published authorities in her writing, but she added her own observations and literary references to make her books appealing and useful to readers. In 1910, Keeler published *Our Garden Flowers*, in which she comments on hellebores. She notes that the Christmas rose is "a stemless evergreen perennial; often blooming in the open air at Christmas, in the climate of New Jersey and Ohio." She adds, "The beauty of the blossom is due to the enlarged sepals—there are indeed petals, rows of them, but they are curiously turned into two-lipped tubes producing nectar. The stigmas mature before the anthers." Either firsthand or through her readings, she is able to relate that "of the genus *Helleborus* eight species are known and most of them have been cultivated. Beside *Helleborus niger*, *Helleborus viridis* [now *H. occidentalis*] is common." Interesting in light of Bailey's 1906 comment that *H. viridis* was seldom grown at that time. Clearly, the popularity and cultivation of certain species was regional and cyclical.

The January 1912 issue of *The Garden Magazine* features an enticing cover painting of *H. niger*. The editor's column "This Month's Cover" says that "The Christmas rose . . . is by all odds the most attractive of winter-flowering plants for a hardy garden. It is the only plant that gives really large flowers throughout the winter. Flowering in January, the expanded blooms, measuring sometimes three inches across, may be gathered after having to brush away the snow. When first expanded they are the purest crystalline white, becoming pinker as they age." Without doubt, the Christmas rose was the darling of early 20th-century American gardens.

In a March 1912 article in *The Garden Magazine*, entitled "More About the Christmas Rose," John Chamblin wrote

> Many people are interested in the Christmas rose (*Helleborus niger*) but it is so seldom to be had or seen that the general knowledge of it is quite small. While I have cultivated the Christmas rose quite a long time I do not even yet claim to know it well, though it is one of the most interesting plants in my garden. The plants came to me as a gift from a friend who kept a sort of old-fashioned garden and it would be hard to trace it beyond that garden. It is by no means the certain bloomer that it is sometimes said to be, though I am sure it would do much better if I knew how to manage it.

The January 1915 cover of *Horticulture* magazine also featured *H. niger*. The article by Richard Roths of Glenside, Pennsylvania, laments that of the 12 hellebore species, "a world-wide distribution and a general popularity in American gardens, however, is enjoyed only by the well known *Helleborus niger*." Roths mentions hybridizing work in Switzerland and Germany involving color lines of "very attractive pink, red, violet and purple shades" of what must be *H. ×hybridus*, noting that "in European gardens ten to fifteen years ago they were extensively cultivated in pots" but that "in America we have confined ourselves principally to the growing of the original white type of *Helleborus niger*." Hellebores appeared often in the pages of *Horticulture* magazine throughout the 1920s and 1930s, but not in the years surrounding World War II. In the early 1950s they re-emerge.

BETWEEN WORLD WARS I AND II

Hellebores figured prominently in American garden literature in the years following World War I. The explosion of interest in gardening was evident in the works of popular writers on both sides of the Atlantic. Stateside, celebrities of the day such as Albert Taylor, Louise Beebe Wilder, and Mrs. Francis King were teaching the emerging middle class how to garden.

Albert D. Taylor used his knowledge and influence to provide practical information to gardeners. Taylor devised *The Complete Garden* (1921) as a "compact reference manual" for amateurs "from which information can be easily obtained." In reality, it is more in the form of a landscape dictionary. *Helleborus niger* is listed in five different charts, offering everything from winter green and ground cover effects to perpetual bloom. Taylor taught landscape architecture at The Ohio State University. In the years following the publication of his book, Ohio emerged as one of the hotbeds of hellebores. From here, Carl Krippendorf would send hellebores to Elizabeth Lawrence, the Luedys would dedicate a volume to the same flower, Wayside Gardens would open its mail-order doors to American gardeners, and Henry Ross would found Gardenview Horticultural Park (more on that later in the chapter).

Taylor's book was short on prose and long on lists. Not so with the writings of Louise Beebe Wilder (1878–1938), however. She was a gifted and prolific writer. Ten books chronicle her experiences tending her Bronxville, New York, garden. *The Garden in Color*, written in 1937, extols the virtues of several hellebore species, among them *H. niger* and *H. orientalis* subsp. *abchasicus*. We read with surprise that "There are numerous forms of *Helleborus niger*, some beginning to bloom towards the end of November or early in December, others in February, or any time during the winter when they are not actually frozen into passivity; and some types have smaller flowers than others." What is the origin of this wealth of forms? She notes that "Several dealers in this country have good collections of Lent roses, so that American gardeners can enjoy plantations of these attractive spring flowers if they want them." Perhaps the same was true for Christmas roses. Her treatment of the genus includes complete and accurate cultural information as well. She also presents a lush photo of a delicious spring arrangement featuring *H. ×hybridus* among anemones, snowdrops, snowflakes, and heather.

Plate 90. EARLY SPRING FLOWERS ARRANGED IN POTTERY JAR

Hellebores excel in vases as well as in the garden. This lovely photograph from *The Garden in Color*, written in 1937 by Louise Beebe Wilder, features primroses, crocus, snowflakes, iris, and hellebores.

John Wister (1887–1982) was a landscape architect with a passion for plants. He served as director of the Arthur Hoyt Scott Arboretum of Swarthmore College from 1930 to 1946. He also maintained an extensive private garden adjacent to the campus.

Over the years, Wister added many hellebores to the gardens at Swarthmore, including a 1937 gift of hellebores from Mrs. Arthur H. Scott. In 1939, William Craig of Weymouth, Massachusetts, sold Wister "*H. niger* var. *altifolius* and *H. niger* var. *praecox*." These two plants were introduced several times between 1948 and 1967 from sources such as Jackson and Perkins. In 1952, *H. orientalis* [now *H. ×hybridus*] was received as a gift from Mrs. Scott. In 1963, plants were received from Elizabeth Lawrence, a personal gift to the Wisters. *Helleborus foetidus, H. argutifolius*, and selections of *H. ×hybridus* were added in 1967 from Lamb Nurseries, which distributed the popular Millet Hybrids. Whether any of these are the direct antecedents of the plants still growing in Wister's garden is anyone's guess.

Wister married for the first time at 73 years of age. His bride, the former Gertrude Smith, was also an accomplished horticulturist. The two shared a love of gardening, and they grew many plants of winter interest, including hellebores.

Today, publications such as The Andersen Horticultural Library's *Source List of Plants and Seeds*, the Royal Horticultural Society's *Plant Finder*, and Timber Press's *The Plant Locator* help gardeners around the world locate plants. It wasn't always so easy to track down a rare or coveted plant. One of the early indices to plant sources was J. Woodward Manning's *The Plant Buyers Index* (1931). Manning listed two varieties of *H. niger* and two colors (pink and maroon) of *H. orientalis*. It seems hellebores were widely appreciated and gaining popularity all the time.

One provider of hellebores to an eager market was Bristol Nurseries, in Bristol, Connecticut. Pierre Benneraup, owner of Sunny Border Nurseries, a wholesale operation nearby, wrote in a letter to us that "In the '20s and '30s, *Helleborus niger* and *H. orientalis* were being grown by the now defunct Bristol Nurseries." At the time, the nursery was one of the largest and most complete in the United States, growing everything from perennials to trees and shrubs. Alec Cumming, co-owner of the firm, and later his son Rod, were instrumental in hybridization of the garden "mum" as we know it today. In his and R. E. Lee's 1960 book, *Contemporary Perennials*, Rod Cumming says only the two above-mentioned species of hellebore are commonly cultivated in the United States. He writes, "True material of *H. niger* var. *altifolius* is vastly preferable to the species; slightly longer scapes bear huge 4–5 inch flowers, and the foliage is more upright and impressive. Under ideal conditions flowering should occur by Christmas. True material is scarce." (Unfortunately, Rod Cumming died a few years after his book was published, and now the once glorious nursery is a housing development.)

AFTER WORLD WAR II

Interest in hellebores was strong after World War II. It finally seemed as though everyone who gardened had a soft spot for hellebores. Gone was George Ellwanger's notion of tolerating the crow until the colorful songbirds returned. People cherished hellebores for all their ornamental attributes. Yes, their precocious bloom was a major factor commented on by all, but hellebores were unqualified favorites, valued for foliage, flowers, and ease of culture.

The Christmas rose, snow rose, or black hellebore was without doubt the darling of the genus. Few could resist those pristine white flowers in the dead of winter and the glowing rose tint of the fading flowers. Every book that mentions hellebores starts with Christmas rose, and some get no further. One such gem is a slim but heartfelt volume entitled *The Christmas Rose*. This loving tribute to a favorite flower was self-published by Arthur E. and Mildred V. Luedy in 1948. The foreword reads, "The authors have set down herein some of their experiences growing The Christmas rose, *Helleborus niger altifolius*, over the past quarter century, in the hope that some who have not known this most enchanting flower heretofore may come to know and grow and prize it." This is the first American book devoted solely to hellebores. Each of its 44 pages is filled with loving prose praising a beloved friend. Chapters discuss history, anatomy, cut flower and garden use, cultivation, and pests and diseases, and the book ends with a fable. Lovely photos by Henry M. Mayer highlight the species' cut flower potential.

The Luedys also shared their enthusiasm for *H. niger* through nursery sales and in the popular press of the day. Mildred penned the article "Christmas Flowers Indoors"

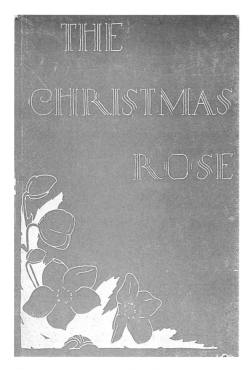

The Christmas Rose, published in 1948 by Arthur and Mildred Luedy, shares one couple's fascination with their favorite flower in both garden and vase.

Christmas roses remain popular as cut flowers. This copy of a beautiful photograph by Henry M. Mayer shows one of Mildred Luedy's creative arrangements.

on the cut flower uses of the plants for the January 1956 issue of *Horticulture*. Hers was one of seven articles on hellebores written by various authors in the magazine's pages in that decade alone. It is interesting to note that only one additional article on hellebores, published in 1965, appears in the pages of *Horticulture* until 1992, when the renaissance of interest in *H. ×hybridus* was well underway in America.

Winterthur, Henry Frances duPont's monumental garden in Delaware, is famous for its naturalistic beauty. Mac Griswold notes in *The Golden Age of American Gardens* (1991) that duPont added hellebores to his woodland garden in the mid-20th century. *Helleborus niger* was in the garden as early as 1928, when duPont writes to several friends on 29 December that he has "been picking Snowdrops, Iris Stylosa and Christmas Roses out of doors!" These plants came from the Luedy Company in Ohio.

A visit to England apparently sparked a more avid interest in hellebores. DuPont writes on 8 April 1956 in a letter to Marian C. Coffin that "I saw Colonel and Mrs. Stern's garden at Goring by Sea, Sussex, which was enchanting with countless crocus species, purple and green Lenten Helleborus, many varieties of snowdrops and some of the early narcissi, cyclamens, etc." After this trip, he corresponded for several years with Stern and adds a number of accessions to the garden, including *H. argutifolius*, *H. ×hybridus*, and *H. lividus*. During this time, he planted the combination of purple

H. ×hybridus with *Rhododendron mucronulatum* that remains one of the hallmarks of his spring garden. On 17 January 1956 he writes to Stern that "I have just made a new walk through my *Azalea mucronulatum*, *Corylopsis*, and *Princepia sinensis*, which always bloom April 1 and I feel the Hellebores would greatly enhance the beauty of my garden."

While northern routes of hellebore introduction at this time may have been through England, many of the hellebores in today's southern American gardens likely came from one of two gardeners: William Lanier Hunt or Elizabeth Lawrence. Both were well known for sharing plants and seeds. Bill Hunt (1906–1996) was a writer and avid gardener who lived and created gardens in North Carolina and Virginia. In the introduction to Hunt's book *Southern Gardens, Southern Gardening* (1982), Lawrence writes nostalgically that he "was born and grew up in the Lindley Nursery in Greensboro, North Carolina." John Van Lindley (1835–1918) established Pomona Nursery in 1877. This venerable institution was a training ground for many aspiring gardeners and provided a wealth of plants to gardeners of the southern United States. Pomona Nursery later became Lindley Nursery and was run by John Van Lindley II when Hunt knew it.

In conversation with Dick and Judith Tyler, Hunt determined that he and Dick Tyler had both attended Woodberry Forest preparatory school near Orange, Virginia. Upon entering Woodberry Forest early in the 1920s, Hunt met the headmaster's wife, Violet Walker, whom he called "Violent Walker" for her enthusiasm over plants and gardens. Hunt remembered an old, very large, and floriferous group of *H. niger* that grew in Mrs. Walker's garden.

Hunt left Woodberry Forest in 1926 for the University of North Carolina at Chapel Hill. He said it took two trucks to haul his plants to his new home. Through a family introduction, Hunt and Elizabeth Lawrence became fast friends and traded both plants and plant people. They introduced one another to gardeners from all over the country. Like Mrs. Walker, Hunt and Lawrence were in correspondence with the garden gurus of the day, among them E. B. and Katherine White and Louise Beebe Wilder.

Hunt settled in Chapel Hill on a wooded hillside, and his garden grew lush, with *H. ×hybridus* spreading freely and *Arum italicum* and cyclamen nestling in tree roots. In 1982, Hunt published his life's accumulated knowledge in a charming and readable book, *Southern Gardens, Southern Gardening*. Hunt praises the hellebores he first discovered in prep school, saying that these "fascinating winter perennials are a joy, even here in the south where we have camellias in bloom in the winter. Along with winter iris, wintersweet, sweet breath of spring, winter jasmine, and Bongoume apricot, they provide us with excitement and a lot to talk about from December to March." He also notes that American specialty nurseries via England are offering new colors. Lawrence, his dear friend and gardening companion, wrote the cover quote. It reads "William Lanier Hunt's *Southern Gardens, Southern Gardening* is a book that has long been looked for and which will be welcomed with delight; it touches upon just about everything in the South and in England and does not neglect the Yankees. It is unique." How right she was.

ELIZABETH LAWRENCE

Elizabeth Lawrence welcomed visitors from far and wide through this gate into her Charlotte, North Carolina, garden. (Photo courtesy of the *Charlotte Observer*)

Elizabeth Lawrence (1904–1985) is indisputably one of America's most beloved garden authors. A shy girl with an exceptionally good mind, she had a keen eye for good plants and a deep love of hellebores. Forever single, but never single-minded, she loved literature, poetry, good food, and good friendship. From her two North Carolina gardens, first in Raleigh and then in Charlotte, she corresponded and traded plants with all the great gardeners of the day, both at home and abroad. She wrote voluminously: books, articles, columns, and letters, letters, letters. Eager readers devoured her words, and in her printed works she praises hellebores on many occasions. Her 1942 classic, *A Southern Garden*, published in three different editions, enthralls readers as much today as it did when it was first published.

Lawrence's writing was as admired abroad as it was at home. Lawrence biographer Emily Herring Wilson (2004) writes that after Lawrence graduated from Bernard College and took a long trip abroad, she rarely traveled again because her Raleigh garden "was so beautiful that she vowed never again to leave it, at least not for long." Lawrence lectured, wrote, and most importantly gardened. She passed on her firsthand knowledge in writing and in person.

We Southerners are lucky. Our winters are mild and relatively short. Lawrence loved having flowers throughout most of the year. She especially favored hellebores and other early bloomers. In her 1957 book, *The Little Bulbs: A Tale of Two Gardens*, Lawrence says that "gardening, reading about gardening and writing about gardening are all one. No one gardens alone." Her words ring as true today as the day they were written. Her plants have been passed from gardener to gardener around the South, and many of us grow descendants in our gardens. Lawrence's hellebores are a cherished link to the past. In her preface to the 1984 edition of *A Southern Garden*, Lawrence wrote, "Gardens are so perishable; they live on only in books and letters; but what is gone before is not lost; the future is the past entered by another door."

In *Gardens in Winter* (1961), Lawrence notes that many of her hellebores, especially garden hybrids, came from her long-time correspondent and friend Carl Krippendorf, an Ohio gardener who "grew them from his own seed. He says he sowed the seed in the fall and pricked out the seedlings in flats in the spring. They were potted in the second fall and sent to me a year later. . . . By their fifth year from seed they were all blooming well. Now they are magnificent clumps up to a yard across." She laments that "none of the other species has prospered for me, though I have tried all I could get hold of."

Like Hunt, both Lawrence and Krippendorf gave seedlings of their hellebores to other gardeners. The plants moved out from their gardens like ripples from a stone tossed in water. A thriving amateur trade in plants and seed was underway. In her books, Lawrence recalls exchanging plants with other gardeners from places as varied as Oregon, New York, and Maine. She regularly corresponded with people from all walks of life. These correspondents included the author Eudora Welty and her agent, Diarmuid Russell, as well as a Mrs. Gladys Stamps, a homemaker from Bogue Chitto, Louisiana.

Lawrence shared her enthusiasm for hellebores with another bookworm, Katharine White, who was a friend and regular correspondent. White began writing about gardening near the end of her professional editing career. She penned a series of 14 pieces for the *New Yorker* over a 12-year period, many from her summerhouse and beloved garden in Maine. Most of her pieces are rambles through garden books and down garden paths. After her death, her husband, E. B. White, collected the essays into the book titled *Onward and Upward in the Garden* (1979). Of hellebores, White developed a fondness influenced no doubt by Lawrence. She writes while extolling the virtues of Lawrence's *Gardens in Winter* that "It is possible on the sub-zero day in February on which I happen to be writing this paragraph that my Christmas rose, *Helleborus niger*, may be putting out its blossoms under the snow drift that buries it." She also notes that their poisonous nature is no reason to shy away from growing them. After all, "even young potato sprouts—and potatoes themselves if their skin is green—are highly poisonous, while just outside the home grounds grow still more dangerous plants."

From Georgia, Connecticut, New York, and Ohio, hybrid hellebores were being traded and promoted. These plants and others were making waves with gardeners and writers around the country. Henry Ross of Gardenview Horticultural Park, Strongsville, Ohio, is a hellebore breeder and avid gardener. In correspondence with us, he recalls meeting Arthur Luedy in the early 1940s: "I did meet Arthur E. Luedy when I was a teenager. He had a great many *H. niger* in cold frames but did not have any *H.* ×*hybridus*. I recall once, his asking me if I would be willing to trade hybrids for *H. niger*, which I have never been able to grow. They always peter out and die for me although I now have about six or eight plants going again and am keeping my fingers crossed." Ross received his original "handful" of *H.* ×*hybridus* seedlings from a Georgia hobbyist, but he cannot remember the man's name.

Helen Van Pelt Wilson (1901–2003) wrote many widely read books between the 1940s and 1970s. She was interested in every aspect of gardening—a true addict! Her books on perennials, shade gardening, and winter gardens all mention hellebores. *Perennials Preferred* (1945) devotes the chapter "Important Winter Flowers" to *H. niger* and *H. ×hybridus*. She notes that "One of the loveliest, *Helleborus niger*, Christmas rose species, as well as the usual mixed varieties of *H. orientalis*, the Lenten rose, are readily available from many growers." Good news for gardeners looking for hellebores after the Second World War. Unfortunately, no sources were listed in the book, so we do not know who provided plants at this time, either locally or by mail.

Wilson gives as complete a treatment as we found in any book. She truly loved hellebores. She laments the scarcity of *H. foetidus* and comments that the small, greenish flowers of *H. viridis* (now *H. occidentalis*) "are attractive only to those who are collecting hellebores." Cut flowers were a passion for Wilson, so naturally winter blooms were coveted indoors as well as out. Much of her winter flower chapter is devoted to the joys of cut hellebore flowers. "It is, indeed, part of the pleasure of growing hellebores that they afford us the special delights of inconsistency. In December, with one hand to reach for galoshes as snow protection and with the other for the picking basket and shears is for most of us a rare experience. Midsummer blooms grown in the open on midwinter plants—therein lies the charm of the hellebores." Wilson elaborated further on her beloved hellebores in her 1978 offering, *Color in Your Winter Yard and Garden*. She adds *H. lividus corsicus* (now *H. argutifolius*) and *H. ×sternii* to her list and provides detailed information on culture and propagation.

Throughout the 1950s and 1960s, Lawrence, Wilson, and other avid gardeners continued to promote the joys of gardening and the merits of hellebores. What *The Joy of Cooking* was to the American kitchen, Louise and James Bush-Brown's *America's Garden Book*, first published in 1939, was to the American garden. Suburban gardeners across America turned to the revised 1958 edition for practical advice on what to plant and how to care for what they planted. This book taught our parents how to garden, and us as well. The book covers the mainstays, which include hellebores in charts but not in the body of the text. Several other garden writers emerged during these years, inspiring a new generation of gardeners. Every serious and aspiring rock gardener read H. Lincoln Foster's influential book *Rock Gardening* (reprinted by Timber Press in 1982). Foster (who died in 1989) notes that although other species are available, "the finest for flower color and size are *H. niger* and *H. orientalis*."

Changing times often produce cultural shifts. America was becoming a fast-paced, busy society with more women in the workforce and more people on the move. Increased wealth for the burgeoning middle class meant more leisure time. When people weren't working, they were relaxing. The suburban lifestyle of cocktail parties and barbecues meant that people were devoting less time to gardening and more time to other pursuits.

Modernism put a damper on the public's enthusiasm for plants. Certainly avid gardeners still grew hellebores and other perennials, but a new way of using the garden was emerging in the American popular culture. Thomas Church's influential 1955 book, *Gardens Are for People*, championed a new garden in keeping with modern architecture, modern lifestyles, and leisure. Church believed that people wanted their gardens to be nothing less than beautiful, but that "None but dyed in the wool gardeners want it to be any work." So, along with many other perennials, hellebores took a back seat to green carpets of turf, pachysandra, and vinca—but not for long.

The 1970s came, and with them, the first Earth Day. Once again, people began to pay attention to their natural surroundings, and the modern environmental movement was born. A new generation opened its eyes to the intricacy and diversity that the landscape provides. People began to fall in love with nature, plants, and gardening all over again. What was old became new. With this renaissance, the popular press soon responded, and many excellent garden books were published. Titles often focused on American natives, but there was ample interest in garden mainstays as well. *Wyman's Gardening Encyclopedia* (1971) describes culture and garden use of five hellebore species. Stanley Schuler's *The Winter Garden* (1972) promotes an appreciation of winter in the northeastern United States. His Connecticut garden became the inspiration for a romp through the snow and a search for satisfaction during the long, white winter. In his section on winter flowers, *H. niger* and *H. orientalis* are mentioned—*H. niger* blooming for Christmas and *H. orientalis* in early spring. Schuler laments, as others before him, that *H. foetidus* is hard to find. This plant is short lived and easily damaged by extreme cold. It was likely much more commonly and consistently grown in the southern United States, where it seeds freely.

Joseph Hudak is a landscape architect with a penchant for good plants. His 1976 book *Gardening with Perennials Month by Month* was widely read among professional and lay audiences. Now revised and updated (Timber Press, 1993), the book holds its own among the excellent encyclopedic works available. Hudak's remarks offer no new perspective, but his contribution is the promotion of hellebores and other perennials in a field that often undervalues herbaceous plants.

By the early 1980s, more Americans than ever were avidly pursuing the joys of gardening. Modern gardeners ascribe to the notion of tending a garden as an enjoyable part of the process. The work of the Washington, D.C.–based design firm Oehme, Van Sweden & Associates helped to popularize perennials with their exuberant public planting. The Perennial Plant Association was founded in 1984 with just more than 300 members (by 2005 it boasted more than 2000). Interest in choice plants was on the rise, and along with that came a renewed interest in hellebores. Gardening books poured from the publishing houses. A new British invasion ensued, fueled by America's renewed interest in anything English.

Two seminal works were published nearly back to back in England. Mathew's *Hellebores* (1989) and Rice and Strangman's *The Gardener's Guide to Growing Hellebores* (1993) exposed Americans to a world of hellebores never before dreamed possible. Not only were we shown firsthand the beautiful hybrids that were far superior to the pale or dull colors found at home, but the pictures and descriptions of the little-known Balkan species excited the imagination and incited lust in the hearts of those with a penchant for subtle, wild beauty.

Hellebores are among the most popular garden plants worldwide. Fine art, knickknacks, merchandizing schemes, and bylines abound.

Such avid American gardeners as David Culp, Glenn Withey, and Charles Price began heading to England to scout out new hybrids. They bought the best plants sold by Elizabeth Strangman at her Washfield Nursery and made the rounds among the other British gurus who offered superior plants. At the top of the list were Helen Ballard at Old Country, Kevin Belcher of Ashwood Nurseries, and Will McLewin of Phedar Nursery.

Though many plants were named, few made their way into the hands of gardeners. The gorgeous colors offered by Ballard and others were sold as named clones. These cultivars were notoriously slow to multiply, as division was the only means of increase. A beautiful, coveted plant was like a precious jewel. It wasn't until the English and ultimately American nurseries began selling selected colors of seed-grown plants that supply began to meet demand. Finally, people could purchase richly colored black, plum, yellow, and pure white plants in flower and be assured of getting exactly what the label claimed the package contained. Seed strains became more reliable, too. Nurseries began to sell color lines. If you wanted to gamble, you could buy seed or plants "from slaty blue," for example, and have a decent chance of getting a flower in the color range you desired. To this day, as good as some of the breeding lines are, if you want a guarantee of a certain shade or pattern, you must buy the plant in flower.

Phedar Nursery and Jelitto Seed Company began selling seeds of species hellebore, which made their way into retail outlets through wholesale nurseries such as Sunny Border. In correspondence with us, Sunny Border's Benneraup recalls that

> We started getting hellebore seeds from Jelitto in the middle '80s. In 1984 we listed only *H. niger* and *H. orientalis* (now *H. ×hybridus*) but added *H. foetidus* and *H. atrorubens* in 1986. The latter two were from Jelitto seeds. In the next several years we added a number of other species, most of which came from Jelitto seeds: *H. argutifolius*, *H. torquatus*, *H. multifidus* subsp. *hercegovinus*, *H. odorus*, and *H. viridis*. We had also been buying two-year-old seedlings of *H. orientalis* (*H. ×hybridus*) from Sam and Carleen [Jones of Piccadilly Farm] starting about that time, maybe a year or two earlier.

He continues

> We never bought seeds from the Wynn-Jones' nor from Jim Archibald, but, starting in the '90s, we did get seeds and still do get seeds of various species from Will McLewin. We first offered seedling *H. ×hybridus* 'Royal Heritage' strain from John Elsley in 1995 and D.L.C. Hybrids from David Culp in 1997. About the same time, we began buying the 'Winter Joy Bouquet' strain from Terry Hatch in New Zealand. He also has supplied us with *H. ×sternii* and some selections of other species such as *H. foetidus* 'Wester Flisk'.

These days, hellebores are the height of fashion. Why? Because they are remarkably beautiful. They open their nodding flowers in the bitter winter chill when few other plants dare to greet the new year. Beauty aside, they are tough, low-maintenance plants, and they are long-lived. It's no surprise in this busy age that hellebores appeal to both beginning and serious gardeners.

Hybrid garden hellebores (*H. ×hybridus*) have attained a level of perfection never before dreamed possible. Gone are the muddy mauves and greenish whites of Beebe Wilder's day. Through breeding programs in England, Holland, and the United States, today's hybrids offer a level of color saturation and form not seen just a few years ago. Hellebores surely occupy a preeminent place in American and European horticulture. May the cult continue to recruit new members!

Gardeners are rediscovering the subtle beauty that wild hellebores such as *H. odorus* add to shaded gardens. They are excellent companions for delicate wildflowers and minor bulbs that are easily dwarfed by larger hybrids.

3
HELLEBORES IN THE WILD

Having had an interest in Hellebores spanning some forty years I have at last
come to the conclusion that this small, loveable, but infuriatingly difficult genus
is almost impossible to classify. My love-hate relationship with Hellebores began
when as a child I found a hybrid of the *H. orientalis* type on a rubbish tip . . .
and brought it back into the garden. This early love of Hellebores led later on in life
to a series of memorable journeys in the Balkans and Turkey to study and
collect them, but inevitably there came a time when identification was necessary,
and this is where the hate crept in, for it is now clear to me that there is no
absolutely foolproof system of classification.

Brian Mathew in *Hellebores* (1989)

The most celebrated hellebore, the Christmas rose (*Helleborus niger*) grows wild on a slope in the Slovenian
Alps.

WE BELIEVE THAT THE BEST WAY to understand the garden requirements of a plant is to see it growing wild in its native haunts. Hellebores are no exception. It was a thrill for us to see their nodding flowers gracing Balkan meadows and woodlands while the first chartreuse blush appeared in the swelling tree buds. Equally compelling were thousands of *Helleborus multifidus* subsp. *bocconei* carpeting dry, rocky oak woodlands in autumn, with flowering drifts of *Cyclamen hederifolium* in the Tuscan hills above Cortona, Italy. That said, we have seen far too few of the species in their native habitats.

The majority of *Helleborus* species are found in a relatively small area of the eastern Mediterranean, in the former Yugoslav republic. The genus is distributed from the British Isles, east through Europe to Asia Minor. One outlying species hails from China. With such a wide distribution, we would expect speciation to have produced distinct *taxa* (any taxonomic category, such as species or subspecies, into which plants are classified). Unfortunately, things are not always so clear. In the eastern Mediterranean, the hellebores are downright perplexing. We asked Brian Mathew, author of the 1989 monograph *Hellebores*, if he would write a key to the species for this book. His reply was simple and given without hesitation: "No!" He said, in fact, that he regretted adding a key to the original monograph, as too many plants do not fit easily into our notions of species. Will McLewin concurs. He states emphatically that for plants in section *Helleborastrum*, which includes *H. orientalis* and other acaulescent species, unless you know the provenance (wild origin) of the plant in question, you cannot assign it conclusively to a species.

To say that the taxonomy of *Helleborus* species is in flux is putting it mildly. Both Mathew and McLewin agree that a "classic" example of each species is easily found in a population of otherwise ambiguously variable individuals. We traveled for two weeks with McLewin in Slovenia, Croatia, Bosnia, and Hungary, where he showed us many populations of plants that do indeed blur the lines between current species designations. Many fervent discussions while driving or sharing meals got us no closer to concurrence or to an answer to the conundrum. These conversations did, however, highlight the breadth of the problem. It seems to us that without a meaningful way to ascribe species, closely related taxa may represent evolving species with a common ancestor.

Traditionally, sexual characteristics, flower color, leaf shape, presence or absence of hairs, and the overall bearing of a plant are some of the characteristics used to designate different species. A species is traditionally described as a population of reproductively or geographically isolated plants. This is a hopelessly ineffective concept for hellebores. Natural variation is the rule in many species as currently described. Leaves vary in number of leaflets and degree of dissection as well as number and extent of marginal teeth. The character of bracts shows similar variation. Flower color is also widely variable. *Helleborus torquatus* is one of the most variable species. Flowers range from deep purple inside and out, purple on the outside with a green interior, to dove colored (soft gray) with green interior, to entirely green. *Helleborus atrorubens* shows similar variation.

WILL McLEWIN

Will McLewin (left), shown with Tim Murphy, led us through the Balkans to see firsthand the variability of wild hellebores.

If we had to choose one person to thank for giving us, and many others around the globe, access to the less well-known hellebore species, the choice would unanimously be Will McLewin of Phedar Research and Experimental Nursery, Stockport, U.K. Will has placed himself in harm's way more than once over the years in his effort to establish a bit of order in the chaos that surrounds the division of the different *Helleborus* species. Throughout the Balkan wars during the 1990s, Will continued to travel the back roads of Croatia, Bosnia, Slovenia, and the surrounding areas, studying the plants in their native locations. His rambles into territories occupied by the gun-toting militia of various warring factions have become the sort of legendary escapades about which folk songs are written. As a result of years spent on roads framed on each side with bombed-out buildings; months of study and writing; days upon days of seed gathering, cleaning, and sorting; and hours on his knees in the cold wet, Will is an unquestioned authority on the hellebore species.

Will did not intend to become the owner of a specialist nursery. He had a previous 27-year career as a lecturer in mathematics at Manchester University, which he abandoned when the lure of the hellebore became too strong to resist. The steeply sloped property he owns in Romiley, Stockport, a suburb of Manchester, England, is more suited to raising goats than raising plants in pots—at least flat-bottomed pots that require level ground to remain upright. Leveled areas are few. It is handy that Will is a runner and has developed his leg muscles by climbing all the major mountains in the European Alps.

Selling *Paeonia rockii* hybrids and other shrubby peonies, hellebore seed and plants, particularly species, from the nursery are only a small part of Will's contribution to the horticultural community. The primary role is the study and documentation of the extremely confusing hellebore taxonomy, which is vitally important. Will has gathered seeds from countless wild plants, and in doing so he has provided gardeners with the opportunity to grow some superb hellebores.

While Will's determination is what makes him such a good plant hunter, the same character traits seem to prevent some of the horticultural elite from hearing what he has to say. He refuses to compromise; he will not tone down his somewhat acerbic comments on other people's ideas, and this trait may prevent publication of his work. He is not going to write what he calls "the kind of pap about hellebores that is served up in most gardening magazines today," and therefore his work may not be read by any but the most dedicated plantsmen. This is unfortunate, since his writing is clear and precise; if you desire exhausting enthusiasm, dogged determination, exasperating exactitude, and argumentative authority, where hellebores are concerned, McLewin is "The Man."

MATHEW'S 1989 CLASSIFICATION OF THE GENUS *HELLEBORUS* LINN

Brian Mathew published the following treatment of the genus *Helleborus* in his 1989 monograph. He ascribed sections into which the different species were grouped based on morphological characteristics that were readily identifiable and observable, such as shape and number of carpels, presence or absence of persistent stems, persistent or deciduous foliage, divided or undivided bracts, and various floral characteristics, including number and size of follicles. Species within these sections closely share characteristics, and most are readily cross-fertile when geographical barriers to crossing are removed. In some cases, plants are cross-fertile between sections (see Chapter 4).

SECTION	SPECIES
Syncarpus	*H. vesicarius*
Griphopus	*H. foetidus*
Chenopus	*H. argutifolius, H. lividus*
Helleborus	*H. niger*
Helleborastrum	*H. atrorubens, H. cyclophyllus, H. dumetorum,*
	H. multifidus, H. odorus, H. orientalis, H. purpurascens,
	H. torquatus, H. viridis
Dicarpon	*H. thibetanus*

Some hellebores take foliage dissection to a high art, especially plants attributed by Mathew to *H. multifidus*. Several varieties are identified based on natural distribution and gross leaf morphology. Variation within the subspecies is rampant. The most dramatic is perhaps *H. multifidus* subsp. *hercegovinus*, which displays linear to threadlike leaflets.

As it is currently described, the genus contains 17 species, though many subspecies and a few forms are recognized. As variation is the rule, two individuals of a species can be distinctly different in the color and size of the flower, as well as in the dissection and serration of the leaves. In the wild, this variation is easily found among a single stand or from valley to valley across the plant's range. Some species are distinctive. Take *H. argutifolius*, for instance. Perhaps its island distribution accounts for its relative uniformity as a species. Why, then, do the Balkan species offer such a headache to botanists keen to place them in neat categories? This is a question that has plagued and fascinated McLewin and Mathew for decades.

Many will say, "Who cares? A good plant is a good plant regardless of name." That philosophy is not tenable for all of us. So as you read through the species descriptions in this chapter, bear in mind that these names are intended to make us conversant, but that many are likely to change in the years or decades to come. These species accounts are drawn from the most up-to-date work of McLewin and Mathew, most of which is serially published in *The New Plantsman*. Our hope is that in time, the collected articles of Will and Brian will become a revision of the genus *Helleborus* published in book form. Species accounts written by Gisela Schmiemann were also consulted. The descriptions and ranges included here are gleaned from their collected works and our limited field experience. This work is continuous, and we are certain that taxonomic revisions published after we go to press will no doubt make this treatment obsolete.

Helleborus argutifolius, Corsican hellebore

Section: *Chenopus*
Synonyms: *H. corsicus*, *H. lividus* subsp. *corsicus*, *H. trifolius* subsp. *corsicus*, *H. triphyllus*

A giant among hellebores, *H. argutifolius* is outstanding, with erect stems topped by open clusters of stiff, three-lobed, coarsely saw-toothed leaves. The foliage is handsome and rivals the flowers in ornamental value. Flower buds emerge from the apex of the overwintering, aboveground stem in winter or early spring. Waxy, nodding, apple-green flowers are carried in dense, multiflowered clusters. Mature plants can reach 2½ to 3 ft. (76 to 91 cm) tall and 3 to 4 ft. (91 to 122 cm) wide. One of the more tender species, references list it as hardy to Zone 7, though it has survived many years under mulch and snow in several Zone 4 gardens. Buds and stems are easily winter-killed below about 10° F (−12° C), though the foliage of flowerless plants is decidedly ornamental in its own right. The old stalks die as the fresh stems emerge for next year's blooms.

Cultivation

Grow in rich but well-drained soil in full sun or light shade. Plants are moderately drought-tolerant and grow vigorously for the first few years, though they can be short-lived where summers are hot and humid. Stems often flop in late summer or autumn, especially in the shade, creating a wide, leafy mass that needs ample room. Cut spent stems to the ground after seeds ripen. Plants self-sow sparingly. This is a plant for regions where winters are mild and summer humidity is low—Zones 7 to 9, or colder with protection.

Propagation

Corsican hellebore and other caulescent species are quite difficult to divide, but fortunately they are very fast and easy to propagate from seed. The central boss of stamens ripens from the outside into the center, and as stamens ripen, they curve outward. In the garden, plants are sometimes in flower when cold temperatures

Even in full sun, the top-heavy flowering stems of *H. argutifolius* form a decumbent ring around the newly emerging spring leaves.

prevent the flight of pollinators; no pollinators means no pollination and consequently no seed. Lightly brush the flowers or hand-pollinate them to ensure seed set.

The seeds of *H. argutifolius* are a bit larger than those of other species, and they are dark brown or black when ripe. As with most species, fresh seed germinates best. Germination occurs later than other species, usually beginning in January or February in our experience.

Cultivars and seed strains

At this time, most cultivars are grown from seed and are variable. 'Little Erbert', a short cultivar that grows from 12 to 18 in. (30 to 45 cm) tall, originated from a seedling that appeared at Ashwood Nurseries. Plants grow into a compact, bushy mound. 'Janet Starnes' is an 18 to 24 in. (45 to 60 cm) variegated selection, produced both by seed and tissue culture. The blue-green foliage is heavily speckled with splashes of cream, often pink-tipped on new growth, but the foliage may not show variegation if grown in deep shade. Flowers are pale chartreuse green. It is often not a strong grower. Large Flowered Form is a seed strain said to be from Bodnant Garden in Wales. The original plant won an award from the RHS in 1960. No doubt it is far removed from the archetype, with flowers that range from semirounded to those that display significant gaps between each sepal. 'Pacific Frost' strain comes from the beautiful garden of Pam Frost, near Vancouver, British Columbia, Canada. This seed strain produces short, 18 to 24 in. (45 to 60 cm) stems with very heavy cream speckles and pink to rose tinted new growth. It is often a weak grower. 'Silver

Lace' is from RD Plants Nursery in Devon (Rodney Davey and Lynda Windsor). First offered as 'RD Silver', this selection displays new foliage with an overlay of cream veins on silvery green. Foliage tends to "green up" when mature.

Description of *Helleborus argutifolius* Viviani

Caulescent. Stem leaves are evergreen, stiff, glabrous, and trifoliate. The outer two segments are each unequal, rounded to the outside, and inwardly flattened; the central leaflet is elliptical with a wedge-shaped base, 3 to 9 in. (8 to 23 cm) long and 1½ to 3 in. (4 to 8 cm) wide. Leaflets are medium green, coarsely serrate to spiny dentate. Petioles are variable, to 8 in. (20 cm). Flowers are 15 to 30 in number at the apex of the stem, pale green, 1 to 2 in. (3 to 5 cm) wide, and broadly bowl shaped. Nectaries are green, 10 to 14 in number, short-stalked, and tubular. Bracts at the base of the inflorescence are simple, leafy, and serrate to entire. Three to five follicles are ¾ to 1 in. (2 to 3 cm) long at maturity. Stems can be 3 to 6 ft. (1 to 2 m) tall. Rootstocks are stout with thin roots, producing new upright to decumbent stems in summer, which die the following year after fruiting. The name was published in 1824 from a specimen collected in Corsica; it has been cultivated since at least 1625.

Range and habitat

Helleborus argutifolius is endemic to the islands of Corsica and Sardinia from sea level to 7500 ft. (2300 m). Plants grow on open, rocky hillsides, in scrub and along the banks of streams. This species is still fairly common in the wild. Rice and Strangman (1993) list *Cyclamen repandum*, *Euphorbia characias* subsp. *wulfenii*, and *Lavandula stoechas* as wild companions.

Helleborus atrorubens

Section: *Helleborastrum*

Synonyms: *H. atropurpureus*, *H. dumetorum* subsp. *atrorubens*, *H. viridis* subsp. *atrorubens*

Horticulture has muddied the identity of *H. atrorubens*, an exquisite and delicate purple to green flowered species from Eastern Europe. Historically, nurseries sold a plum-flowered selection of *H. orientalis* under this name, which some call "atrorubens of gardens," signifying that the plant is not the true species. Its true identity is *H. orientalis* subsp. *abchasicus*. *Helleborus atrorubens* is a delicate, quietly sophisticated plant, 12 to 18 in. (30 to 45 cm) tall, with rather open scapes bearing ¾ in. (2 cm) flowers on short pedicels if the tips of long, straight peduncles. In select forms, the flowers are deep violet-purple with sea-green interiors. Flower color varies among individuals from purple-black or pale red-violet to green. Mixed colonies with green, dull red, and intermediate flowers occur. The deciduous, pedately divided leaves have three elongated, oval leaflets, toothed above the middle. The paired, outermost segments are often further dissected into three to five narrow divisions each. New leaves are

In the wilds of Slovenia, *H. atrorubens* varies in color from plum-purple to red.

In the garden, *H. atrorubens* forms a full-crowned, richly colored plant of exceptional beauty.

sometimes tinged with purple in spring. Until recently, this species was scarce in cultivation but is now regularly listed in catalogs of specialty nurseries.

Cultivation
Plants require humus-rich, well-drained, circumneutral soil for best growth. Choose a spot in sun or shade, as plants are widely adaptable. Mature clumps exhibit many tightly packed stems and form leafy summer clumps. Though often one of the first species to go dormant, foliage may persist into winter where soil moisture and nutrition are ample. In the U.S. Pacific Northwest and other winter-wet areas, plants are susceptible to black spot and botrytis. This species is hardy from Zones 4 to 8.

Propagation
Collect ripe seeds in early summer just as the capsules begin to split, and sow the seeds without delay. Germination begins in approximately six months, after several weeks of cold temperatures. For full germination details, see Chapter 7.

Description of *Helleborus atrorubens* Waldst. & Kit.
Acaulescent. The basal leaves are deciduous, glabrous, and pedate with three primary segments. The central segment is undivided, 4 to 8 in. (10 to 20 cm) long and ¾ to 1 in. (2 to 3 cm) wide. The outer two segments are each divided into three to five additional segments for a total of seven to eleven. Segments are broadly lance shaped to elliptical and somewhat thin textured. Margins are coarsely serrate. The petiole is 6 to 10 in. (15 to 25 cm) long. Two to three, and occasionally five, flowers appear per scape and are purple, violet, red, or pale green, with a green interior that is sometimes striped or rarely spotted with violet. Flowers are 1½ to 2 in. (4 to 5 cm) wide and saucer to cup shaped, unscented. Nectaries number 15 to 20, are entire, and green, stalked, funnel shaped, and curved outward. Bracts are leafy, deeply divided into three to five serrate segments. The five to six follicles are ¾ to 1 in. (2 to 3 cm) long at maturity. Scapes are from 10 to 12 in. (25 to 30 cm) tall. The rootstock is stout, with thick roots. Its name was first published in 1812 from a specimen collected in Croatia.

Range and habitat
This species has a limited range in eastern Slovenia and northwestern Croatia west of Zagreb, where it grows in open woods, fields, and pastures in low mountains. Plants persist after the forest is cleared but are often obscured by bracken and other summer vegetation. At one site we visited in Slovenia, plants were short in stature and produced more leaves than flowers due to the influence of regular mowing. At other sites, many clumps were extremely robust. Wild companions include *Allium ursinum*, *Anemone nemorosa* and *A. ranunculoides*, *Corydalis solida*, *Galanthus nivalis*, and *Pulmonaria saccharata*. In dense woods, we found smaller plants growing with *Cardamine enneaphyllos*, *Epimedium alpinum*, *Erythronium dens-canis*, *Hedera helix*, and *Scopolia carniolica*. Plants were more vigorous in rough grass at the edge of the woods in more sun.

Green-flowered plants of *H. atrorubens* may result from intergrades or from lack of anthocyanin pigments that tint the flowers red.

Plants of *H. atrorubens* often persist in pastures and other agricultural lands where they are avoided by cows. The foliage varies between individual plants.

Though similar in size and flower color to *H. atrorubens*, plants of *H. croaticus* usually have fine hairs on the pedicels and bracts of the inflorescence.

Helleborus croaticus

Section: *Helleborastrum*
Synonym: *H. atrorubens* subsp. *croaticus*

This Croatian endemic is one of the newest taxa described at the rank of species. On first glance, the cultivated forms available in America appear indistinguishable from some forms of *H. atrorubens*. Many of the distinguishing characters are apparent only at the cytological level. Provenance is an important factor in distinguishing these two taxa. There are, however, a few characteristics that are generally, though by no means consistently, visible that a keen observer can use to distinguish distinctive individuals of the two species. Keep in mind that *H. croaticus* and *H. atrorubens* are closely allied, and like many Eastern European species, they are likely evolving into or away from truly distinct taxa.

The flowers of *H. croaticus* are generally purple to violet, occasionally sea-green on the outside, and green on the inside. Flower color and shape can help with identification, but look first to the pedicels. The pedicels and peduncles of *H. croaticus* are often hairy. Hairs are sometimes found on the bracts and veins on the undersides of the leaves. As for flowers, purple staining is often present on the inside of the sepals and usually occurs along parallel lines starting at the center of the sepal and decreasing in length and intensity of color as they move outward toward the sepal edge. The overall effect is like a starburst, similar to the pattern present in some clones of *H. torquatus*.

Cultivation

Plant in sun or partial shade in humus-rich loam or clay soil. Plants go dormant by the end of summer. This easy and beautiful plant produces a full, rounded crown of leaves when mature. Once clumps reach flowering size, they mature quickly, becoming multistemmed in two to three years. Leaf spot and botrytis are sometimes problematic in winter-wet regions such as the U.S. Pacific Northwest. It is hardy in Zones 4 to 8.

Propagation

Propagation is similar to that of *H. atrorubens*. See the section dealing with that species for information.

Description of *Helleborus croaticus* Martinis

Acaulescent. The basal leaves are deciduous, sparsely pubescent, and pedate with three primary segments. The outer two segments are each divided into five additional segments. Segments are lance shaped to narrowly elliptical, and slightly leathery; they are 4 to 8 in. (10 to 20 cm) long and ¾ to 1 in. (2 to 3 cm) wide. Margins are finely serrate. The petiole is 6 to 10 in. (15 to 25 cm) long. Flowers grow two to four per scape; are purple, red, or green; 1½ to 2 in. (4 to 5 cm) wide; cup shaped; and unscented. Bracts are leafy; divided into three to five slender, serrate segments; and pubescent. Pedicels and peduncles are pubescent. The five to six follicles are ¾ to 1 in. (2 to 3 cm) long at maturity. The scape rises up to 15 in. (38 cm) tall. The rootstock is stout with thick roots. Its name was first published in 1789 from a specimen collected in Croatia.

Range and habitat

Helleborus croaticus is limited to a few locations in a small area of northern Croatia, where it grows in open woods and fields, often in floodplains or terraces in wide stream valleys. We observed plants at two stations. The first was wooded with a closed canopy of *Carpinus betulus* and occasional *Fagus*. The soil was rich and loamy, with a good humus layer. Herbaceous companions included *Allium ursinum*, *Anemone*

Magnification reveals the fine hairs that usually cover the pedicels and bract veins of *H. croaticus* at flowering.

Helleborus croaticus has a very limited range in northern Croatia, where it grows in woods and meadows. Plants also persist after clearing in pastures and fields.

nemorosa, *Corydalis cava*, *Lathyrus vernus*, *Vinca minor*, and *Caltha* in the low places adjacent to the scattered plants. The second station was an open field with low grass trimmed by grazing. Individual plants were large and often grew in dense colonies. Few companions were present, presumably due to grazing.

Helleborus cyclophyllus
Section: *Helleborastrum*
Synonym: *H. viridis* var. *cyclophyllus*

Helleborus cyclophyllus is a commanding and gardenworthy species with large, apple-green, often outfacing flowers on multistemmed clumps. We love green flowers, and to our eyes this species is the showiest "greenie" of the genus. It is closely allied to *H. odorus*. In fact, some botanists consider it a southern expression of that species. The visible characteristics botanists use to distinguish this species are variable and of dubious merit according to some. Most often mentioned is the fully deciduous foliage of *H. cyclophyllus*, which, unlike *H. odorus*, emerges in spring coated in silken, silvery hairs. In addition, the carpels are free at their bases, while those of *H. odorus* are usually fused.

The apple-green flowers of *H. cyclophyllus* are often outfacing and showy in their own right. They also contribute green and yellow flowers to garden hybrids.

Outfacing, 1 to 2 in. (3 to 5 cm), deep green flowers make this a good breeding parent, potentially passing these traits to offspring. The scent is variable and vanishes after plants are pollinated. The fragrance varies from somewhat sweet to slightly "skunky."

The black hellebore of antiquity may have been *H. cyclophyllus*. This species grows on Mount Parnassus, Mount Helicon, and Mount Olenos, classic localities mentioned in the ancient Greek literature. The name black hellebore is said to arise from the dark nature of the roots, which dry to black. Another theory purports that the name comes from its poisonous, or black, nature. In any case, this is likely the plant described by the ancients, though it is possible that *H. orientalis* deserves the moniker.

Cultivation

Helleborus cyclophyllus is easy to grow but a bit slow to reach full size. It blooms heaviest in sun or light shade but tolerates partial deciduous shade in summer. It does not perform well in dense shade, as the foliage is absent in winter. It grows best in deep, rich circumneutral loam or clay soil. This species is less hardy than other acaulescent species, to perhaps Zones 5 to 8, or colder with protection.

Propagation

Its propagation is similar to that of *H. atrorubens*. See the section dealing with that species for information.

Description of *Helleborus cyclophyllus* (A. Braun) Boissier

Acaulescent. Its basal leaves are mostly deciduous, pubescent on the underside, with veins fully pubescent beneath, and pedate with three primary segments. The central segment is divided or not, 6 to 8 in. (15 to 20 cm) long and up to 2 in. (5 cm) wide. The outer two segments are each divided into five to seven additional segments, which are broadly oblanceolate to elliptical, and thick textured; their margins are finely serrate. The petiole is up to 16 in. (40 cm) long. Scented flowers number three to seven per scape, are a deep apple-green, 2 to 3 in. (5 to 7 cm) wide, and bowl to saucer shaped. The nectaries are green, stalked, and widely funnel shaped with slightly toothed margins. The leafy bracts are divided into three to five serrate segments. Three to six follicles are free at the base and ¾ in. (2 cm) long at maturity. The scape is 8 to 16 in. (20 to 40 cm) tall. The rootstock is stout, with thick roots. Its name was first published in 1867 from a specimen collected in Greece.

Range and habitat

This more southern species is found from Greece north to Montenegro, southern Bulgaria, and Albania. It intergrades in range and character with *H. odorus*; hence, the contested validity of this plant as a distinct species. *Helleborus cyclophyllus* is often found near sea level, whereas *H. odorus* is most often an upland and mountain species. McLewin postulated that this species may be an intermediate between *H. odorus* and *H. orientalis*, but extensive fieldwork is required before this or any other classification theory can be proposed. Plants grow in open woods and mountain pastures, also on rocky limestone slopes in scrub or in the open. We have not seen this plant in the wild, but the literature reports *Colchicum triphyllum*, *Corydalis cava*, *Crocus biflorus*, *Muscari botryoides*, and *Scilla bifolia* as companions.

Helleborus dumetorum

Section: *Helleborastrum*
Synonyms: *H. pallidus*, *H. vaginatus*, *H. viridis* var. *dumentorum*

Many consider *H. dumetorum* a collector's plant, grown for a complete hellebore collection rather than for horticultural prowess. We are very fond of this delicate green-flowered species, though it is far from showy in the traditional sense. It has a quiet charm reminiscent of some of our native spring wildflowers. The small apple-green flowers are occasionally pale-edged, almost like a frosted picotee. Flowering scapes bear conspicuous leafy bracts that add to the early display. Double-flowered selections occur. The divided leaves superficially resemble *H. atrorubens*, but this plant is not as robust. This is one of the few Balkan species that is usually recognizable by its foliage alone. The leaves often, but not consistently, resemble a horseshoe; their overall structure brings maidenhair fern (*Adiantum pedatum*) to mind. Emerging leaves are occasionally stained with deep red, but mature foliage is green. The leaves are soft and thin textured and do not overwinter. Plants bloom in late winter and early spring. The fresh leaves often obscure the flowers as the seed ripens.

Though small and green-flowered, *H. dumetorum* is a charming and gardenworthy species. Flowers seem to smother the dense leafy clumps.

Cultivation

Plant this understated species in humus-rich, well-drained clay or loam soil in sun to partial shade. In gardens, it seems to thrive in lighter soil than others. Avoid dense shade as plants are deciduous and need spring and summer sun to set good bloom. Plants may go dormant in late summer. This species is hardy from Zones 4 to 8.

Propagation

Its propagation is similar to that of *H. atrorubens*. See the section dealing with that species for information.

Description of *Helleborus dumetorum* Waldst. & Kit.

Acaulescent. Its basal leaves are deciduous; glabrous to finely puberulent on the underside of veins; pedate, and horseshoe shaped with three primary segments. The outer two segments are each divided into three or more segments. Segments are narrowly lance shaped to nearly elliptical, but generally linear, thinner textured than other species, 2 to 4 in. (5 to 10 cm) long and ⅜ to 1 in. (1 to 3 cm) wide. The margins are finely serrate. Petioles are 4 to 8 in. (10 to 20 cm) long. Two to four flowers appear per scape, and are pale green, ⅜ to 1 in. (1 to 3 cm) long, and somewhat funnel shaped. Eight to twelve nectaries are green, short-stalked, out-curved, and funnel shaped with unevenly toothed margins. Bracts are leafy, divided, and serrate. Two to five follicles are about ¾ in. (2 cm) long at maturity. The scape is 6 to 10 in. (15 to 25 cm) tall. The rootstock is stout, with thin roots. The name was first published in 1809 from material collected in "Hungaria."

The distinctive foliage of *H. dumetorum* punctuates a carpet of *Anemone nemorosa* and *Cardamine eannophyllos* in a Croatian woodland.

Range and habitat

Helleborus dumetorum grows in scattered colonies in northeastern Slovenia, southwest Austria, Croatia, and Hungary—in woods and fields, occasionally on flat land at the bases of slopes. We saw many colonies of this favored species, usually at the bases of rocky slopes with limestone outcroppings and scattered talus. Plants generally grow adjacent to streams in wide, flat floodplains. Often the plants form dense drifts, accented by *Ajuga reptans*, *Anemone nemorosa*, *Corydalis cava*, *Galanthus nivalis*, *Hacquetia epipactis*, and *Leucojum vernum*. Plants are often swamped by tall vegetation in summer, but in many cases, they grow in fairly open, groomed hornbeam (*Carpinus*) and birch (*Betula*) woods with little understory of shrub layer. In one field we visited, plants grew along side *Anemone ranunculoides*, *Fritillaria meleagris*, and *Urtica dioica*.

Helleborus foetidus, stinking hellebore, bear's foot
Section: *Griphopus*
Synonyms: *Helleboraster foetidus*, *Helleborus nemoralis*

The early flowers of *H. foetidus* never fail to delight gardeners. This voluminous species, with its spidery black-green foliage and bright chartreuse bracts and flowers, may stand nearly 3 ft. (1 m) tall on succulent green stems. Pedate leaves display five to ten narrow, toothed segments—the outermost with three or more divisions. Don't let the name "stinking hellebore" dissuade you from growing this beauty. The undeserved name refers to the slightly musky odor of the crushed leaves. Uncrushed,

The early green flowers of the misnamed stinking hellebore, *H. foetidus*, are scentless to slightly musky and carried in beautiful, dense terminal clusters above the black-green foliage.

the leaves emit little or no scent. The flowers run the gamut from sweetly scented to slightly skunky or scentless. The large flower trusses are carried at the top of year-old stems. Each nodding, cylindrical flower is chartreuse to apple-green, often with a red-brown lip. Mature clumps are multistemmed and several feet wide. The bracts become conspicuous before the new year, and branched flower clusters begin to elongate in early winter. In a warm winter, buds appear early, though late winter to early spring (February and March in North America) are the main flowering months.

Cultivation

Plant *H. foetidus* in light to partial shade in humus-rich, well-drained soil. This species has a very small root system compared to other caulescent species, especially in proportion to its height. These shallow roots often provide a poor foundation for a plant that can reach 3 ft. (1 m) or more in height. Perhaps this is one of the reasons *H. foetidus* is prone to leaning or even toppling over in some garden situations, particularly in moist soil. We lose more *H. foetidus* to overwatering than any other cause. The roots seem to be very susceptible to rot; dry soil certainly seems to help prevent this problem. It is hardy from Zones 6 to 8, though it is often reported as hardy to Zone 4 or 5. In our experience, the growing point, which never seems to go fully dormant, is damaged in areas colder than Zone 6, even when protected by snow.

Plants are easy to grow and free-seeding. They often bloom the second year from seed. Though they are often short-lived, plants can shrivel and die with no warning, their fecund nature assures a ready supply of replacements. Cut old stems to the ground after new foliage appears to keep the clump vigorous. After three years of bloom, plants often lose vigor; the lower portions of the stems become bare, and the remaining foliage is often undersized and ratty. Remove underperforming plants to make way for vigorous seedlings. Recruits are easy to move when young. Use self-sown plants to fill in gaps or create new plantings. Display this species in drifts for best show, as single plants usually look forlorn. Plants seem indifferent to soil, as long as it is not sodden, especially in winter. In their native haunts, they usually grow on calcareous soils.

Propagation

Helleborus foetidus is easily grown from seed; fresh seed gives the best germination. In our experience, seed stored for several months does not germinate until the second year after planting. When the ripe carpels open and the fresh seeds are exposed, they are often connected along the spine like peas in a pod. They separate as they dry. A word of warning: the alkaloids in this species are more potent than in others. The follicles contain irritating oil that can make fingertips numb or tingly.

Cultivars and seed strains

All of the currently available strains of *H. foetidus* are grown from seed and as a result plants are variable. Seedlings of golden forms vary from bright gold to a green-gold color. Variegated forms are also variable from seed. Some are lightly spotted with yellow or cream, while others are so heavily spotted that little green is visible. All show their best colors on newly emerging foliage; the color tends to fade as the leaf ages.

All seed strains of *H. foetidus* are cross-fertile. Different seed strains with different ornamental attributes, when planted together, produce offspring with a variety of traits. Many seed strains come relatively true from seed if kept in reproductive isolation—that is, if not planted near other selections and allowed to cross-pollinate. If you wish to keep seed strains as pure as possible, plant them in different areas of the garden or restrict your garden to the one strain you like best. Common practice is to rogue out any seedlings that do not visually match the characters of the named strain, and regard the rest as true to type.

'Bowles' is an older strain said to have originated in Italy and grown at Myddleton House, the garden of E. A. Bowles. It has very divided foliage similar to plants listed as Italian Form. 'Chedglow' strain is one of the first golden forms, from Martin Cragg-Barber's Natural Selection Nursery. This strain may "green-up" in summer in warm-weather gardens. 'Chedglow Variegated' strain is the speckled form of 'Chedglow'; its spotting varies from plant to plant. 'Curio' strain is another Natural Selection Nursery introduction from Cragg-Barber. This selection is variegated in creamy white. 'Gertrude Jekyll', sometimes known as 'Miss Jekyll's Scented', is a fragrant strain. As with all other scented hellebores, the fragrance of these plants varies from nose to nose. On a warm day, plants are abuzz with insects, indicating that they find them desirable even if we do not always catch the scent.

Silver foliage is common among certain strains of *H. foetidus*, and plants come fairly true from seed when isolated. 'Wester Flisk' is an old strain still popular today.

'Gold Bullion' is an extremely variable commercial seed strain. Foliage varies from all gold, to gold variegated, to green tipped and speckled with gold. Blooms are a very light primrose yellow. This strain is possibly a reselection of 'Chedglow Variegated' strain. It was introduced in the U.S. by Pine Knot Farms. 'Golden Showers' strain was introduced by Plant Delights Nursery and selected from a seedling in their gardens. Its foliage is green streaked with gold that extends up the petioles into the flowers. 'Green Giant' strain from Phedar Nursery produces tall, 4 to 5 ft. (1 to 1.5 m) stems with light green foliage that is cut into many fine segments; its flowers are pale green. The Italian Form is a large, 5 ft. (1.5 m) plant that produces many clusters of flowers; it is grown originally from seed collected in Italy.

'Piccadilly' strain is a Pine Knot Farms selection; the 3 ft. (1 m) tall plants have silvered foliage and red stems, similar to the 'Wester Flisk' strain. It is vigorous and adapted to warm-weather areas. Pine Knot Variegated Form was produced from crossing seedlings of variegated plants grown from Phedar Nursery seed. The plants reach 18 to 24 in. (45 to 60 cm) and are heavily spotted and blotched with yellow and cream. New and cold-weather growth is often infused with pink. 'Pontarlier' is a midsized strain with medium-green foliage; it may bloom early in some climates. 'Red Silver' strain, from Northwest Garden Nursery in Eugene, Oregon, is shorter than most, 24 to 30 in. (60 to 75 cm), with very silvery foliage and red stems and petioles, with red extending into the base of the flower.

'Ruth' strain is a Phedar Nursery selection with deep, dark green cut foliage and heavy flower production. 'Sienna' strain is another Phedar Nursery introduction, from seed collected near Sienna, Italy. Plants have black-green foliage and pale chartreuse flowers. 'Sopron' strain is a Phedar Nursery selection from seed collected near Sopron, Hungary, with dark foliage overlaid with silver. 'Tros-os-Montes' is a seed strain from near the Spanish/Portuguese border, with dark green serrate leaves, and whose flowers do not have the red lip. 'Wester Flisk', a group of seed strains from the Firth of Tay, Scotland, has gray-green foliage and red stems and petioles, especially in winter. As with all seed strains, plants can vary greatly.

Description of *Helleborus foetidus* Linn.

Caulescent. Stem leaves are evergreen, leathery, glabrous, and pedate, with seven to eleven segments. The central leaflet is lanceolate, 8 in. (20 cm) long, and ¾ to 1 in. (2 to 3 cm) wide, with divided outer segments. Leaflets are a deep black-green to silvery green, serrate to nearly entire. Petioles are variable, to 8 in. (20 cm). Flowers are numerous at the apex of the stem, pale green, about ¾ in. (2 cm) wide, and bell shaped, unscented or scented. Nectaries number 8 to 12 and are short-stalked, tubular, and toothed at the apex. Bracts at the base of the inflorescence are simple to weakly divided, leafy, and entire. Three follicles are about ¾ in. (2 cm) long at maturity. Stems can reach up to 30 in. (75 cm) tall. The rootstock is small without well-developed rhizomes, and roots are thin and fibrous, producing new upright stems in summer that die the following year after fruiting. Plants are often short-lived. It was introduced from the native range "Germania, Helvetica, Gallia" in 1753.

Range and habitat

Helleborus foetidus is widespread in Western Europe, from Portugal east to Hungary, north to Britain and Germany, in a variety of woodland areas. This species prefers limestone-derived soils and grows from sea level to 7000 ft. (2135 m). We have seen plants in oak and mixed oak-pine woods in Tuscany and Umbria, Italy, growing with *Cyclamen hederifolium* and *Helleborus multifidus* subsp. *bocconei*. In England, plants grow in coppice woodlands of *Carpinus* with *Hyacinthoides non-scripta* and *Hedera*.

Helleborus lividus

Section: *Chenopus*
Synonyms: *H. corsicus* subsp. *lividus, H. trifolius* (not *H. trifolius* Linn., which is *Coptis groenlandica*), *H. triphyllus*

This most tender of the hellebores is marginally hardy in Zone 7, and the flower buds are killed at 10° F (−12° C), though the plants usually survive. Some believe hardy individuals of this species represent *H.* ×*sternii*, a hybrid with *H. argutifolius*. The stiff, three-lobed, slaty green leaves are glossy and attractively mottled with cream or silver. The petioles and undersides of the leaves vary from rosy red to green. Outfacing, bowl to saucerlike flowers are rose-pink to madder, occasionally silver-green. Flowers flatten as they age. In areas where hardiness is a factor, containerized plants are often placed in the garden for the summer.

Though *H. lividus* has limited hardiness, plants respond well to container culture in areas where they are not hardy.

Cultivation

Plant in rich, well-drained soil in full sun to light shade. Protect plants from extreme cold with a light mulch of straw or chopped leaves. Take care not to smash or smother plants with a dense cover; they need light and good air circulation even in winter. Plants grow easily in containers kept in a cool, bright greenhouse or a garden room during the winter. In cold zones, container culture is preferable to winter damage. It is hardy from Zones 8 to 9 and marginally hardy in Zone 7.

Propagation

While difficult to divide, *H. lividus* is perhaps the easiest of all the hellebore species to grow from seed. It is the first to begin to germinate, often as early as mid-October at Pine Knot Farms. Plants often bloom approximately 18 months from sowing, beginning to flower in late winter (February at Pine Knot) the year after germination. While *H. lividus* does not seem to produce as many stamens as some of the other species, plentiful pollen on the flowers assure pollination.

Helleborus lividus seedlings grow rapidly. Shortly after germination, they produce their first true leaves, which are more prominently veined than the mature foliage, with sharp teeth along the edges. Seeds are quite a bit smaller than other species—¹⁄₁₆ in. (2 mm)—with a well-developed elaiosome. *Helleborus lividus* has shallow roots and often dies in overly moist soil. Leaves are susceptible to black spot and sooty mold.

Cultivars and seed strains

Despite its frost-tenderness, plants are used extensively in hybridization. Two outstanding crosses are available. *Helleborus ×sternii*, with *H. argutifolius* as the second parent, is fertile and excels in its stiff, mottled foliage and its spreading trusses of soft green to creamy rose flowers. Crosses with *H. niger* produce the sought-after *H. ×ballardiae*, noted for its black-green leaves with light veining and rose-tinted flowers in clusters of three. (See Chapter 4 for more information.)

Description of *Helleborus lividus* Aiton

Caulescent. Its stem leaves are evergreen, somewhat stiff, glabrous, and trifoliate. The outer two segments are each unequal, rounded to the outside, and inwardly flattened; the central leaflet is elliptical with a wedge-shaped base, 4 to 8 in. (10 to 20 cm) long, and 2 to 4 in. (5 to 10 cm) wide. Leaflets are a deep gray-green, often stained with purple and marked with cream to silver reticulate venation, and entire or weakly serrate. Petioles are variable, to 4 in. (10 cm). Five to ten flowers appear at the apex of the stem and are a pale sea-green, often suffused with a dull rose-purple, 1 to 2 in. (3 to 5 cm) wide, and broadly bowl shaped. Ten nectaries are green to plum, short-stalked, and tubular. The three-lobed bracts at the base of the inflorescence are leafy, serrate to entire. Follicles usually number three to five and are about ½ in. (1 to 2 cm) long at maturity. Stems are 18 to 24 in. (45 to 60 cm) tall. Rootstocks are stout, with thin roots, producing new upright to decumbent annual stems that die the following year after fruiting. Its name was published in 1789 from an illustration in *Curtis's Botanical Magazine*.

Range and habitat

This species is endemic to Majorca and now quite rare in the wild. Plants persist in out-of-the-way places, often in rock crevices and dense thickets in the mountains. We have not seen this plant in nature.

Helleborus multifidus
Section: *Helleborastrum*

This variable but beautiful species is noteworthy for its delicately divided foliage and its apple- to lime-green, occasionally purple-tinged, flowers. The emerging leaves of *H. multifidus* are often tinted red. Several subspecies are recognized that vary in height, flower size, and degree of leaf dissection. Considered more a collector's plant than one that provides dramatic garden display, it is nonetheless enchanting. Some of the subspecies are quite showy. McLewin and Thomsen are currently overhauling the species (see "The Future of Hellebore Taxonomy" at the end of this chapter); since the work is not yet published as of this writing, we decided to maintain Mathew's classification.

We fell in love with this species in Croatia. The plants we saw belong botanically to what is currently classified as subspecies *multifidus*. They were common and

Many Croatian populations of *H. multifidus* subsp. *multifidus* contain plants with flowers ranging from pure green to purple. This variation may result from hybridization with *H. torquatus* from nearby Bosnian populations.

A thin lip of red graces the sepals of this putative plant of *H. multifidus* subsp. *multifidus* growing in the loamy soil at the base of a limestone sinkhole in Croatia.

widespread in some areas and always beautiful. The base color was green, but many individuals had red-edged or dark-tinted flowers. In one region, in a deep limestone doline (sinkhole), we found plants with deep purple flowers indistinguishable from *H. torquatus* growing nearby in Bosnia. These populations may be distinct species. Leaf dissection was extremely variable, with many of the old, dried leaves showing sixty or more segments, while others had just nine. We believe that these plants are underutilized in gardens. As more seed is distributed and more plants become available, we hope to see this group of species more widely appreciated and grown.

On the beautiful Adriatic Coast, we saw *H. multifidus* subsp. *istriacus* growing in scrubby woodlands with huge old clumps of *Cyclamen repandum*, which were in full bloom. The hellebore foliage was well expanded and widely diverse in the number and width of segments as well as in the degree of serration. In the adjacent coastal mountains, plants were in full bloom, surrounded by a recent snowfall. No new foliage was evident, although the flowers were large and attractive.

The large-flowered *H. multifidus* subsp. *bocconei* is a beautiful garden plant that deserves wider cultivation. The flowers are green to creamy white, saucer shaped, and nearly as large as some forms of *H. orientalis*. The coarsely toothed foliage is quite attractive and makes a bold summer statement as a ground cover under open-crowned shrubs such as beautyberry (*Callicarpa*).

The prize for gorgeous foliage undoubtedly goes to *H. multifidus* subsp. *hercegovinus*. The thin, spidery segments form a beautifully tattered parasol held flat atop the stout petioles. The flowers are smallish and yellow-green, attractive enough but certainly not as commanding as the foliage. Plants bloom early with nodding, slightly cupped flowers on 8 to 14 in. (20 to 36 cm) stems. Old clumps are quite large, with eight to twelve scapes laden with flowers. The elegantly divided foliage is a real summer asset that fades away in autumn.

Cultivation
Sun to partial shade suits this species, which seems to require more sun than others for best growth and flowering. Plants tolerate a wide range of soils, but best growth is attained in deep, rich loam or clay soil that stays evenly moist. That said, plants are widely tolerant of summer dryness. This early bloomer is occasionally damaged by late frost, making it susceptible to bacterial and fungal diseases. In winter-wet regions, plants may underperform. Provide good drainage and perhaps a bit of shelter from overhanging evergreen branches that

Helleborus multifidus subsp. *bocconei* is dramatic in both foliage and flower.

shed some of the moisture. It is hardy in Zones 4 to 8, though subspecies *bocconei* may be less hardy.

Propagation
Its propagation is similar to that of *H. atrorubens*. See the section dealing with that species for information.

Description of *Helleborus multifidus* Visiani
Four subspecies are currently recognized, but this geographically and morphologically diverse species will likely be broken up into four or more separate species.

Helleborus multifidus subsp. *multifidus* Visiani
Synonyms: *H. angustifolius, H. odorus* subsp. *multifidus, H. viridis* var. *multifidus*

Acaulescent. Basal leaves are deciduous to partially evergreen, glabrous to sparsely pubescent, and pedate with all segments divided into multiple additional segments, for a total of 20 to 45. Segments are lance shaped and leathery, 5 in. (12 cm) long and about ½ in. (1.5 cm) wide. Margins are coarsely serrate. The petiole is up to 12 in. (30 cm) long. Three to eight green flowers appear per scape, each ⅜ to ¾ in. (1 to 2 cm) wide and somewhat conical to cup shaped, scented or unscented. Bracts are leafy, divided into two to eight narrow, serrate segments. Ten nectaries are green, stalked, and funnel shaped with wavy or serrate margins. Three to four follicles are

Though exposed to the full spring sunshine, putative colonies of *H. multifidus* subsp. *multifidus* growing on a Croatian roadside are cast in summer shade by bracken.

approximately ¾ in. (2 cm) long at maturity. Scape is 8 to 12 in. (20 to 30 cm) tall. The rootstock is stout with thick roots. Its name was published in 1829 from a specimen collected in the former Yugoslavia.

This plant grows in a variety of habitats, from open pasture to scrubby woods. In Croatia, it seems to favor open ground on rocky, wooded, and treeless slopes; in pastures; and in the deep, rich soil of limestone dolines. Bracken often obscures the plants in summer. Early bloom no doubt accounted for the paucity of companions we saw at some sites, though *Arum* was often common. On the edges of woodlands, *Asarum europaeum*, *Crocus*, *Hedera*, *Hepatica nobilis*, and *Lamium maculatum* were common. In dolines, *Crocus*, *Galanthus nivalis*, and *Primula vulgaris* fight it out with the dense grass and bracken.

Helleborus multifidus subsp. *bocconei* (Tenore) B. Mathew
Synonyms: *H. bocconei*, *H. intermedius*, *H. siculus*, and *H. viridis* var. *bocconei*

Acaulescent. It is similar to *H. multifidus* subsp. *multifidus* but its basal leaves are nearly glabrous, and it is pedate with segments divided only half their length. Segments are lance shaped, leathery, and less than ¼ in. (6 mm) wide. Margins are coarsely serrate-dentate. Three to eight green, fragrant flowers appear per scape and are 1½ to 3 in. (4 to 7 cm) wide, showy, and saucer shaped. Bracts are conspicuous and coarsely toothed. Its name was published in 1913 from a specimen collected in southern Italy.

As it is currently classified, this subspecies grows wild in central and southern Italy and Sicily on rocky, wooded, and scrubby slopes. *Cyclamen hederifolium* is a constant companion in the oak woods of Umbria and Tuscany, where this plant forms nearly a solid ground cover.

It is likely that the showy, pale-flowered *H. multifidus* subsp. *bocconei* will be elevated to species status—one of many forthcoming changes in this complex group.

The deeply dissected foliage of *H. multifidus* subsp. *hercegovinus* upstages the subtle green flowers in the spring garden.

Helleborus multifidus subsp. *hercegovinus* (Martinis) B. Mathew
Synonym: *H. hercegovinus*

Acaulescent. It is similar to *H. multifidus* subsp. *multifidus* but its basal leaves are pubescent, pedate, with many thin segments for a total of 45 to 100. Segments are lance shaped, leathery, and less than about ¼ in. (6 mm) wide. Margins are serrate. Its three to eight yellow-green flowers are 1½ to 2 in. (4 to 5 cm) wide and cup shaped. Its name was published in 1913 from a specimen collected on Mount Orjen in Herzegovina.

This subspecies has a distinct range in the southern coastal mountains of Herzegovina and Montenegro and possibly in adjacent Albania, on rocky, wooded, and scrubby slopes and in meadows.

Helleborus multifidus subsp. *istriacus* (Schiffner) Merxmuller & Podlech
Synonyms: *H. istriacus*, *H. laxus*, *H. odorus* var. *istriacus*, and *H. viridis* var. *laxus*

Acaulescent. It is similar to *H. multifidus* subsp. *multifidus* but its basal leaves are pubescent, clearly pedate, with 10 to 14 lance-shaped, finely to coarsely serrated segments. Segments are broadly lance shaped, leathery, and ¾ to 1½ in. (2 to 4 cm) wide. Margins are serrate. Its three to eight flowers per scape are apple- to yellow-green and showy, 1½ to 2 ¼ in. (4 to 5.5 cm) wide, and cup shaped. Its name was published in 1961 from a specimen collected in Istria, Croatia.

A pastiche of foliage characterizes this stand of *H. multifidus* subsp. *istriacus* growing on the Croatian island of Krk.

High in the Vojack Mountains above the Croatian Adriatic, *H. multifidus* subsp. *istriacus* blooms through the spring snow.

This subspecies grows at sea level as well as in coastal mountains of northwestern Croatia, Slovenia, and northeastern Italy, on open rocky slopes. in pastures, and in the deep, rich soil of scrubby forests. Companions include *Arum italicum, Cyclamen repandum, Euphorbia characias, Hedera helix, Muscari* spp., *Ruscus aculeatus* at lower elevations, and *Galanthus nivalis* on mountain slopes. Bracken and grasses often obscure the plants in summer.

Helleborus niger, Christmas rose, snow rose
Section: *Helleborus*

The Christmas rose is celebrated in song and story. No wonder. Its perky, glistening white flowers open in winter, as early as January where the climate is benign in North America, and a few even open in late autumn. Unlike most hellebores, the flowers are borne on short, often naked stalks and they face outward. The sepals open white and slowly fade to green or burnished pink. When bracts are present, they are undivided and lack teeth.

Helleborus niger seems to evoke memories. A nonagenarian who spent most of her life in Manhattan shared with us her recollection of an ice skating party in New York in the 1920s. A long, rainy spell had flooded a local pond and caused it to overflow its banks; then a sudden hard freeze just after Christmas turned the pond into a skating rink. More than 75 years later, she continued to wonder at an awe-inspiring sight she and her friends shared that day. Under the ice they saw flowers blooming, the perfect white stars of *H. niger* completely encased in solid ice. Evidently the hellebore was planted in the floodplain near the edge of the pond.

The thick, evergreen leaves have seven to nine rounded entire or toothed segments. The leaves are black-green to medium-green and are mottled with cream in plants sold commercially as *H. niger* subsp. *macranthus*. Plants grow from knobby crowns with thick, fleshy roots, which are rarely more than 6 in. (15 cm) long and grow in a somewhat horizontal fashion. One should not remove the leaves of *H. niger* in late winter or the plant's vigor could suffer.

In their article published in the June 1995 issue of *The New Plantsman*, McLewin and Mathew state that "There are strong arguments for regarding it as acaulescent and strong arguments for caulescent." Further study, no doubt accompanied by spirited discourse, is needed before definitely assigning *H. niger* to one group or another. Its been suggested that *H. niger* may be a "bridge" between the two groups. We continue to use the acaulescent designation for *H. niger*.

This species has an extensive natural range, so variation in bloom time and flower size is common. Flowering times also vary year to year, depending on weather conditions, climate, health, and age of the plant. Some forms seem to bloom at approximately the same time each year, while other forms bloom for Christmas one year and for Valentine's Day another year. During our research, we heard from an American gentleman who has a plant that has never flowered later than early

The flowers of many plants of *H. niger* turn pink as they age. Cool nighttime temperatures intensify the anthocyanin pigments that give the flowers their rosy color.

November since the early 1940s! It was brought to the United States from the Netherlands by a World War II refugee and is perhaps associated with All Saint's or All Soul's Day—a "Halloween rose."

We grew several forms of *H. niger* from commercial seed, producing almost 5000 1 qt. (1 l) pots that we observed for more than two years. These plants had foliage in every size and shape—from long, narrow leaves to very short, rounded leaves; some marbled and veined like *H. ×ericsmithii*, some blued, and others an unusual yellow green. Some leaves were toothed while others were entire. The flowers also varied from 1 to 2 in. (3 to 5 cm), rounded, pure-white blooms to creamy flowers that measured more than 5 in. (12 cm) across. In some forms, the blooms turned pink very shortly after opening, while other forms remained white until aging to tan. Some forms had purple-red stems and raspberry-red styles, while others had green or spotted stems. Individual plants from each strain bloomed early, late, and everything in between. In fact, we had something in flower every month of the year.

Helleborus niger is a popular cut flower. Crops are grown for markets in Europe, where they are sold in shops and on stands. New crosses at Ashwood Nurseries in

Despite its alpine origins, in the garden, *H. niger* thrives over a wide range of climatic, soil, and moisture conditions.

the U.K. and Heuger in Germany produce plants with extended pedicels and two to three flowers per stem, which increases their potential for cuts.

Cultivation

Plant in fertile, loamy to humus-rich soil in light to full shade. Plants tolerate evergreen shade and still bloom well. Many gardeners consider this tough and beautiful plant difficult to grow. *Helleborus niger* is slow to mature, so time and patience are needed until your plant reaches full size. In its native haunts, *H. niger* generally grows in limey soil. It also thrives in acidic duff under conifers, underlain with calcareous rocks. Gardeners on intensely acidic soils report that an annual sprinkling of ground limestone or watering with Epsom salts increases vigor and promotes flowering. Mature clumps will reward you with more than 20 flowers. Plant *H. niger* with the crown a bit deeper than that of *H.* ×*hybridus*. This montane to alpine plant may languish in hot, humid weather. Gardeners in hot, humid climates (as in the U.S. South) should try such heat-adapted selections as the 'Wilder' and 'Nell Lewis' strains. While not the only selections that thrive in the southern U.S., they seem to establish easily and grow quickly. *Helleborus niger* is hardy in Zones 3 to 7.

Propagation

The seeds of *H. niger* are black or dark brown, ³⁄₁₆ in. (5 mm) long, with a definite elaiosome running down one side. Freshly collected seed germinates well after the required periods of warm then cool temperatures; old or dried seed usually takes an extra year. A friend advised us to harvest seeds while the carpels are still green; the immature seed supposedly germinates faster than ripe seed when planted immediately. A seedling's first true leaf is distinctive, with the shape of a clover. Seedlings grow slowly, often taking six months to reach 2 in. (5 cm) tall.

Cultivars and seed strains

Cultivars and strains are selected for certain genetic characteristics deemed attractive. To preserve the exact characteristics, the plant must be clonally propagated by division or tissue culture. Most of the currently available selections of *H. niger* are seed-grown. While strains should produce similar plants, they are variable.

Ashwood Form was selected for its vigorous growth and pure-white midseason, rounded, cup-shaped flowers on strong stems. Ashwood Marbled Form is a midseason selection with light green foliage veined with silver and cup-shaped flowers held well above the foliage. Ashwood Silver Leaf Form is a midseason selection with silver-pewter foliage with no marbling. Petioles and flowering stems are shorter than other Ashwood selections, but the flowers are large and cupped. 'Blackthorn' strain is Robin White's superb midseason seed-grown form with red stems. The red pigment sometimes continues into the petiole. Buds are pink and open to creamy white flowers with pink reverses; flowers age to pink. They were produced by crossing 'White Magic' with 'Louis Cobbett'. Crûg Hybrid is a midseason seed strain developed by Crûg Farm Plants in Wales; it features large, 15 in. (38 cm) multiflowering plants.

'Eco Potter's Wheel' was developed by Don Jacobs at Eco Gardens in Decatur, Georgia. This large-flowered, early to midseason form is propagated by division. 'Double Fantasy' is produced by tissue culture in Japan, possibly from an offspring of 'Marion'. Midseason blooms have an outside ring of large, ruffled, white sepals, with an inner ring consisting of varying numbers of petals. Some plants are fully double while others sport only a few extra petaloid nectaries. The plants appear to be fertile. Harvington Hybrids is a vigorous, long-flowering (midwinter to midspring) seed strain selected by Liz and Hugh Nunn and available from several sources in the U.K. Stems are 9 to 12 in. (23 to 30 cm) tall with rounded, white flowers. 'Louis Cobbett' is an older midseason selection, no longer routinely available, and noted for its pink-flushed flowers and tall stems. 'Madame Fourcade' is another old, early-flowering selection with short stems and small, rounded flowers. Growers in the Netherlands offer this selection. 'Maximus' is a seed strain from the late 19th century, possibly a selected form of *H. niger* subsp. *macranthus*, with very large, 4 to 5 in. (10 to 12 cm), star-shaped flowers that turn pink with age. It produces new flowers over a long period.

The 'Nell Lewis' strain was selected by Pine Knot Farms from the garden of Nell Lewis of Greensboro, North Carolina. It is a vigorous strain with two rounded, white,

2 in. (5 cm) flowers per 10 to 12 in. (25 to 30 cm) stem. It continues to produce blooms from January to May in North America. 'Potter's Wheel' is a horticultural legend from the garden of Major Guy Tristram, introduced by Hilda Davenport-Jones of Washfield Nursery. The original plant was described as having exceedingly large, 4 to 5 in. (10 to 12 cm), midseason white flowers with overlapping sepals and a distinguishing green eye. Although the original plant was subsequently lost to commerce in the undiluted form, a number of nurseries sell seed strains purportedly derived from the original plants. 'Praecox' is an early to midseason seed strain that produces medium-sized white flowers that open around the time of the winter solstice and continue into early spring. 'Saint Brigid' was originally from a garden in Ireland. This older mid- to late-season selection was said to have dark green foliage that covered the flowers. Plants are not commonly available.

'Sunrise' (WM9113) and 'Sunset' (WM9519) are McLewin's collections from wild material in Slovenia, and the names are to be used only for plants grown from seeds collected at the site. The mid- to late-season flowers at the 'Sunrise' site change from white to deep red-pink with age. The 'Sunset' site had plants flowering in a wide range of colors from white to pale and dark pink; unusual yellow and striped forms also appeared. 'White Magic' is an early to midseason seed strain from New Zealand that arose when Pat Stuart was fortunate enough to be given a seedling that was "a little different." This plant was the beginning of 'White Magic' according to Kate and Ken Telford of Clifton Homestead, Stuart's daughter and son-in-law. The plants feature strong stems, 15 to 17 in. (38 to 43 cm) tall, with bright green leaves and white flowers. Finally, 'Wilder' strain seed is selected from the North Carolina garden of Bobby Wilder; the original source is lost to the mists of time. Plants are early to bloom and continue to produce flowers over a period of several months, with very large star-shaped white flowers that age to pink.

Description of *Helleborus niger* Linn.

Two subspecies are currently recognized, though ultimately they may not be maintained when the species is overhauled by botanists.

Helleborus niger subsp. *niger* Linn.
Synonym: *H. niger* var. *typicus*

Acaulescent. This it the type species for the genus *Helleborus*. Basal leaves are evergreen, leathery, glabrous, and often waxy; 2 to 8 in. (5 to 20 cm) long, and 1 to 3 in. (3 to 7 cm) wide, pedate, with seven to nine segments. Segments are broadly lanceolate to oblanceolate, occasionally elliptical, and often toothed at apex. Petioles are 4 to 10 in. (10 to 25 cm) long. Flowers, from one to three per scape, are white, often fading to pink, 2 to 3 in. (5 to 7 cm) wide, and usually flat. Nectaries are green, number 12 to 20, and are stalked, tubular, and curved outward. Sometimes they are notched. Bracts are small, rounded, and entire, found below the flowers. Five to eight follicles are about ¾ to 1 in. (2 to 3 cm) long at maturity. The scape is 2 to 8 in. (5 to

20 cm) tall, usually at or below the leaves. Snow often flattens the leaves, so flowers rise above them. The rootstock is stout, with thick roots. Its name was published in 1753 from a specimen collected in Austria.

Helleborus niger subsp. *niger* is widespread in the Alps of Central and Eastern Europe, from Croatia and Italy north to Switzerland and Germany. Plants grow from middle elevations to above tree line in mixed coniferous and deciduous forests. We observed plants in meadows and rocky pastures and along road cuts. In Croatia, we found plants growing in deep, mossy spruce woods with *Anemone nemorosa*, *Asarum europaeum*, *Cyclamen purpurascens*, *Hepatica nobilis*, and *Primula vulgaris*. Plants may begin blooming under the snow, and they open as the snowpack recedes. Blooming plants are frequently buried by late snowfalls. In *Fagus* and *Carpinus* woods at lower elevations in Slovenia, plants grew with *Anemone nemorosa*, *Cardamine enneaphyllos*, *Corydalis solida*, *Daphne cneorum*, *Hacquetia epipactis*, *Helleborus odorus*, *Isopyrum thalictroides*, *Pulmonaria saccharata*, and *Scilla bifolia*.

H. niger subsp. *macranthus* (Freyn) Schiffner
Synonym: *H. macranthus*

Acaulescent. Plants are similar to *H. niger* subsp. *niger*, but with broadly lanceolate, slightly serrate segments. Leaves are blue-green to slightly glaucous, sometimes mottled with transverse cream bands. Flowers are 3 to 4 in. (8 to 10 cm) in diameter. Its name was published in 1889 from a specimen collected in Italy.

This taxa is found in open woods; dense, mossy evergreen forests; and meadows in northern Italy, Slovenia, and Croatia.

Helleborus occidentalis
Section: *Helleborastrum*
Synonym: *H. viridis* subsp. *occidentalis*

This delicate species was split by McLewin and Mathew in 2002 from the more robust *H. viridis*. Once considered a variety of the latter species, it now has specific rank. The plants differ morphologically and geographically, thus the separation. Overall, plants are smaller in stature and have a more northern and western distribution.

In the garden, this species offers a bit less punch than other green-flowered species, yet it still has its charms. One of only two species native to Britain, it has a place in the hearts of gardeners and nature lovers there. In America, it was one of the first widely cultivated green-flowered acaulescent species. An early and long medicinal history indicates that this was perhaps the first hellebore cultivated in America, and the plant was widely naturalized by the mid 1800s. Jinksie Burnum of Mountain Brook, Alabama, introduced *H. occidentalis* to contemporary American southerners. Burnum moved to her gardener's paradise in the late 1940s, and this hellebore, identified for her by Brian Mathew, was among the treasures she found.

The charming and widespread *H. occidentalis* has been recognized as a distinct species. Long associated with gardens, plants were once highly valued medicinally but are now enjoyed purely for ornament.

The emerging buds of *H. occidentalis* cluster close to the mossy ground near Cologne, Germany.

A woodlot near Cologne, Germany, shelters a small colony of *H. occidentalis* on a mossy slope.

Cultivation

For best growth, plant in light to partial shade in rich, loamy soil. The foliage is often ratty by midsummer, but it remains well into winter despite its disheveled state. This plant seems more susceptible to frost damage than others. Frozen flowering scapes can develop rot, but the problem does not seem to affect the crown or new foliage. It is hardy from Zones 4 to 8.

Propagation

Its propagation is similar to that of *H. atrorubens*. See the section dealing with that species for information.

Description of *Helleborus occidentalis* Reuter

Acaulescent. Basal leaves—usually two—are deciduous, glabrous to sparsely pubescent, and pedate, with three primary segments. The central segment is narrowly elliptical, 2 to 4 in. (5 to 10 cm) long and ⅜ to 1 in. (1 to 3 cm) wide. The outer two segments are each divided into three to six additional segments, for a total of seven to thirteen. Segments are deep green and slightly glossy, somewhat thin textured, with margins serrate to coarsely dentate-serrate. The petiole is 4 to 8 in. (10 to 20 cm) long. Two to four pale green, unscented flowers appear per scape and are 1 to 2 in. (3 to 5 cm) wide and somewhat cup shaped. Nine to twelve nectaries are green, stalked, and funnel shaped, with unevenly toothed margins, curving outward. Bracts are leafy, divided into three to five coarsely serrate segments. Follicles number three to four, rarely two, and are about ½ in. (1 to 2 cm) long at maturity. The scape is 8 to 16 in.

(20 to 40 cm) tall. The rootstock is stout with thick roots. Its name was published in 1889 from a specimen collected in "Gallia occidentali, Pyrenaeis, Hispania boreali."

Range and habitat

This northern species is found from Spain and France, northeast to Germany, and northwest to England in open or rocky woods and the margins of pastures. We saw few companions with this early bloomer in England or in Germany. Plants grew in mossy, sheltered woods under linden, ash, and oak. This plant is naturalized in Europe and in northeastern North America.

Helleborus odorus

Section: *Helleborastrum*
Synonyms: *H. decorus*, *H. viridis* var. *odorus*

Beauty and fragrance go a long way in creating a flawless plant. Add chartreuse flowers, and perfection is attained. This tantalizing combination makes this fragrant hellebore a must for collectors and enthusiastic gardeners. The 2 to 3 in. (5 to 7 cm) luminescent flowers nod from leafy scapes up to 20 in. (50 cm) tall. The flowers vary in fragrance from sweet to slightly skunky, a scent we happen to like. Some plants are completely scent free. The carpels within the flower are fused for a few millimeters at the base. The mostly persistent basal foliage has five main, oval, segments, with the outer further divided variously to make up to eleven segments. Each leaflet is toothed on the upper third of its length. The newly emerging leaves are glabrous, or sparsely clothed in hairs.

This species is easily confused with *H. cyclophyllus*, which is similar in many respects. However, the carpels within the flowers of *H. cyclophyllus* are not fused at the base and the leaves are usually deciduous.

The deep green to chartreuse flowers of *H. odorus* are sweet-scented when fresh and with age become musty but never unpleasant. This photo pictures the Slovenian form, which may be a distinct species.

Cultivation
Deep, rich soil in sun to partial shade allows this beautiful species to develop to full potential. The coarse foliage overwinters but may get tattered by cold and wind. Cut old leaves before the flowers emerge. This is often the first hellebore, after *H. niger*, to bloom in Cole's Virginia garden. It is hardy in Zones 4 to 8.

Propagation
Its propagation is similar to that of *H. atrorubens*. See the section dealing with that species for information.

Description of *Helleborus odorus* Waldst. & Kit.
Acaulescent. Its basal leaves are mostly evergreen, pubescent, and pedate, with three primary segments. The central segment is undivided, 6 to 8 in. (15 to 20 cm) long and up to 2 to 3 in. (5 to 7 cm) wide. The outer two segments are each divided into three to five additional segments, for a total of seven to eleven. Segments are elliptic to broadly oblanceolate, thick textured, with coarsely serrate margins. The petiole is 5 to 11 in. (13 to 28 cm) long. Five to six flowers appear per scape, are occasionally single, and are colored a rich lime green to chartreuse. They are 2 to 3 in. (5 to 7 cm) wide and bowl to saucer shaped, outfacing, and scented. Nectaries are green, stalked, and widely funnel shaped with slightly toothed margins. Bracts are leafy but often small, divided into three to five serrate segments. Three to five, and sometimes six, follicles are fused together at the base, ¾ in. (2 cm) long at maturity. The scape

can reach 8 to 12 in. (20 to 30 cm) tall. The rootstock is stout with thick roots. Its name was published in 1809 from a specimen collected in Hungary.

Range and habitat
Helleborus odorus is a wide-ranging species found from Slovenia east and south to Hungary, Romania, and Bosnia. Slovenian plants may represent a distinct species. It is found in open woods, along roadsides, and in meadows, where it is often obscured by summer foliage. We really like this plant and were thrilled to see colonies in Slovenia, Croatia, and Bosnia. Plants grew under *Carpinus* with

Helleborus odorus is fairly consistent in flower form, though the foliage is often quite variable.

Corydalis solida, Cyclamen purpurascens, Lamium maculatum, Primula vulgaris, Pulmonaria saccharata, and *Ruscus aculeatus*. In meadows, bracken (*Pteridium aquilinum*) dominated and often swamped the plants. In Slovenia, plants grew in open beech woods with *H. niger, Hepatica nobilis*, and *Cardamine enneaphyllos*.

Helleborus orientalis, Lenten rose
Section: *Helleborastrum*

Arguably, the most colorful and floriferous hellebore species is *H. orientalis*. The visual impact of this species in full flower in the garden is apt to upstage all others. Nodding bells dangle from the scapes like the satin pulls on a Victorian window shade. That's not to say they are fey beauties. Quite the contrary, they are sturdy, serviceable plants that offer months of elegance for little effort.

The three subspecies vary in flower color and native range. All are gardenworthy but devilishly hard to find in their pure forms, as they hybridize freely in the garden. There is much overlap in characteristics, especially between *H. orientalis* subsp. *orientalis* and *H. orientalis* subsp. *guttatus*, which may not be distinct. Subspecies *orientalis* has large, white to creamy flowers, usually fading to green at the center. Some flowers are pale yellow. Flowers of subspecies *guttatus* are white with maroon spots. *Helleborus orientalis* subsp. *abchasicus*, which is sometimes incorrectly referred to as "atrorubens of gardens," is represented in American and English gardens by the plants known as the 'Early Purple' Group, which sports red-tinged spring foliage and 1 to 2 in. (3 to 5 cm) flowers that open plum and fade to dusty mauve. The plants known as 'Early Purple' are likely hybrids, diluted from purity by years of garden hybridization.

Mature clumps of *H. orientalis* are quite large, with leathery evergreen leaves with wide leaflets. Crowns become quite thick and woody, with extensive root masses that firmly anchor the plants. The leafy flower stalks rise from the center of the clump, with one to three flowers each. Plants are variable in flowering time, often starting in late January and continuing through April in North America.

Cultivation
Plant in rich, evenly moist but well-drained clay or loam soil in light to partial shade. Plants are very robust when mature, and some wild forms rival the beautiful garden hybrids so coveted today. The evergreen foliage adds visual interest to the winter landscape; it also helps protect the emerging flowers from late frost. Excessive cold and dry winds can burn the leaves; they are often damaged or tattered at flowering time. Remove the leaves in early spring to allow the flowering scapes to expand without getting tangled. It is hardy in Zones 4 to 8, with reports of success in Zone 9.

Propagation
Its propagation is similar to that of *H. atrorubens*. See the section dealing with that species for information.

'Early Purple' is believed to be a group of old selections of *H. orientalis* subsp. *abchasicus* that are still popular in gardens today, more than 100 years after its introduction.

Description of *Helleborus orientalis* Lamarck

This species has a wide distribution in the wild. Three subspecies are commonly recognized to make up this species, though current thinking is that characteristics used to define the subspecies are not defensible.

Helleborus orientalis subsp. *orientalis* Lamarck

Synonyms: *H. caucasicus, H. kochii, H. officinalis, H. olympicus*

Acaulescent. Its basal leaves are deciduous, glabrous to sparsely pubescent, and pedate, with five to nine and occasionally eleven segments. The central segment is undivided, 4 to 10 in. (10 to 25 cm) long and up to 4 in. (10 cm) wide. Outer segments are each divided into two to five additional segments, which are elliptical to oblanceolate and thick textured, with margins evenly serrate. The petiole is 6 to 14 in. (15 to 36 cm) long. Two to four creamy white to green flowers appear per scape. They are unscented, about 2½ in. (6 to 7 cm) wide, and somewhat cup shaped. Nectaries are green, stalked, tubular, and curved outward, with wavy or toothed margins. Bracts are leafy and divided into three to five serrate segments. Four to seven follicles are free at the base and ¾ to 1 in. (2 to 3 cm) long at maturity. The scape rises to 14 in.

Helleborus orientalis subsp. *orientalis* contributes large flowers to many hybrids but is a showy, gardenworthy plant in its own right.

(36 cm) tall. The rootstock is stout with thick roots. Its name was published in 1789 from a specimen collected in Turkey.

Helleborus orientalis subsp. *orientalis* is found in northwest Greece and Turkey, north to the Ukraine, and in the Caucasus to Georgia in deciduous and mixed coniferous woods and meadows. This plant has an extensive geographic range and exploits a variety of habitats from sea level to 6600 ft. (2011 m). Rice and Strangman (1993) report the following wild companions: *Cornus mas, Cyclamen coum, Daphne pontica, Fritillaria pontica, Galanthus plicatus, Paeonia mascula* subsp. *aretiana, Rhododendron luteum,* and *Trachystemon orientale.* We have not seen this species in the wild.

H. orientalis subsp. *abchasicus* (A. Braun) B. Mathew
Synonyms: *H. abchasicus, H. colchicus*

This subspecies is similar to *H. orientalis* subsp. *orientalis* but with pink to plum-colored flowers, often with tinted green interiors. Flowers are occasionally spotted with deeper purple. Nectaries are also plum to dark purple. Its name was published from a specimen in Berlin Botanic Gardens collected in the Western Caucasus.

This species has a limited range in Georgia and perhaps in Romania, where it grows in open woods.

MORE ON *HELLEBORUS ORIENTALIS* SUBSP. *ABCHASICUS* IN AMERICA

Bailey's 1906 edition of *The Cyclopedia* lists "*H. orientalis* var. *atrorubens*" as distinctive from "*H. orientalis* var. *abchasicus.*" The confusion perpetuated here likely started with early nursery listings. Perhaps the names used in nursery listings by Ellwanger and Barry in 1860 (*atro-rubra*) and Manning in 1887 (*atrorubens*) were drawn from early English literature. M'Mahon (1806) lists *H. atrorubens* as a species. George W. Johnson, author of *The Cottage Gardner's Dictionary* (1865), says that *H. atrorubens* was introduced to Britain from Hungary in 1820. He describes the flowers as purple, blooming on a 1 ft. (30 cm) scape, in March. This is likely actually *H. orientalis* subsp. *abchasicus,* but it is curious to note that neither species grows in Hungary.

H. orientalis subsp. *guttatus* (A. Braun & Sauer) B. Mathew
Synonyms: *H. guttatus, H. intermedius*

This subspecies is similar to *H. orientalis* subsp. *orientalis,* but its flowers are white to cream, spotted with red or deeper purple. Its name was published in Berlin Botanic Gardens from a specimen collected in the Caucasus.

This subspecies has a very limited range in the Ukraine, where it grows in open oak-beech-hornbeam woods. Garden literature reports that it grows with *Cyclamen coum, Erythronium caucasicum, Galanthus ikariae, Paeonia caucasica, Primula vulgaris* subsp. *sibthorpii,* and *Ruscus.* We have not seen this plant in the wild.

Once considered a distinct taxon, the subspecies *guttatus* likely represents a spotted variant found in most populations throughout the range of *H. orientalis*.

Helleborus purpurascens

Section: *Helleborastrum*

Synonym: *H. viridis* var. *purpurascens*

Foliage alone is reason enough to grow *H. purpurascens*. The deeply divided palmate leaves are like origami parasols. Some sport as many as 30 segments, while others have only 10. They form circular caps on stiff petioles 12 in. (30 cm) or more tall. The leaves are deciduous and are completely gone by late winter. As lovely as the foliage is, the flowers are the true sirens of this species. Dusty-plum, saucer-shaped, 1 to 2 in. (3 to 5 cm) blooms borne singly or in threes open as soon as they pierce the cool soil surface. Flower color varies from rich plum-purple to sea-green. The insides of the flowers are generally green but may match the outer surface. Bloom occurs as early as December in mild American climates. In Cole's Minnesota garden, this was the first species to bloom, often sending up its buds under the snow and winter mulch in early March.

Cultivation

Give *H. purpurascens* full sun to partial shade for best growth and flowering. Plants tolerate deep deciduous shade. Rich, loamy soil with abundant organic matter suits this species best. This woodland denizen thrives in closed canopy deciduous forest in spite of its deciduous nature. In the garden, plants with ample water and nutrients

The flowers of *H. purpurascens* open as they are emerging from the chilly spring soil. In the wild, plants are sparsely flowered.

often hold their foliage into winter. British gardeners report a propensity for botrytis during wet winter weather. In the American Pacific Northwest, where winters are also wet, plants are more susceptible than other species. In general, this species is pest-free throughout most of North America. Early flowering seems to limit seed set in some areas, as pollinators are at a premium. We find few self-sown seedlings in the garden. It is hardy in Zones 4 to 8.

Propagation
Its propagation is similar to that of *H. atrorubens*. See the section dealing with that species for information.

Description of *Helleborus purpurascens* Waldst. & Kit.
Acaulescent. Basal leaves are deciduous, sparsely pubescent, and palmate, with five primary segments. Segments are each divided into three to six additional segments. Segments are broadly lance shaped to narrowly elliptical, somewhat thick textured, 4 to 8 in. (10 to 20 cm) long and ⅜ to 1½ in. (1 to 4 cm) wide. Margins are finely serrate. The petiole is 6 to 10 in. (15 to 25 cm) long. One to three, and rarely four, appear per scape and are plum-purple, reddish, or celadon to pale green, often with a grayish bloom; they are 2 to 3 in. (5 to 7 cm) wide, cup shaped, and unscented. Nectaries number 15 to 20 and are green to purple tinted, stalked, widely funnel shaped, ragged, and curved outward. Bracts are leafy, divided into three to five serrate segments. Five to seven follicles are ¾ in. (2 cm) long at maturity. The scape is to 2 to

In cultivation, flowering scapes of *H. purpurascens* eventually grow 8 to 12 in. (20 to 30 cm) high, holding three to five fully open flowers well above the newly emerging foliage.

In the Pilis Mountains north of Budapest, *H. purpurascens* grows in open woods under a canopy of hornbeam, linden, and beech.

8 in. (5 to 20 cm) tall. The rootstock is stout, with thick roots. Its name was published in 1802–1803 from a specimen collected in Hungary.

Range and habitat

This charming species is found in rocky woodlands and scrub from Hungary, Slovakia, and Romania, north to Poland. We saw this plant in the Pilis Mountains north of Budapest. It grew on the upper reaches of the slopes in closed canopy *Carpinus*, *Fraxinus*, *Quercus*, and *Tilia* woods. The native woods were highly managed with constant grooming, leaving little understory or shrub layer. The plants grew singly or in clusters of up to 10 plants. Most were small and blooming just above the leaf litter. They seemed most common near exposed limestone ledges that were scattered through the woods. Few companions were evident except for *Galanthus nivalis*, but a few *Anemone nemorosa* were emerging.

The pale rose-pink flowers of *H. thibetanus* lend their color and crepe-paper texture to the beautiful hybrid known as 'Pink Ice'.

The early flowers of *H. thibetanus* never fully open until the seed is ready to disperse.

Helleborus thibetanus

Section: *Dicarpon*

Synonyms: *H. chinensis*, *H. viridis* var. *thibetanus*

Until the mid-1990s, *H. thibetanus* was virtually unknown and completely unobtainable. Imports from China, mostly from wild collections but some from propagated plants, markedly increased the plants' availability. Today, domestically propagated and imported plants are readily available. Though popular among enthusiasts, like most species, it has been slow to catch on in the trade. This blowsy plant has white to pink, nodding to outfacing flowers with pointed sepals that deepen in color as they age. Red-veined selections are sometimes listed; while the flowers are deeper pink, they do not approach red.

The flowering scapes sport several flowers, accented by large, leafy bracts. The erect, sea-green to silvery green leaves have seven to eleven toothed divisions. Each leaf may reach 12 in. (30 cm) across. The overall effect is reminiscent of *Glaucidium palmatum*. This species has just two follicles, but abundant seeds are usually produced. Plants self-sow freely in Cole's garden on clay loam. The seedlings produce no visible cotyledons. The first true leaf emerges from the seed and persists the first year. In subsequent years, the crowns may produce multiple leaves, though a single leaf is most common. Multiple crowns make up mature clumps. It takes three to four years before the first flowers emerge. Plants go completely dormant in summer after flowering.

Cultivation

Plant in rich loam or clay soils in full sun or light shade. Plants tolerate winter-wet conditions, as they grow wild in low meadows where water often collects. Plants are summer dormant, so spring sunshine is essential for growth and flowering. Plants emerge very early and are easily damaged by late frost. The flowers are hardy enough, but repeated freezing of the stem can cause crown rot. Damaged flowering stems may collapse, and in some cases the entire crown may rot. For this reason, select a protected spot or place plants on a gentle slope so water does not stand around the crowns. It is hardy in Zones 4 to 8.

Propagation

The propagation of *H. thibetanus* is similar to that of other species with a few differences. *Helleborus thibetanus* usually takes two full seasons to germinate. The seedlings lack visible cotyledons, which stay inside the seed, and instead rely on a three-lobed true leaf for photosynthesis the first season. Seedlings are slow to mature and take a number of years to reach blooming size.

Description of *Helleborus thibetanus* Franchet

Acaulescent. The basal leaves are early deciduous, glabrous, and pedate with three primary segments. The outer two segments are each divided into three to four additional segments for a total of seven to ten. Segments are narrowly elliptical, somewhat thin textured, 6 in. (15 cm) long and ¾ to 2 in. (2 to 5 cm) wide. Margins are coarsely serrate to dentate. The petiole is 4 to 8 in. (10 to 20 cm) long. Two to eight unscented flowers appear per scape; they are pale pink with deep pink veins, 1½ to 2 in. (4 to 5 cm) wide or occasionally larger, somewhat bell shaped, and thin textured. The leafy bracts are divided into three to five serrate segments. Nectaries are green, 8 to 10 in number, stalked, and curved outward. Two, rarely three, follicles are ¾ in. (2 cm) long at maturity. The scape is 12 to 20 in. (30 to 50 cm) tall. The rootstock is stout, with thick roots. Its name was published in 1885 from a specimen collected in Sichuan, China.

Range and habitat

This plant is uncommon in the wild within a limited area of central China, where it grows in open woods and low meadows. Plants are often overgrown by ferns and grasses in summer. We have not seen this species in the wild.

The Bosnian *H. torquatus* plants are slender and smaller flowered than those from Montenegro and may represent intergrades with *H. multifidus* subsp. *multifidus*.

Helleborus torquatus

Section: *Helleborastrum*
Synonyms: *H. intermedius*, *H. serbicus*

Finding a nursery that offers the exquisitely beautiful *H. torquatus*, let alone getting hold of a good color form, is more difficult than choosing a winning lottery ticket. Well, not quite. This plant is proudly displayed in the gardens of collectors, but mere mortals must search nurseries and the Internet long and hard to find a source. But take heart, because more nurseries than ever are importing seed and growing plants. It just takes a while to get them to flowering size. The elegantly divided, rounded leaves are pedate rather than palmate. Each of the three segments is intricately divided into many linear, toothed segments. The leaves are completely deciduous, even in mild winters.

Like most hellebore species, this plant is extremely variable in size, form, and flower color. At its best, the flowers are a deep plum-purple inside and out. Most plants are rich purple outside and sea-green inside with flaring sepals. The flowers may be dull gray-green. They hang or face outward on leafy, 12 in. (30 cm) stalks that are overtopped after flowering by the upright foliage. The name *torquatus* comes from the Latin meaning adorned with a collar, referring to the pale collar at the

The stripes at the center of some forms of *H. torquatus* show up in many hybrids, especially picotees.

center of the flower around the carpels. This characteristic, when present, is passed along to dark-flowered garden hybrids that include *H. torquatus* as a parent. The hybrids' flowers often present a pale central halo outlined in red against a deep purple background. Plants with interior striping on the sepals also readily pass this trait to their progeny. This plant is a major player in hybridizing programs, contributing deep purple color as well as the metallic sheen that creates "black" flower color.

Cultivation
Give this species rich, well-drained, fertile loam or clay soil. Full sun to partial shade is best. Plants are slow to establish but are worth the wait. Plants grown from wild-collected seeds are more likely to yield the true species. Garden seed is usually contaminated by blood from other species. In winter-wet climates such as the American Pacific Northwest and Britain, plants are susceptible to diseases that disfigure flowers and foliage. It is hardy in Zones 4 to 8.

Propagation
Its propagation is similar to that of *H. atrorubens*. See the section dealing with that species for information.

'Aeneas' is one of two *H. torquatus* cultivars with double flowers discovered by Elizabeth Strangman.

Cultivars and seed strains
'Dido' and 'Aeneas' are two double-flowered selections from Montenegro.

Description of *Helleborus torquatus* Archer-Hind
Acaulescent. Basal leaves are deciduous, sparsely to regularly pubescent on the underside veins, and pedate, with three primary segments. The central segment is entire or divided. The outer two segments are each divided into three to six additional segments for a total of thirty or more. Segments are lance shaped to narrowly elliptical, thick textured, and 4 to 6½ in. (10 to 17 cm) long and ⅜ to 1½ in. (1 to 4 cm) wide. Margins are coarsely serrate. The petiole is 6 to 10 in. (15 to 25 cm) cm long. Two to seven flowers appear per scape and are deep purple, reddish purple, or pale green stained or streaked with red; inside is paler purple to green, often streaked. Flowers are 1½ to 2 in. (4 to 5 cm) wide, occasionally smaller or larger, somewhat bell to cup shaped, nodding or outfacing, and unscented to faintly clove scented. Ten to twenty nectaries are green, stalked, funnel shaped, and curved outward with fine marginal teeth. Leafy bracts are divided into three to five thin, serrate segments. Three to five follicles are about ¾ in. (2 cm) long at maturity. The scape is 8 to 16 in. (20 to 40 cm) tall. The rootstock is stout, with thick roots. Its name was published in 1884 from a cultivated specimen of unspecified origin.

Range and habitat

In the wild, plants are found in thin mountain woods and scrub, occasionally in the open. Northern populations from Bosnia and Croatia are smaller flowered, while the southern plants from Serbia, Herzegovina, and Montenegro are often larger flowered. Most horticultural selections are from this region, including two doubles, 'Dido' and 'Aenaeus', found by Elizabeth Strangman in Montenegro. We observed a large colony of a northern population in Bosnia. Flower color varied from deep purple to apple-green, and everything in between. Most plants closely resemble *H. multifidus* subsp. *multifidus*, which was growing on the other side of a mountain range in Croatia. The plants were spread widely across a grassy pasture, growing among bracken in dolines and in low grass. Plants grew between the scattered thickets of *Corylus*, *Prunus*, and *Crataegus*. Few companions were in evidence so early in the season, but crocus was in bloom, and *Fragaria* and *Potentilla* rosettes were greening. The dried heads of *Carlina* were common.

Helleborus vesicarius

Section: *Syncarpus*

Seedpods, rather than flowers, are the charm of *H. vesicarius*. Inflated follicles hang like Chinese lanterns from the 10 in. (25 cm) scapes. The effect is both curious and handsome yet seldom achieved in gardens. The small green flowers are attractively banded in brick red, but they are often muddled with the leafy bracts. Soft, dissected leaves set off the flowers and seedpods. When seeds ripen in early summer, the pods fall off and roll away like tumbleweeds rather than split to disperse the seeds. Once dispersal is complete, the plant goes completely dormant.

This species, taxonomically distinct and the sole member of section *Syncarpus*, has basal leaves as well as true stem leaves. All other hellebores have one or the other. These leaves are stalkless and divided. The deep, penetrating roots are fleshy and serve as water reservoirs to carry the plants through the dry summer.

Cultivation

A mercurial nature makes *H. vesicarius* the Holy Grail of collectors. This species is difficult to grow. The summer dormancy presents many problems for gardeners in summer-wet regions. Being native to arid regions, it must remain dry though not parched throughout the dormant period to survive. It is best treated like a spring-flowering bulb. Plants perform better in containers than in the open ground, but they must never dry completely. In the garden, plants demand excellent drainage and a dry summer crown. Plant in circumneutral loam or clay soils. Humidity is sure death, so the steamy U.S. South, where we garden, is not a region where this species is usually successful. Slugs and snails are problematic indoors and out. Many are called, but few are chosen. It is hardy in Zones 7 to 9 and by trial in other zones, but there are few successes in the open garden.

Helleborus vesicarius is as lovely as it is difficult to grow. Most who attempt to grow it fail, but they keep trying.

Propagation

The seeds of *H. vesicarius* are rounded, brown, and approximately ⅛ in. (2 to 3 mm) in diameter, with three to six seeds in each swollen follicle. The radicle begins to emerge a month or more before the cotyledon leaves. In late autumn to early winter (November to December in North America), a pair of large, rounded cotyledon leaves emerge, sometimes only one leaf. Only the cotyledons develop the first year, but occasionally the first true leaves form as well. These are bright green and curled, rather like celery. Plants begin to go dormant as weather warms in early summer, and only the dormant bud remains under soil level until the foliage begins to arise in late autumn.

The cotyledons are unusually long and continue an inch (3 cm) or more underground, where they meet the young vegetative bud. The newly formed bud remains dormant until the following late autumn, at which point the plant breaks dormancy. It is very important to keep these dormant buds from becoming too dry. If growing in the open garden, this is not a problem, but in pots they must never completely dry out. It is best to leave these seedlings in the sowing flat until the second year before transplanting.

Cultivars and seed strains

This species was crossed with *H. niger* at Ashwood Nurseries to produce 'Briar Rose', an attractive plant with open, cream-colored flowers banded with pink. This plant is not fully tested in the garden, but it makes a handsome container plant.

Description of *Helleborus vesicarius* Aucher

Acaulescent. The basal leaves are deciduous, glabrous to sparsely pubescent, and pedate, with three thin-textured primary segments. The outer two segments are each divided into two lobes with many thin, jagged divisions. Margins are toothed. Basal leaves are 3 in. (8 cm) long and 6 in. (15 cm) wide. The petiole is 3 to 10 in. (8 to 25 cm) long. Cauline leaves are sessile or with short winged petioles; they are glabrous to sparsely pubescent. The pale green, unscented flowers number two to four per scape and are about ¾ in. (2 cm) wide and somewhat bell shaped. Five green nectaries are stalked and funnel shaped with reflexed lips. Bracts are leafy, divided into three-toothed segments. Three follicles are inflated and three are ribbed and indehiscent, 3 in. (8 cm) long at maturity. The scape is up to 24 in. (60 cm) tall. Plants die down completely in summer after seed dispersal. The rootstock is stout, with thick, fleshy roots. Its name was published in 1841 from a specimen collected in Turkey.

Range and habitat

This species is native to southern Turkey and northern Syria, in dry, rocky montane terrain. It is found in open oak woodlands or scrub, in rocky, alkaline clay soil. We have yet to see this in the wild, nor have we grown it successfully in our gardens.

The kelly-green flowers of the aptly named *H. viridis* are among the greenest of any species.

Helleborus viridis
Section: *Helleborastrum*
Synonym: *Helleboraster viridis*

We love green flowers, so were naturally thrilled to acquire *H. viridis*. A variable species distributed in western and southern Europe, the outstanding forms are gorgeous. Nodding, deep apple-green flowers are 1 to 2 in. (3 to 5 cm) across in groups of two to four. The stiff, lustrous, deciduous foliage has up to 13 divisions and is coarsely saw-toothed. The leaves stand up to a foot (30 cm) high and are perfect with sedges and ferns in the summer garden. Until recently, two subspecies were recognized: *H. viridis* subsp. *viridis* and *H. viridis* subsp. *occidentalis*. The work of McLewin, published in *The Plantsman* in September 2002, proposes elevation of *H. viridis* subsp. *occidentalis* to species status. This species, though similar in some respects, is no longer considered to belong to *H. viridis*.

Helleborus viridis is currently rare in cultivation in the United States, though it is more widely grown in Europe. We hope that its designation as a species in its own right speeds up introduction by seed and plants.

Cultivation
Plant in humus-rich clay loam for best growth. This species seems to tolerate more moisture than others. It is early-blooming and attractive, though the leafy bracts may compete with the flowers. It is hardy in Zones 4 to 8.

Like all hellebores, *H. viridis* is variable. Flower color ranges from deep green to chartreuse.

Propagation
Its propagation is similar to that of *H. atrorubens*. See the section dealing with that species for information.

Description of *Helleborus viridis* Linn.
Acaulescent. Its usually two basal leaves are deciduous, glabrous, and weakly pedate, with three primary segments. The central segment is narrowly elliptical, 2 to 4 in. (5 to 10 cm) long and ⅜ to 1 in. (1 to 3 cm) wide. The outer two segments are each divided into three to six additional segments for a total of seven to thirteen. Segments are deep green and slightly glossy, somewhat thin textured, with coarsely serrate margins. The petiole is 4 to 8 in. (10 to 20 cm) long. Two to four unscented deep green flowers appear per scape and are 1½ to 2 in. (4 to 5 cm) wide and somewhat flattened. Nine to twelve green nectaries are stalked and funnel shaped with unevenly toothed margins, curving outward. Bracts are leafy, divided into three to five coarsely serrate segments. Three to four, and rarely two, follicles are about ¾ in. (2 cm) long at maturity. The scape is 8 to 16 in. (20 to 40 cm) tall. The rootstock is stout, with thick roots. Its name was published in 1753 from a specimen collected in France (Vienne) or Italy (Euganeis).

Range and habitat
This species is native to Spain, France, Italy, and Switzerland in open woods in deep, loamy, calcareous soils. We have yet to see this attractive species in the wild. Mathew reports *Arum dioscoridis*, *Crocus* spp., *Cyclamen coum*, *Fritillaria* spp., and *Hyacinthus orientalis* as companions.

MATTHIAS THOMSEN

We are green with envy because our friends in Europe do not need an eight to twelve-hour plane ride to visit Balkan hellebore sites. Matthias Thomsen lives in southern Germany, but he would probably find a way to visit the species hellebores even if he weren't so centrally located. His ease of accessibility permits car trips over a long weekend, both during the flowering period and later for seed collecting.

Matthias has always been very interested in botany and gardening. He has grown and hybridized daylilies for more than 20 years, with contacts all over the world. He was cofounder of Hemerocallis Europa, the first internationally based perennial plant society in Europe.

His main focus has always been botany and wild plants in their native habitats, so sooner on later he had to end up with hellebores, because they grow not too far away from his doorstep. He told us his interest in species hellebores was sparked when he found wild *H. cyclophyllus* near the Vicos Gorge in northeastern Greece in 1995. A few years later, he made an exploratory trip to northern Italy to find and study *H. multifidus* subsp. *bocconei* in its wild habitat. Since that time, Matthias has visited more than 80 different colonies of wild hellebores in Italy.

As his interest grew, Matthias contacted other people interested in species hellebores, exchanging the locations of various sites in Italy and the Balkans. Friendship developed and led to joint explorations with Will McLewin. Together they have studied the complex situation of several populations of Italian hellebores. The first is a large population in central Italy that Matthias discovered in 2000. The plants at this location are very different from anything the two have seen anywhere else in Italy. Matthias told us that, unlike *H. multifidus* subsp. *bocconei*, many of the plants in this location have very finely divided leaves, some with as many as 200 individual segments. These are attractive foliage plants with flowers that are large and green to yellow.

Matthias found another site in coastal Italy, where the plants appear to fit into neither *H. multifidus* subsp. *bocconei* nor *H. viridis*. This group has very large evergreen leaves with just a few wide segments and early, strongly fragrant whitish flowers on tall flower stalks. Both men believe that these two distinct populations represent two new species.

He is working toward a better understanding of the questionable Balkan species *H. multifidus* subsp. *multifidus* and *H. torquatus*. New findings in the wild, ideas, proposals, and results are constantly discussed with McLewin and others. His approach to understanding and classifying these plants is based on morphological, genetic, and evolutionary aspects of the genus.

Matthias collects seeds on his expeditions and grows the plants on to test them in his garden. He offers a seed list of species seeds from controlled garden crosses as well as wild-collected hellebore seed to those who would like to grow their own.

THE FUTURE OF HELLEBORE TAXONOMY

The goal of taxonomy is to classify organisms so that people can be conversant about them. Yes, science for science's sake is perhaps the ultimate triumph, but when pointing to an organism, in order to talk about it, something more than "that plant over there with the green flowers" was, and still is necessary. If we assume that we need plants to have names, it stands to reason that we would try to name them at all cost. As Will McLewin points out, this point of view creates problems. He proposes throwing out existing concepts of many of the species and starting from scratch. While this is theoretically the best approach, it falls short of being a practical and useful alternative. Returning to the premise that, from a gardener's standpoint at least, we need to put a name to the plants in our gardens, then what are we to do? It seems to us that the existing species as outlined in Mathew's monograph *Hellebores* are a useful starting point. Using them as the basis upon which to start the discussion, we begin to say how certain plants or populations differ or concur with those descriptions of species.

Cytological analysis is helping to shed light on some of the species, but interpreting the genetic differences is also problematic. "What does all this mean for gardeners?" you might ask. "Why worry about the taxonomy of the genus?" We believe that proper identification of the plants we grow is important. Perhaps of greater significance, though, is the fact that the species are uniquely beautiful garden plants. Our love of American native wildflowers, as well as wild plants from around the world, compels us to grow the wild forms of hellebores as well. In doing so, we want to identify them as accurately as possible.

Much has been learned since 1989 when *Hellebores* was published. The current taxonomy is being closely examined by McLewin, Matthias Thomsen, Tim Murphy, and Brian Mathew. "The structure of the genus *Helleborus*" (facing page) is a synopsis of the changes that are afoot. We cannot say with precision when and how the new species will be described. Our intent is to illuminate the changes. Time will tell. *The Plantsman* will continue to be the best source for advances in hellebore taxonomy published in English.

Helleborus niger, *H. thibetanus*, and *H. vesicarius* do not fit neatly into the current descriptive terminology of caulescent or acaulescent. It is likely that a new series of terms will be proposed for describing the nature of stems of hellebore species. The species in all sections other than *Helleborastrum*, as published by Mathew, seem to be fairly consistent with current taxonomic thinking. The only exception is

THE STRUCTURE OF THE GENUS *HELLEBORUS*

Will McLewin created the accompanying chart, which presents the current relationship of species and hybrids. Several new species which seem defensible are presented, especially elevation of the subspecies of *H. multifidus* to specific rank.

THE STRUCTURE OF THE GENUS *HELLEBORUS*

SPECIES   **HYBRIDS**

Caulescent (= with stem)
{2} *foetidus* G

[1]   [2]
{3} *argutifolius* G ——————— ×sternii ————— ×nigercors
{3} *lividus* G+P ——————— ×ballardiae ————— ×ericsmithii

....

C/A {4} *niger* W ——————— 'Briar Rose'

....

{1} *vesicarius* G+P

———————————————————————————————————————

Acaulescent (=without stem)
{6} *thibetanus* W/Pi★ ——————— 'Pink Ice'

~~~~~~

"few, large" leaflets
[3]   **"large" flowers**
orientalis/caucasicus
o. guttatus W★★★
o. abchasicus P
odorus G/Y   'Snow White'
cyclophyllus G
purpurascens P
viridis G
istriacus G
"small" flowers
dumetorum G
croaticus P★★   *Helleborus* ×*hybridus*
atrorubens P+G★   wrongly called "orientalis hybrids"
occidentalis G★   or even simply "orientalis"

                                         [4]

{5}   **"many, small" leaflets**
"large" flowers
bocconei G+Y   Flower color
"small" flowers   G = green   P = purple
hercegovinus G   Pi = pink   W = white
multifidus G★   Y = yellow
torquatus P+G★★   ★rarely
WM 9531 G+P G/Y/W   ★★frequently/usually
                                      ★★★spotted and/or veined inside

....

Sections   { } botanical, B. Mathew   [ ] horticultural, W. McLewin

{1} *Syncarpus*   [1] caulescent species
{2} *Griphopus*   [2] (interspecific) caulescent hybrids (named)
{3} *Chenopus*   [3] acaulescent species
{4} *Helleborus*   [4] *Helleborus* ×*hybridus*, acaulescent hybrids (unnamed)
{5} *Helleborastrum*
{6} *Dicarpon*

H. niger, which is currently broken into two subspecies which may not be maintained over time.

Section *Helleborastrum* is the focus of current revisionary taxonomy, and what is held to at the time we write this will change. Already, *H. occidentalis* has been split from *H. viridis* and given specific rank. Following are some of the potential changes to this large and diverse group of hellebores.

Helleborus atrorubens seems like a distinct species as it is currently described. On the southeastern part of its range, *H. croaticus* was separated based on the presence of hairs on the pedicels and bracts. At the southwestern end, a large number of green-flowered plants are found, often mixed with red flowers and some green stained with red, which may represent intergrades.

Helleborus cyclophyllus (described in 1867) may be simply a southern expression of *H. odorus*, which was named in 1809. The rules of botanical nomenclature give precedence to the older name, so if the two species are combined, the name of *H. odorus* would be maintained.

Helleborus multifidus is the most complex species as it is currently described. Each of the four currently recognized subspecies will likely be elevated to species status. This would create *H. bocconei*, *H. hercegovinus*, *H. istriacus*, and *H. multifidus*. Within Italy, plants once considered to belong to *H. bocconei* show the same degree of difference from that species as *H. istriacus* does from *H. bocconei*. In light of this, it seems likely that two additional species from Italy will be named. In addition, some populations of *H. multifidus* in Bosnia and Croatia that show affinity with both *H. multifidus* subsp. *multifidus* and *H. torquatus* may in fact be described as an entirely new species.

Helleborus odorus, as mentioned above, may be combined with *H. cyclophyllus* as one species. Northern populations of *H. odorus* in Slovenia differ from typical species in having thin textured, fully deciduous foliage and smaller stature. These plants may represent a new species.

Helleborus orientalis is a relatively homogeneous and distinct species with flower color being the only significant variation. Differences in flower color and range are currently used to maintain three subspecies. The trait of spotting, used to separate out *H. guttatus*, has been observed in populations of *H. orientalis* subsp. *orientalis*, making *H. guttatus* seem less distinct and perhaps an artificial designation. *Helleborus orientalis* subsp. *abchasicus* is more geographically isolated and consistent in flower color. The native range of this species is difficult to access due to political strife. Until further field work is possible, no decisions can be made on the future of these plants.

Helleborus torquatus seems distinct, but at the northern extent of its range in Bosnia it seems to intergrade with the plants currently described as *H. multifidus* subsp. *multifidus*. These plants may represent an entirely new species.

Helleborus viridis no longer includes the more northern and western *H. occidentalis*. In northern Italy, *H. viridis* is usually distinct and easily recognizable.

ITALIAN AND BALKAN HELLEBORES: CHANGES AND PROBLEMS

Matthias Thomsen

In mainland Italy, hellebores are widespread from the southern Alps down to western Sicily. They are found in woodlands and, at higher altitudes, in open grazing land on fertile soils over limestone formations. They extend from the western coastal regions to the higher hills and mountains of the Apennine range. In addition to *H. foetidus* and *H. niger*, existing literature mentions two species of the section *Helleborastrum*, namely *H. viridis* in the north and *H. multifidus* subsp. *bocconei* in central and southern Italy. Fieldwork in Italy, which took more than seven years with more than 80 colonies thoroughly explored, revealed a more complex situation. Two new candidates for species status were found and proposed, which are very distinct from both *H. viridis* and *H. multifidus* subsp. *bocconei*.

One candidate is a mountain plant that grows in open meadows or very light woods with high light levels and sufficient moisture due to fairly frequent summer rains. This plant has large, saucer-shaped green to yellow flowers, and the leaves can be very strongly dissected into narrow or very narrow segments. A plant has been found with 200 narrow segments on one leaf. This candidate species is an attractive garden plant both for flowers and ornamental foliage effect. The other plant is found in hot and dry evergreen woodlands of the coastal region and the lower hills in northwestern Italy. In its mild natural habitat the foliage lasts through the winter, and the whitish to white strongly fragrant flowers on tall stalks begin to appear around Christmas. The leathery leaves are very robust with few broad segments. This is a fantastic garden plant for mild winter climates.

In the Balkans, acaulescent hellebores (section *Helleborastrum*) are widespread over limestone, and existing taxonomy gives us some good, undisputed species for large regions there. For many years, there has been a lot of confusion and discussion over plants from northwestern Croatia and northwestern Bosnia-Herzegovina, namely *H. multifidus* subsp. *multifidus* and Bosnian *H. torquatus*. Whenever botanists or gardeners visit colonies within the range of these two, some of them invariably report how indistinguishable these plants are from each other apart from predominant flower color.

Colonies of plants with reasonably uniform flower color do not exist, neither within what is presently called *H. torquatus* in Bosnia nor within what is supposed to be *H. multifidus* subsp. *multifidus* in northwestern Croatia. One widely accepted theory is that many of those colonies represent intermediate forms between both species. This thesis is unsatisfactory, however, because if clean, separate species do not exist in northwestern Croatia, how can there be intermediates between them?

The whole complex is presently explored and discussed on the basis of thorough observation on many levels. As fieldwork continues and more data is collected, discussions will also go on for a few more years with open end. A satisfactory future taxonomy of this complex must be consistent with the true situation in the wild; it must make things less contradictory in terms of biology, and it must give us all a good language in which to address these wonderful plants.

4

THE INTERSPECIFIC AND INTERSECTIONAL HYBRIDS

'Briar Rose' has all the charm of a boil on Madonna's bum.

Tony Hall, Eastern Winter Study Weekend (2002)

The intersectional hybrid *Helleborus* 'Pink Ice' set a new standard for flower size, shape, and color.

ONE OF THE MOST PERPLEXING, exciting, or annoying (depending on your outlook) facets of hellebores is that so many of the species interbreed. While hybridization occurs in the wild, the interspecific and intersectional hybrids discussed in this chapter are created for ornamental effect. Crossing two different species produces most hybrids. A few, such as *Helleborus ×ericsmithii*, involve three species. The majority of site-specific hybrids produce sterile offspring, but a few hellebore crosses produce fertile offspring.

Helleborus ×hybridus is the most familiar interspecific hybrid, and we have devoted Chapter 5 to these plants. Most of the hybrids we discuss in this chapter involve species that fall into different botanical sections within the genus *Helleborus*, thus the name *intersectional* hybrids. A few, such as *H. ×sternii*, are interspecific crosses of two species within the same section but are not included in *H. ×hybridus*, so they are discussed here. Most other intersectional and interspecific hybrids are relatively unknown horticulturally as of this writing, though they are eminently gardenworthy. Hybrid vigor makes them robust and floriferous. The availability of *H. thibetanus* and *H. vesicarius*, which were once extremely rare in cultivation, has provided breeders with material from which to create new hybrids. While the ultimate gardenworthiness of new crosses is surely determined by time, the prospect of untried crosses is a veritable candy shop to the kid in every hybridizer.

Two terms are important for any discussion of hybrids: *pollen parent* and *seed parent*. The pollen parent plant donates pollen to a cross. The seed parent serves as the female, or seed-bearing plant, onto which the pollen is placed. In any cross, such as *H. niger* × *H. argutifolius*, convention dictates that the seed parent is listed first. (For a more detailed discussion, see Chapter 7.)

Helleborus ×nigercors Wall

Helleborus niger crosses with *H. argutifolius* to produce *H. ×nigercors*, a very tough and floriferous plant. First exhibited at an RHS show in 1931 by J. E. H. Stooke, this hybrid is particularly attractive, vigorous, and amazingly hardy. A number of clones of *H. ×nigercors* have been introduced in both the U.K. and U.S. since the mid-1990s.

The foliage of these hybrids often favors the *H. argutifolius* parent in size and shape, with the flowers almost always resembling the *H. niger* parent. The foliage on 18 in. (45cm) tall plants is usually heavily toothed and very sturdy. The leaves of some forms are blue-green or even veined with white when the foliage is young, although the older leaves often darken with age. Flowers of the best forms are large, roughly 2 to 4 in. (5 to 10 cm) wide, and creamy white. Some forms are tinted pink, a trait inherited from anthocyanin-rich *H. niger* selections such as the 'Sunset' strain. Flowers with a blush of green down the center of the sepal are also common.

Like most hybrids, the offspring of *H. ×nigercors* vary in flower size and leaf coloration.

The carriage of flowers on *H. ×nigercors* is unusual, combining both caulescent and acaulescent traits. Some flowers are produced from the top of the stem, as with *H. argutifolius* (section *Chenopus*), and others are borne on stems from soil level, similar to the forms of *H. niger* (section *Helleborus*) that bear more than one flower per stem. The combination produces a bouquet of long-lasting blooms, some plants producing several dozen flowers at a time.

The full hardiness of *H. ×nigercors* is unknown; both parents are hardy over much of North America, and consequently the hybrids are likely hardy as well, but further testing is required before generalizations are made. The demonstrated range is Zones 6 to 9. As with most hellebores, *H. ×nigercors* plants appreciate well-drained and fertile soil, tolerating sun or shade and easily adapting to pot culture.

This cross is traditionally sterile, although reports of fertile plants come from both the United States and Europe. Propagation from division in autumn is quite easy, as the stem and root delineations are easily discernible. New plants bulk up quickly and bloom much more rapidly than most other hellebores do after division. *Helleborus ×nigercors* has responded to production by tissue culture. Several selections are in culture in both the United States and Europe, creating the potential for thousands of plants.

The variability between individual plants of *H.* ×*nigercors* is quite pronounced.

Cultivars and seed strains

'Alabaster' from Washfield Nursery was one of the first forms offered for sale. Using *H. niger* 'Potter's Wheel' as a seed parent contributed to the large, creamy white flowers with a touch of green. 'Blackthorn' strain seed strain is produced by making the cross each year; plants are pure white or white with green. 'Green Corsican' is produced by tissue culture and has green-white flowers that age to pure green. 'Honeyhill Joy' was bred by Jim and Audrey Metcalfe of Portland, Oregon. It has gray-green leaves and many cream-colored blooms; it is produced by tissue culture. 'Silver Moon' is a tissue-cultured cultivar with cool white flowers over silvery foliage. 'Valentine Green', a micropropagated form from Japan, offers a large white flower with a faint green blush running down the center of each sepal. Flowers fade to lime-green as they age; it is produced by tissue culture. 'Vulcan Beauty' is a tissue-cultured cultivar from the Netherlands, with cream-colored flowers over gray-green foliage. 'White Beauty', also listed as *H.* ×*nigercors* 'Micha White Beauty' or simply *H.* 'White Beauty', has cream-colored flowers that fade to green.

JIM AND AUDREY METCALFE

Jim and Audrey Metcalfe are lifelong hellebore enthusiasts. Their garden features hundreds of plants, including the exceptional *H. ×nigercors* 'Honeyhill Joy', which they introduced.

The garden at Honeyhill, Jim and Audrey Metcalfe's home in Portland, Oregon, is abuzz with talk of hellebores. Longtime hellebore fans, they became serious after Jim retired from his cardiology practice to become an avid breeder of both *H. ×hybridus* and intersectional hybrids.

Their first plant was a white-flowering *H. ×hybridus* that Jim received from a Native American medicine woman in 1964 in trade for a pot of goutweed, *Aegopodium podagraria*. Having made this most fortunate exchange, Jim began to divide his plant, increasing the numbers each year until he had a bank of white flowers to enjoy. When retirement provided the time necessary to begin experimenting with more hellebores, Jim and Audrey began to purchase seed from Gisela Schmiemann and Will McLewin. It did not take the pair long to discover they were producing more plants than they needed for their garden, and Honeyhill plants became available for retail sale. Correspondence with Schmiemann led to a trip to Germany and the first pink double-flowering *H. ×hybridus* that began their double strain.

Although much of their work is devoted to producing double-flowering plants in a range of colors, Jim and Audrey also enjoy the other hybrids. One of their plants, a *H. ×nigercors* named 'Honeyhill Joy', was micropropagated by Terra Nova for commercial release. Jim and Audrey believe that 'Honeyhill Joy' is endowed with the vigor of *H. argutifolius* and the beauty of *H. niger*. The plants are among the sturdiest and most striking in their garden.

Helleborus ×sternii Turrill

Helleborus argutifolius and *H. lividus*, both in section *Chenopus*, cross with one another to produce the fertile hybrid called *H. ×sternii*. The cross was named for Sir Frederick Stern, in whose garden it originated. *Helleborus ×sternii* is a very attractive plant, and nurseries in the United States, Japan, and Europe produce dozens of lovely strains. This interspecies cross can be made using either species as the seed parent.

The showy foliage of *H. ×sternii* varies from green to silver, depending on the amount of *H. lividus* blood expressed by the cross.

The best forms of *H. ×sternii* have bronzy flowers above silvery mottled leaves.

Helleborus ×sternii is widely grown and makes an attractive garden plant. Evergreen boughs protect plants from frost and excessive moisture at Ashwood Nurseries.

Individual plants of this caulescent hybrid vary considerably in size, shape, foliage color, and bloom size. Some are tall, up to 24 in. (60 cm), with green foliage. Others are very short, about 6 in. (15 cm), and resemble *H. lividus*, with deep purple-rose on the back of the leaves. Foliage is exceedingly varied and often combines parental traits. For example, they may possess the toothed edges and intricate veining of *H. argutifolius* and the silvery blue color and purple reverse of *H. lividus*. The flowers of *H. ×sternii* range from 1 to 2 ½ in. (3 to 6 cm) wide. Clumps produce multiple stems, each bearing up to a dozen flowers.

Plants respond to rich, well-drained soil in either sun or shade once established. Cold tolerance varies between individuals of this cross. Generally, plants with greener foliage exhibit greater hardiness than those with silver, silvery blue, or silvery marbled foliage. Plants are root hardy into USDA Zone 6, possibly colder if provided with good drainage. Where the plants are root hardy but the stems are frozen, fresh foliage emerges in spring and remains attractive throughout the season. Individual gardeners must decide whether or not the loss of flowers is acceptable.

Plants are susceptible to black spot and frost damage if grown outdoors near the limits of their hardiness. *Helleborus ×sternii* makes a very attractive container plant. Given protection when temperatures are below 15° F (−10° C), this hybrid may provide attractive blooms for Valentine's Day in much of North America.

A very easy cross to execute, all forms are fertile and produce seedlings similar to the parents. If gathered when ripe and sown fresh, seeds begin to germinate in late autumn or early winter. *Helleborus* ×*sternii* germinates readily even after the seed has dried. Shortly after germination, seedlings develop their first true leaves, which are quite like the mature foliage, only in miniature. Breeders are then able to rogue out any plants that do not reflect the characteristics of the selected form. Seedlings of *H.* ×*sternii* are so like those of *H. lividus* it is often impossible to tell them apart.

Plants grow rapidly and often flower the first winter after germination. Like other stemmed species, division does not produce healthy plants. Micropropagation by tissue culture is possible with this species but is not financially practical since the cross is easily executed and seedlings mature quickly. Perhaps a new hardy or disease-resistant selection will have enough value to make tissue culture profitable.

By backcrossing *H. lividus* onto *H.* ×*sternii*, Pine Knot Farms now grows selections of *H.* ×*sternii* that are hardier than either of the parent plants, with some keeping the silvery blue foliage, which sets this group apart. While the preliminary results are interesting, a detailed study of the varying forms is needed to determine horticultural usefulness. We asked Peter Brandham of the Royal Botanical Gardens, Kew, about the hardiness of plants resulting from crosses of *H.* ×*sternii* with *H. lividus*. His reply helped us understand that when backcrossing *H.* ×*sternii* onto *H. lividus*, many of the offspring are genetically very close to *H. lividus*, so they naturally resemble that species in color and hardiness:

> Here the two species *argutifolius* and *lividus* evidently do not show strong dominance, so the F1 is intermediate between the parents, i.e., taking all the genes together (where H or h = all the genes in a species) and expressing them as four copies as above, HHHH *argutifolius* × hhhh *lividus* gives HHhh *sternii*. As many genes are involved, most of the progeny of selfing the F1 *sternii* will still be almost exactly intermediate between the parental species, *argutifolius* or *lividus*, but some will tend towards one or other of those species, with decreasing frequency towards the extremes. *Helleborus sternii* ×*lividus* is genetically HHhh × hhhh. Because of the wide range of genetic structure of the gametes of the F1, which contributes to variability, the offspring must be at least half *lividus* in character, but also it will extend to almost wholly *lividus*, again with decrease in proportion of individuals as pure *lividus* is approached. Again, selection for the character combinations that are desirable will be of use here.

Cultivars and seed strains

There are many forms of *H.* ×*sternii*, and each specialist hellebore nursery has its own. Some are selected for silvery foliage, others for exceptionally strong teeth along the edges of the leaf, and some for height, bloom color, or hardiness. All are grown from seed and therefore variable.

'Ashwood' strain, dwarf form, is 12 to 15 in. (30 to 38 cm) tall, with gray-green marbled foliage that is heavily toothed and green blooms flushed pink. The Blackthorn Group has very blue foliage and cream and dusty pink flowers. 'Boughton Beauty' has gray foliage with red reverse, rose-red stems, and cream flowers flushed pink. 'Bulmer's Blush' has narrow marbled leaves, red stems, and chartreuse flowers aging to dusty pink. 'Clifton Grey', from New Zealand, has gray leaves with heavy veining. 'Fire and Ice' (sometimes listed as *H. argutifolius*) is a variegated selection with red-flushed stems. 'Montrose' strain has green-gray foliage and chartreuse flowers blushed pink; it is quite hardy. 'Pine Knot' strain is silver-gray with rose-pink flowers. 'Rachel', from Tasmania, is very silvery, with toothed leaves, red reverse, and chartreuse and rose-colored blooms.

Helleborus ×ballardiae B. Mathew

Helleborus lividus (section *Chenopus*) crosses with *H. niger* (section *Helleborus*) to produce *H. ×ballardiae* (previously known as *H. ×nigriliv*), which is named for Helen Ballard, whose work with these species is recognized by this epithet. At a petite 12 to 15 in. (30 to 38 cm) tall, this selection is much smaller in all its parts than *H. ×nigercors*. In most forms, the foliage is more reminiscent of *H. niger* in shape, although sometimes having more divisions in the leaflets. Quite often foliage shows the veining or marbling inherited from the *H. lividus* parent and perhaps a rose color is displayed on the backs of the leaves.

The flower stems are often reddish rose and support several 2 to 4 in. (5 to 10 cm) flowers per stem. Flowers of *H. ×ballardiae* are a rose tone, similar to those of *H. lividus* in bud, and on the reverse open to a creamy white inside, sometimes blushed with pink and resembling *H. niger* in size and shape.

Although the full extent of the hardiness of this plant is not yet known, Judith has grown it outside in her Zone 7 garden for more than 10 years. Since this plant has the tender *H. lividus* as one of its parents, it is best used as a container or alpine house plant in much of North America. Fortunately, this hybrid responds well to pot culture, assuming the prerequisite of well-drained, fertile medium is met. In soil or in pots, *H. ×ballardiae* is tolerant of a wide range of light conditions, growing well in full sun to partial sun, partial shade, and full shade.

Helleborus ×ballardiae is generally considered sterile, although Ballard's published notes say that *H. niger × H. lividus* is often fully fertile and can even be self-fertilized. However, this discrepancy is possibly due to a translation or printing error. For most breeders, the plant is sterile. Producing this plant requires repeating the cross each year. Larger plants are easily divided.

Note that because *H. lividus* crosses so freely with *H. argutifolius*, much of the commercially available stock of *H. lividus* is likely *H. ×sternii*. Plants should be given the name *H. ×ballardiae* only when they are created from pollen of *H. lividus* of known wild origin. Otherwise, plants are actually *H. ×ericsmithii*.

Helleborus ×ballardiae is a robust and attractive hybrid with outfacing flowers and deep green foliage.

Helleborus ×ericsmithii B. Mathew

Helleborus ×sternii, when crossed with *H. niger*, produces *H. ×ericsmithii*. This hybrid, previously known as *H. ×nigristern*, was named for Eric Smith, one of the first to make the cross. Traditionally a small plant 10 to 14 in. (25 to 36 cm) tall, with foliage that is often quite blue, *H. ×ericsmithii* can resemble each of the plants involved in this three-way cross. In some forms the foliage is toothed, while in others it is more rounded. Veining is common, but the foliage is sometimes pure green. It is not unusual to find completely rose-colored stems and petioles. Flowers are borne in clusters atop short stems, each cluster having multiple buds. Each flat-faced cream to rose-tinted flower is roughly 2 to 4 in. (5 to 10 cm) wide.

As with the other intersectional hybrids, the full hardiness range remains undetermined until plants are tested in a wide range of conditions. Demonstrated hardiness range is from Zones 6 to 8. With a long flowering period and extremely attractive foliage, *H. ×ericsmithii* is certainly worth considering as a container plant, responding well to being grown in a freely draining medium with adequate nutrition, in both sun and shade.

Cultivars and seed strains
Helleborus ×ericsmithii responds to micropropagation, assuring that superior forms eventually become widely available at reasonable prices. A selection of *H. ×ericsmithii*

Three distinct forms of *H. ×ericsmithii* illustrate the variability inherent in this complex cross.

from Ashwood Nurseries was the first to be produced by tissue culture, with good blue-green foliage with cream venation and rose reverse. Cream-colored flowers are blushed rose pink on reverse and stems. Blackthorn Form has blue-green leaves with silvery veins. Flowers are cream to dusty rose. It is not micropropagated. Heronswood Form has attractive foliage characteristic of *H. ×ericsmithii*, with large ivory flowers with red stems; plants may be fertile. 'Pink Beauty', also known as 'Micha Pink Beauty', shows typical forms of *H. ×ericsmithii* with dusty rose flowers; plants are produced by tissue culture. 'Sun Marble' from Sunshine Farms is a representative cultivar of *H. ×ericsmithii* with cream-colored veins on blue-green foliage. It is produced by micropropagation or division.

OTHER INTERSECTIONAL HYBRIDS

We are experiencing an explosion in the number of intersectional hellebore crosses, as hybridizers seem to delight in pollinating the most unlikely plant pairs with one another. The availability of formerly rare or unusual species has provided new breeding material. Most of the work involves *H. niger*, which crosses with the species listed previously in this chapter as well as with *H. vesicarius* and *H. thibetanus*, and quite possibly with other species.

Helleborus 'Ivory Prince'

'Ivory Prince' was bred by David Tristram, son of Major Guy Tristram, who named *H. niger* 'Potter's Wheel'. The cross was made using a seedling of 'Potter's Wheel' and Tristram's form of *H. ×ericsmithii*. Plants are similar in appearance to a good form of *H. ×ericsmithii*, with cream-colored buds flushed pink, opening to outward-facing blooms that are streaked with green and with rose on the reverse. Sterile plants develop many flowers. Produced by tissue culture, plants should show very little variability.

Helleborus 'Pink Ice'

Kevin Belcher of Ashwood Nurseries crossed *H. niger* with *H. thibetanus* (section *Dicarpon*) to produce 'Pink Ice'. When presented at an RHS winter show in London, it created quite a stir. The first recorded cross of these two species, 'Pink Ice' is the result of eight years of work. After repeated crosses were made over several years, one finally produced fertile seed, and the seedlings took four or five years to bloom. 'Pink Ice' inherits its silvery pink color, darker pink veining, and ruffling along the edge from *H. thibetanus*. The broad, flat flower face comes from *H. niger*. The apparently sterile flowers are produced in branched clusters, with each flower approximately 2 in. (5 cm) across on plants that reach 12 to 15 in. (30 to 38 cm) tall. Propagation depends on repeating the cross for each crop of seed, or by division, until tissue culture becomes a reality. (*Helleborus* 'Pink Ice' was illustrated and cited in the March 2001 issue of *The Garden*, the journal of the Royal Horticultural Society.)

'Pink Ice' has been turning heads since its introduction by Ashwood Nurseries in 2001.

The diffused pink rim of *H.* 'Briar Rose' comes from *H. vesicarius*.

Helleborus 'Briar Rose'

Belcher was also the first to cross *H. niger* and *H. vesicarius* (section *Syncarpus*), producing the plant he named 'Briar Rose'. *Helleborus vesicarius*, the unusual hellebore from Turkey, has mystified growers for years. It is difficult to cultivate in the open garden. 'Briar Rose' has the bright celery-green foliage of *H. vesicarius*, which darkens with age, and is evergreen like *H. niger*. The flowers are larger than those of *H. vesicarius*, approximately 1 to 1½ in. (3 to 4 cm), and are creamy white with a wide rose rim around the outside. This hybrid is an exciting container plant but is virtually untested in the garden at this time. Time will tell whether 'Briar Rose' makes a suitable garden plant. (*Helleborus* 'Briar Rose' was profiled in the March 2002 issue of *The Garden*.)

Helleborus 'Snow White'

The Yokoyama Nursery in Japan introduced a hybrid from a white-flowering *H. ×hybridus* and *H. niger*. 'Snow White' has large, outward-facing flowers that open out flat as with *H. niger*. Foliage is intermediate between the parents. The previously undocumented cross between these two species is the result of a "bee hybrid." The Yokoyama plant, which occurred in the late 1990s, is a seedling of *H. ×hybridus* with *H. niger* as the pollen parent. 'Snow White' is sterile and is being produced by tissue culture.

Helleborus multifidus × *Helleborus ×hybridus*

A number of breeders in the United States and Europe continue to experiment with crosses involving *H. multifidus* (section *Helleborastrum*) with divided leaves and good color forms of *H. ×hybridus*. The aim is to produce plants with excellent flower form and color with lush, dissected foliage.

The cross *H. niger* × *H. ×hybridus* was rare until tissue-cultured plants named 'Snow White' became available.

WORKING WITH INTERSPECIFIC AND INTERSECTIONAL HYBRIDS AT PINE KNOT

Judith Knott Tyler

Working with intersectional hybrids can be both exciting and extremely frustrating. After pollination, we must wait to see whether seed forms. If seed begins to form, we must wait to see whether it matures and ripens. If so, it still may not be viable. If the viable seed germinates, we must wait until the seedlings are mature enough to determine whether the cross has worked.

Plants from intersectional crosses can be deceptive in the seedling stage. The foliage of the hybrid can be so similar to one parent that the results of hybridization will not be apparent until the seedlings bloom. Some crosses may take several years to develop their true flower and foliage form; patience is a definite asset. No standard is used to verify crosses. DNA studies would perhaps provide definitive documentation that the offspring is, in fact, a product of the intended cross, but the expense of this procedure is prohibitive.

Until recently, we have never produced viable seed from any of our intersectional crosses. Seed often began to form on *H. ×ballardiae*, *H. ×ericsmithii*, and *H. ×nigercors*, but it was seldom viable. It either aborted during formation or formed incompletely. It is possible to stimulate the plant's hormones with a chemical or use a technique called *embryo rescue* (removing the embryo for tissue culture in a sterile medium), but we have never attempted these extreme measures.

In 2004, a *H. ×nigercors* plant, which has been in the garden for several years, produced seed voluntarily from a random pollination. How annoying, after all the years we have spent unsuccessfully backcrossing pollen from *H. niger* onto *H. ×nigercors* and *H. ×ericsmithii* plants by hand, that the first successful seed was produced by bee feet. We must monitor the resulting seedlings for several more years before we can make any decision about the gardenworthiness of these plants; however, it is always exciting to work with a new cross.

When attempting to create an intersectional hybrid, we must use a plant of one species for the seed parent and at least pollen from the other species, the pollen parent. The seed parent is emasculated prior to fertilization. (See Chapter 7 for more information on the complete operation of emasculation.) Neutering of the seed parent should prevent self-fertilization, but pollen grains are tiny and can cling unnoticed to fingernails, forceps, or other tools, so random fertilization is still possible.

Some species seem to set seed more easily than others, and this is often one of the criteria we use when selecting the seed parent. If, for instance, we are attempting to cross *H. niger* with *H. argutifolius* to produce *H. ×nigercors*, we will usually use *H. niger* as the seed parent. *Helleborus niger* plants set seeds that ripen reliably for us, and we know what to expect from this cross. It is often interesting to work the cross both ways, using *H. argutifolius* as the seed parent. This is especially valuable if we are trying to incorporate a particular trait from the chosen mother plant.

One particular hybrid we have attempted for several years is crossing *H. niger* with one of the variegated forms of *H. argutifolius* with the intention of producing a variegated form of *H. ×nigercors*. We have done this cross using both *H. niger* and the variegated *H. argutifolius* 'Pacific Frost' as the seed parent. Performing the cross both ways improves the chances of producing the desired seedlings. Our final hurdle, once the cross takes, is to grow the seedlings to flowering size for evaluation without some fatal accident befalling them.

A "super niger"

We noticed an unusual feature when working with *H. niger* in intersectional crosses over the years. If a cross of *H. niger* and *H. argutifolius* fails, and the cross does not produce *H. ×nigercors*, the seedlings from this cross usually grow more rapidly and vigorously, and they ultimately produce larger plants than seedlings from other flowers of the same plant that were not interfered with and allowed to form seed in the usual way.

We discussed this phenomenon with other breeders and found that many of them observe similar reactions in their plants. None of us quite knows why this happens, and eventually we decided to consult an expert. Peter Brandham of the Royal Botanical Gardens, Kew, told us this:

The two species are genetically close enough to produce a fertile F1, which happens in many plants. In the hybrid, many of the shape/colour-inducing genes (controlling the characters used in species differentiation) are therefore the same genes, but from the data supplied, these genes seem to exist as dominants in *niger* and recessives in *argutifolius*. In common with all hellebores, both species are tetraploid with 32 chromosomes and have four copies of every gene. Thus AAAA BBBB CCCC DDDD etc. gives pure-breeding *niger*, while aaaa bbbb cccc dddd etc. gives pure *argutifolius*. The F1 hybrid will be AAaa BBbb CCcc DDdd etc. and will be uniform, as are all F1 hybrids between pure-breeding lines. In the F1, the dominant *niger* forms (alleles) of each gene will override the effect of the *argutifolius* recessives to give a *niger* appearance. Being a hybrid, the plant will also show the well-known phenomenon of hybrid vigour (as noted).

On selfing the F1, or by crossing two of the F1 plants (which is the same thing genetically) the next (F2) generation will still have many dominant alleles and will tend to resemble *niger*. On further selfing, the F3, F4 etc. generations will at last produce a few combinations in which at least one gene is in the totally recessive form. An example is AAAa BBbb cccc dddD, in which the recessive c gene will be expressed in the individual as an *argutifolius* character.

5

THE HYBRID LENTEN ROSE,
HELLEBORUS ×HYBRIDUS

"The Lent Hellebores . . . have become," said Miss Gertrude Jekyll, who had a
famous Nut Walk bordered with them, "much mixed by hybridization, both natural
and intentional, and though they are no doubt kept distinct in botanical gardens,
those to be found in private places are for the most part hybrids." This is all to the
good from the gardener's point of view, for we find among these hybrids many
lovely colors—soft ruddy, purplish tones, greenish tints, cream, blush, even pure
white ones and some with spotted flowers, or they may be suffused with other hues.

Louise Beebe Wilder in *The Garden in Color* (1937)

The exquisite colors and full forms of double, semidouble, and single hellebores are beautifully displayed
in this bowl at Ashwood Nurseries.

The only sure way to get the exact color that you want is to buy your plants in bloom.

IF JEKYLL AND WILDER COULD SEE today's garden hybrid hellebores, they would no doubt be stunned. Their lovely "soft ruddy, purplish tones" have been replaced with rich burgundy, plum, and deep black-purple. The "greenish tints," perhaps euphemistically describing pink or white flowers more green than not, have given way to deep apple-greens, many of which are gorgeously spotted with deep red. The purity of the pinks, from soft shell-pink to deep rose, is unbelievable by comparison. Perfectly shaped flowers with overlapping, rounded sepals; deep, pure colors; and, above all, voluptuous double flowers have thoroughly transformed the Lenten rose. How did we get to this level of perfection? To answer that question, we travel to England and Europe to explore the work of a handful of hybridizers who changed the face of garden hybrid hellebores.

HUMBLE BEGINNINGS

The Lenten rose (*Helleborus orientalis*) arguably lays claim to the showiest flowers in the genus. By *showiest*, we don't necessarily mean the largest. The Christmas rose can give its cousin a run for its money on that account. Showy is more a combination of traits rather than any one single attribute. The Lenten rose has poise. The flowers nod gracefully or in rare cases are outfacing, held well free of the leaves on branched stalks. The flowers are by no means small, many stretching to 3 in. (7.5 cm) across. The clincher is that they are colorful. Though white is common, spotted, pink, plum, and dusky purple flowers abound. Taken together, these characteristics give *H. orientalis* and its hybrids preeminent status among hellebores.

Long referred to as "orientalis hybrids," modern garden hellebores are complex hybrids involving many species. Most include *H. orientalis* blood, but they incorporate the genes of other species. The rich purple and black flowers take their color from *H. torquatus* and *H. purpurascens*. The yellows owe a debt to *H. odorus*, while the greens are derived from *H. cyclophyllus*, *H. odorus*, and others. Some garden hybrids do not involve *H. orientalis* at all.

So what should we call these garden hybrid hellebores? Nomenclature of garden plants is confusing in the best of circumstances. To retire the misnomer "orientalis hybrids" once and for all, and to acknowledge their complex origins, McLewin and Mathew published a paper in *The New Plantsman* in June 1998 in which they proposed that all acaulescent plants (section *Helleborastrum*) of hybrid origin, including those involving *H. orientalis*, should be known as *H. ×hybridus*. This seems a satisfactory solution to the confusion. The name *Helleborus ×hybridus* Hort. ex Vilmorin was first published in 1894. The following description of *garten-nieswurz*, or garden hellebores, was published by Siebert and Voss in Vilmorin's *Blumengärtnerei* and translated in *The New Plantsman* article by McLewin and Mathew:

> Under this name are included the hybrids that have resulted from the crossing of individual species and which occur in various colours, often being also spotted and veined. . . . Properly named sorts [that is, *cultivars* in modern parlance] can also be found in trade catalogues. The garden hellebore differs from the above [acaulescent] species partly in its non-evergreen leaves that usually appear in the spring at the same time as the flowers and then only last for one growing season, and partly in the color and size of its blooms which are excellent as cut flowers. As hardy and early flowering as the other species, even when not pampered. To be thoroughly recommended.

Opinions differ on whether or not this description is sufficiently detailed to validate the name. McLewin and Mathew believe that the intent of the description, coupled with the illustration included in the original book, applied to the name *H. ×hybridus* is sufficiently clear to indicate acaulescent species of hybrid origin. The authors proposed reinstating the name to refer to all hybrids "past, present and future" between acaulescent species. Many of the plants, but by no means all, contain *H. orientalis*. The fact that garden hybrids can exclude *H. orientalis* is the reason that "orientalis hybrids" is no longer a useful or acceptable name.

According to the rules set down by the International Code of Botanical Nomenclature, a hybrid species name such as *H. ×hybridus* can be given only when a plant is the result of crossing two species, such as A × B. If A is crossed with C, the plant cannot bear the name *H. ×hybridus*, as that name refers only to A × B. Most hybrid, acaulescent hellebores are of complex parentage and contain genes from many species or other complex hybrids. While the name does not truly conform to the rules, McLewin and Mathew believe historical precedent is enough to maintain the name, and we concur.

Elizabeth Strangman raised this lovely hybrid with white and red-speckled sepals.

THE CULTIVAR QUAGMIRE

While we firmly believe that one does not need named cultivars to get exceptional plants, some historic named selections bear mention. Many of the first hellebores that were taken into breeding lines by England's influential hybridizers were unnamed plants of exceptional quality. A few of the early stock plants were named. As superior plants appeared, many new selections were given cultivar names. Far too many were named in most cases, including inferior plants as well as some nearly identical to others produced by the same or different breeders. And their slow vegetative propagation meant that the named plants were never readily available. Asexual propagation was so slow, in fact, that many nonclonal plants of similar flower color and form were sold under the name of the cultivar they resembled. This so muddied the water as far as the true identity of the named plants that most named selections are no longer extant. Those that remain hold historical significance but have largely been superseded.

THE MODERN ENGLISH LINES

English breeding lines provide us with a new standard. The U.K. is home to a number of hellebore breeders. Washfield Nursery in Kent, an area of southeast England aptly called the "Garden of England," was where Elizabeth Strangman created myriad lovely hellebores. Building on a firm foundation, Strangman introduced a number of interesting plants. One of these was 'Pamina', an apricot-colored hybrid named in

The dark petaloid nectaries of this semidouble Ashwood hybrid set off the picotee edge to great effect.

1987. This arose from a bit of bee-dispersed pink pollen deposited by chance onto a primrose-colored flower, producing the first of what became the 'Apricot' strain.

Strangman's excellent color strains set her plants apart from those being marketed elsewhere. The Washfield pinks are still among the clearest, and the blacks are robust and deeply colored. Her 'Picotee' strain developed from 'Violetta', and her doubles based on 'Aeneas' and 'Dido' became the foundation for the exceptional work carried on by many breeders.

ELIZABETH STRANGMAN OF WASHFIELD NURSERY

Many of the *H.* ×*hybridus* plants available today owe their existence to a sprightly bright-eyed lady with a strong will and a determined attitude. Elizabeth Strangman is known not only as one of the most significant hybridizers of hellebores but also for the information she has shared with other breeders throughout the world. Tall and slender with a quick wit and firm opinions, she remains recognized as an authority on the breeding of hellebores, although Washfield, the nursery she owned, is now closed.

Strangman's training, while impressive (she received a diploma in horticulture from Studley College and worked at Cambridge Botanic Gardens), is secondary to her inborn eye for good plants. She is one of the chosen few with the ability to visualize not only the apparent physical aspects of a plant but also what that plant can produce when bred with another member of the kingdom Plantae.

In 1961, the young Strangman began working at Washfield Nursery, a respected specialist nursery located in the village of Hawkhurst, Kent. At the time, the nursery was owned by the inspiring Hilda Davenport-Jones. An excellent plantswoman herself, Jones had worked with hellebores, particularly *H. niger*, introducing the legendary 'Potter's Wheel' strain, well known at the time for having huge white flowers held on long, sturdy stems. When Strangman asked if she could begin a breeding program, "Boss," the designation she still uses when referring to Davenport-Jones, agreed. In 1964, Strangman began systematically breeding hellebores, eventually producing plants so beautiful their celebrity eclipsed the many other unusual plants produced at the nursery.

In the traditional English fashion, the original stock plants came from some of the more noted gardeners of the day, with the list of donors reading like a horticultural who's who. Amy Doncaster, one of the legendary grande dames of

Hybrids produced by Elizabeth Strangman at Washfield Nursery set a new standard for hellebores in the 1980s. Her warm smile greeted enthusiasts from around the globe, who flocked to Washfield to acquire plants and knowledge.

the British gardening world, had a reputation of keeping very select garden plants in her unusual garden. During a visit to Doncaster's garden, Strangman spotted an interesting hellebore whose white flowers had a bit of color along the edge. This unusual trait intrigued her, and she was kindly given a bloom to work with at Washfield. Pollen from that one flower was placed onto a good white, and one of the seedlings was selected and named 'Violetta'. After several generations, the 'Picotee' strain ensued, a breakthrough in breeding that remains one of the most unusual forms ever created.

Rita Maxted, another discerning lady gardener of the same generation as Doncaster, was well known for her selection of unusual plants. It is said that she was somewhat terrifying, always dressed in black with one hooded eye. Among the treasures in the Maxted garden were some especially nice pink-flowering hellebores. Strangman received much encouragement from Maxted, and she was allowed to choose a pink-flowering plant from the garden for her work at Washfield. After years of breeding and selecting the very best plants, Strangman's pale-pink hybrids became known throughout the gardening world as having the most beautiful pure colors, remaining unsurpassed to this day.

Though improvements are made each year in the colors of garden hybrid hellebores, the pink strains produced by Strangman remain among the best.

Hellebores continued to attract customers to Washfield after Strangman inherited the nursery from "Boss." As the nursery prospered and the hellebore breeding program progressed, stock began to come in from other breeders. Helen Ballard at Old Country had set a standard of excellence with her crosses that Strangman admired. Ballard's plants were well known for their very rounded, bowl-shaped flowers. Chris Brickell provided a yellow plant descended from 'Bowles'Yellow' that was incorporated into the primrose strain, which began by crossing *H. odorus* and a cream-colored plant from Davenport-Jones. With plants from these celebrated gardeners and others whose names are not as universally recognized, Strangman produced the Washfield strains, select colored strains of *H. ×hybridus*, coming almost 100 percent true from seed. Hellebores from the seedling Washfield strains were known as vigorous, relatively inexpensive plants that grew much faster than the usually very small divisions of named cultivars sold at some other nurseries. These seedlings were sold in bloom, allowing customers to choose their favorite colors and flower forms. Washfield became one of the sources of many of the best hellebore plants available in the world today.

As hellebores became popular throughout the world, breeders began making pilgrimages to Washfield. Every single breeder of hellebores we interviewed gave Washfield as a source of some of their original plants. Strangman's breeding techniques are featured in *The Gardener's Guide to Growing Hellebores*, which she wrote in 1993 with Graham Rice. This book showed the world that there was more to Lenten roses than dingy or muddy colored blooms, and it excited gardeners who had never before heard the word *hellebore*.

Washfield Nursery is now closed; the gate in the gray wooden fence along Horn's Road no longer opens to display the scrumptious banquet of chlorophyll that once was offered to plant-hungry customers. Strangman experienced a stroke and needed to concentrate her energies on healing. Rather than compromise the reputation of excellence she had built at Washfield, she made the hard decision to sell up and begin anew.

In the garden she is building beside the ancient walls of her new home in East Sussex, Strangman and her two cats scamper about with an equal degree of grace and nimbleness, showing fortunate visitors around. One pair of treasures growing under a gnarled old fruit tree is from a 1971 collecting expedition to the former Yugoslavia. In Montenegro, Strangman's expert eye spotted two

Strangman discovered 'Dido', one of two important double-flowered *H. torquatus* that have given us many fine double-flowered hybrids.

double-flowering *H. torquatus*, a most exciting find. Small pieces of these plants were collected and named 'Aeneas' and 'Dido', which became the start of the 'Montenegran Doubles', one of the first double-flowering strains. The double-flowering hellebores named Party Dress, Westwood, and Wolverton Hybrids, as well as many thousands of unnamed double- and semidouble-flowering *H. ×hybridus*, are descendants of these two plants.

During her supposed retirement, she occasionally helps the RHS trials committee at Wisley judge new ornamental plants. She also supervises the production of Washfield color strains. Strangman is still very much interested in good new plants, trying out many of her latest acquisitions in her rapidly filling garden. She also enjoys the company of other keen gardeners, offering help and advice to younger gardeners and meeting up with friends and colleagues at Snowdrop lunches in February.

Elizabeth Strangeman is celebrated not only for the plants she raised and sold at Washfield, but also for the advice she so freely gave to other breeders. Rather than shutting away the knowledge garnered from her 30 years of growing, she has always been keen that the work with these plants should continue. Because she has so generously allowed others to build on her experience, the quest for the "perfect" hellebore continues, with breeders all over the world hearing her voice in their heads offering her favorite maxim, "Put the best with the best."

Across the country at Elmstead Market, Essex, Beth Chatto and David Ward have grown and sold hellebores for years at Beth Chatto Gardens. While in the next county, Suffolk, Roger Harvey of Harveys Garden Plants breeds the 'Bradfield' strain of *H. ×hybridus*, offering a wide range of colors in both single- and double-flowering plants with a special emphasis on early flowering. In Yorkshire, Ann Watson's Rarer Plants list a number of hellebores, species and hybrids. Southward outside of Manchester is Phedar Research Nursery, where Will McLewin grows many unusual hellebore species.

To the west, in Wales, are more breeders, including Graham Birkin, whose former location, Thirty Nine Steps, was perched on a hillside so steep that visiting goats would need to bring their climbing gear. The new nursery is much flatter, smaller, easier to find, and full of interesting single- and double-flowering hellebores. Not too far away in Llandysul, Carmarthenshire, are two more hellebore sources, Farmyard Nursery and Jim and Jenny Archibald. They offer both hybrids and species. In Scotland, enthusiasts flock to Buckland Plants.

In the Midlands lies Ashwood Nurseries, the current leader in *H. ×hybridus* breeding. Ashwood's program, like so many others, started with the best plants available—some named, such as 'Violetta', but many exceptional unnamed seedlings or strains such as Strangman's Picotee hybrids. Many of Ballard's best plants came into the mix early on. Each successive generation produced improvements, and always the best plants were kept and the rest sold. The Ashwood lines are exceptional. One such strain, descended from a picotee crossed with a yellow, is named for a uniquely British dessert called "Rhubarb and Custard." This delicious seed strain has a bowl-shaped, creamy, pale yellow base with dark pink veining. It is hard to imagine anything as luscious, but the next generation of "Rhubarb and Custard" is even more exciting. Deep yellow with egg yolk–yellow nectaries crossed with "Rhubarb and Custard" produced a line humorously named "Neon." The flowers on this cross are saturated deep yellow, accented with rich claret.

The results of each year's crosses produce something new and exciting at nurseries all over the U.K., creating new forms while building on the work of previous generations. Breeders like Robin White and Kevin Belcher continue to push the envelope.

JOHN MASSEY AND ASHWOOD NURSERIES

Ashwood Nurseries is truly a *nursery* in the very best sense of the word. The hellebore program at Ashwood began in 1989 and became world famous in a relatively short period of time, due in no small part to the dedication and persistence of owner John Massey.

As the hellebore program at Ashwood began, Massey visited the best breeders, specialist hellebore nurseries, and keen hobbyist growers of the time—McLewin, the Whites at Blackthorn, Strangman at Washfield, and Ballard, among others. Whenever he was permitted, Massey purchased plants or seeds for the fledgling breeding work at Ashwood, sometimes returning home on the train with muddy plastic bags containing large hellebore plants freshly dug from the fields of Kent. At the time,

Ashwood Nurseries is a mecca for hellebore enthusiasts worldwide. A full-service garden center, Ashwood features its diverse line in elegant displays both indoors and out.

almost all hellebores were grown in soil beds in the traditional way: plants were lifted and divisions made as a customer required. Many growers believed that hellebores would not grow in pots, and Ashwood was perhaps the first to do this successfully.

Massey, a gifted speaker with a keen sense of humor, tells groups how he visited Old Country, in Mathon, Malvern, Worcestershire—Ballard's home and famous garden—armed with gifts of fruitcake and whiskey, favorites of Dick Crandon, who helped grow the Ballard plants. The small divisions, which Ballard called "cutlets," an eye or node with roots and a flower, grew well at Ashwood, and these plants, handed over to breeder Kevin Belcher, were crossed with others to help produce the Ashwood Garden Hybrids.

Unlike Ballard and many other breeders, Massey does not name the Ashwood hellebores, choosing to concentrate on color strains. It is his belief that each year's crosses are better than those from the year before—always improving—and a named plant would quickly become obsolete. Rather than produce a very limited number of plants through clonal propagation, the Ashwood *H. ×hybridus* are grown from seed each year and the plants are sold in bloom.

The hellebores of Ashwood are often featured with two other Ashwood specialties, hepaticas and cyclamen, at RHS winter flower shows in London, in displays that are models of perfection, both for the consummate flawlessness of the displays and the unusual variety of the plants. The RHS has honored Ashwood with numerous gold medals for its plants and presentations. While accolades are always welcome, the pleasure of the job, the creation of the displays, and the actual work itself is reward enough for Massey, Belcher, Phillip Baulk, and the Ashwood staff. They are a team, whether working on the nursery, on the displays in London, or around the extensive display gardens that make up Ashwood.

The Party Dress Hybrids developed by Blackthorn Nursery are based on the *H. torquatus* doubles such as 'Dido'.

DOUBLES

Doubling occurs when the nectaries of a flower become petaloid. This phenomenon occurs in a number of species, most importantly *H. torquatus* and *H. orientalis*. In Hampshire, Robin and Sue White at Blackthorn Nursery began working with double-flowering hellebores using Strangman's *H. torquatus* 'Dido'. Some of the first double-flowering hellebore plants offered for sale in the U.K. were the Wolverton Hybrids, which clearly show their *H. torquatus* heritage, producing short plants with flowers in shades of green and pale yellow-green, sometimes streaked with purple. The Whites also bred the Westwood Hybrids, a similar *H. torquatus* strain with enlarged nectaries and *H. ×hybridus* blood. This group produces flowers that are semidouble in shades of reds and purples as well as the more common greens.

By introducing blood from selected hybrids into the double *H. torquatus* selection, a group of plants with larger flowers arose. The Whites named this strain Party Dress Hybrids; the flowers bloomed in shades of mauve, pink, cream, and green, and the flowers were ruffled and frilled like the skirts of a young girl's fancy dress. Party Dress hellebores are still popular today.

Doubles from *H. torquatus* are generally slower to mature and are not usually as robust as those created from double *H. ×hybridus*. When hybrid plants from German breeders were included in the bloodlines, new forms of double-flowering hellebores began to appear. Some of the first double-hybrid selections from Germany were

The newer doubles bred from *H. ×hybridus* are vigorous and large-flowered. This red Ashwood hybrid is exceptional.

'Snow Queen' and 'Günter Jürgl'; this group is taller, with larger flowers and more vigorous growth habits, leading to the lovely, strong, many-flowered plants we know today.

HELLEBORUS ×HYBRIDUS IN EUROPE

A number of European nurseries are producing high-quality plants. Building on 150 years of work of German and English hybridizers, Gisela Schmiemann in Germany and Hans Kramer in Holland provide plants in a full range of colors. Schmiemann, a keen gardener with a love of snowdrops and hellebores, befriended Ballard in 1983. By the early 1990s, Ballard was no longer able to carry on her breeding work. In her long life, she had seen many gardens and the plants they contained decay and eventually disappear; she knew well that the same fate could befall her garden and plants. To insure their perpetuation, she entrusted them to Schmiemann, who moved the entire collection to Germany. In 1997, two years after Ballard's death at age 86, Schmiemann honored her friend by publishing *Helen Ballard: The Hellebore Queen*. Sensual photos by Josh Westrich accompany the text. Schmiemann has continued to breed hellebores, using Ballard's plants and others acquired from England and closer to home. Seed from some of Schmiemann's plants infused the red line developed by the O'Byrnes at Northwest Garden Nursery in Eugene, Oregon, who still offer the best reds available anywhere.

GISELA SCHMIEMANN

Gisela Schmiemann poses in her garden where Helen Ballard's plants as well as many excellent hybrids from her own crosses grow among bulbs and other choice perennials.

The cover of *Helen Ballard: The Hellebore Queen* sports a gorgeous purple hybrid. (Photo by Josh Westrich)

We arrived in Cologne, Germany, on a January day when the wind howling down off the steppes penetrated our coats and sliced into our bones. The soil was frozen. Although our teeth were still chattering, Gisela Schmiemann's welcoming smile and a chance to see the famous Ballard plants generated an excitement that warmed us from within.

When Gisela and Klaus Schmiemann bought their house in the mid-1980s, they wanted a garden for all seasons to surround it. Gisela loved hellebores and began breeding them in her garden, later adding a piece of land where she grows her stock plants. A good eye is a necessity for plant breeders, and she certainly has 20/20 vision. Klaus says, "She can find a four-leaf clover from inside the car." Gisela also has an interest in history, particularly in older gardeners and horticultural texts from previous generations. These interests led her to visit Ballard the first time as translator for two hellebore breeders, Heinz Klose and Günther Jürgl. The group visited other breeders, too, including Strangman. Gisela was not able to buy plants during that trip, but she knew her turn would come, and come it did. She and Ballard became friends, and as age overcame Ballard's ability to continue her breeding work, Gisela was selected to become the custodian of her plants.

The plants are settled in and flourishing. Gisela grows everything in the open ground and has no access to poly houses or greenhouses. There were years when some of her work was lost, seeds did not form, or they were aborted when cold temperatures or icy weather ruined the flowers. But some did grow and she began to sell both plants and seeds. Since seeds meet importation requirements more easily than plants, seeds from her plants are sent all over the world.

Schmiemann learned that dividing hellebores again and again weakens them, and tissue culture was not feasible. To provide good plants, she began to breed color strains. After reaching a point when a high percentage of the strains bred true to color, Schmiemann and Georg Uebelhart of Jelitto Seed Company became partners in the production of the Lady series. The "ladies" are brought to market as seeds in a full range of colors under the names *H. ×hybridus* 'Red Lady', 'White Lady', and so on. Each year, the series becomes more stable. The groups are rigorously culled and any unsatisfactory plant is removed from production. Ultimately, they hope to achieve more or less 100 percent true color strains. This series is commercially available to gardeners and nurserymen all over the world, giving people in remote areas access to excellent plants founded on some of the finest bloodlines available.

HANS KRAMER OF DE HESSENHOF

The nursery and gardens at de Hessenhof, just outside the charming town of Ede, The Netherlands, are filled with *H. ×hybridus* and other species hellebores as well as many other interesting and unusual perennials and shrubs. The complexity of the plant palette means something is blooming at all times of year. The nursery and gardens are delightful to visit. A good time to see hellebores is on one of the open days the nursery hosts at the end of February.

Like almost every other hellebore breeder of his time, Hans Kramer began growing hellebores with plants from Strangman, Ballard, the Whites, Ashwood, and McLewin as well as plants from Belgium and Germany. He credits Strangman, Ernst Pagles, and Barbara Keuning for helping him get started. He began to make his own crosses and has developed his own strains of both single- and double-flowering selections of *H. ×hybridus*.

Kramer has also traveled widely in the Balkans to see species in the wild and to collect exceptional forms to incorporate in his breeding lines. With a gift for growing and a keen eye for selecting unusual perennials, he has made his nursery, de Hessenhof, a destination for nurserymen and gardeners from all nations.

The hellebores of de Hessenhof are grown from hand-pollinated crosses, and a full range of colors is available from deep purple to the pure whites and the pale pinks associated with the Strangman breeding program. Kramer has developed several very nice forms, a lovely reverse picotee strain in which the inside of the flower is dark and the edge is a light color. An unusual double-flowering bicolor shows flowers of red-purple on the reverse and cream colored inside, displaying a fine tracery of colored veins. His lines are some of the purest we know.

In addition to the open days at the nursery, plants from de Hessenhof are displayed at the annual Internationale Helleborusdagen at Arboretum Kalmthout in Belgium. This annual event is put together by a number of the most skillful hobbyist breeders and nurserymen in continental Europe. Specimen plants in flowering containers are brought into a building where many large windows provide exceptional natural light. The hellebore plants at this particular exhibition are quite ingeniously displayed on tables and along benches, their soil covered with moss, and small round mirrors are mounted under particular flowers so their interiors are easily viewed without the viewer touching the blooms. A trip to see the exceptional plants at Arboretum Kalmthout and those at de Hessenhof provides not only a lovely day out but a chance to see some of the latest additions to horticulture.

In 2005, Hanneke van Dijk and Harry van Trier, in association with Kramer, Thierry van Paemel, and Koen van Poucke, published a new book in the Netherlands entitled *Helleborus: Winterroos* (*Helleborus: Winter Roses*). As of this writing, the book has not been translated from Dutch to English.

THE HELLEBORE REBIRTH IN AMERICA

Long before the modern European hellebores came ashore, American breeders were selecting exceptional plants from existing domestic stock. Avid gardeners had traded good forms for nearly a century, improved from time to time by the infusion of new blood from abroad. Good plants came and went, but by and large, spotted white, dusky plum, pink, and almost pure white were stock in trade. The Slate Select Hybrids were one of the early lines. George L. Slate (1899–1976) of the Geneva Experiment Station in New York had an interest in breeding. Upon his death, his plants went to Cornell Plantations of Cornell University, where they are displayed today. Slate hybrids in mixed colors of pink, creamy white, and plum are still grown in New York and other places.

The Millet Hybrids, sold by Lamb Nurseries, formerly of Spokane, Washington, came in mixed soft colors. This line was sold as early as the 1930s and was offered for sale until the nursery closed in the mid 1990s. While not exceptional by today's standards, they were among the first American-bred plants that were sold as named selections. Carl Purdy (1861–1945), a nurseryman from Ukiah, California, and best known for his work with native bulbs, was a great fan of these hybrids. In the January 1935 issue of *Horticulture* magazine, he wrote in "New Colors in Hellebores" that "The Millet hybrids comprise quite a varied range of colors and markings. Some are white . . . others are apple blossom, near pink, and from that through varying shades to ruby crimson, all with a beautiful penciling, flecking, or mottling of various shades from rose to deep maroon." He listed five named selections as "a few instances of the colors."

Henry Ross at Gardenview Horticultural Park in Strongsville, Ohio, began growing hellebores with plants from Georgia. He received a few seedlings from a hobbyist in about 1950. From these, he collected seed from plants he preferred and grew them on, repeating the process for some 50 years. Henry also grew hellebore species from seed obtained from Leon Doyen and Will McLewin. Although Henry does not sell plants, the plants on view in the garden today are descended from more than a half century of hellebore history.

Don Jacobs of Eco Gardens in Decatur, Georgia, has been growing and selecting hellebores since the 1960s. His original stock was augmented with plants grown from superior *H. ×hybridus* selections received from a German friend in 1974. In the 1970s the Eco hellebore collection grew to include a number of species as well as hybrids when Jacobs brought home plants from two trips to Europe. He returned from a visit to China in 1983 with seeds of *H. thibetanus*. Jacobs has produced a large number of named *H. ×hybridus* over the years, each with the appellation *Eco* beginning the name.

Many American enthusiasts and breeders started bringing home exceptional hellebores in the 1980s. Like their European counterparts, they began breeding programs with some named plants and many others that were unnamed. The usual suspects—Ballard, Strangman, Ashwood, Schmiemann, and others—provided plants to fuel the growth. Today's spectacular hybrids in shades of purple-black, plum, burgundy, lime-green, shell-pink, and white are the result of hybridization with many wild species. Most of the best hybrids available in America today are seed strains, some developed by making controlled crosses each season, while others come more or less true from open-pollinated plants.

SAM AND CARLEEN JONES OF PICCADILLY FARM

In the early 1980s, Sam and Carleen Jones began growing hellebores on their farm near Bishop, Georgia. At that time, Sam was a botany professor at the University of Georgia, and Carleen was a biology teacher. The first hellebores in the Joneses' garden came from an historic home in Georgia, where the plants had naturalized. They planted 12 clumps, the first of many thousands of hellebores that now grow in the rolling woodland at Piccadilly Farm, a favorite of hellebore enthusiasts in the U.S. South.

When they began their nursery, very little was known about growing hellebores in a nursery situation, and little information was available. The Joneses tried different production methods; some failed, while others were successful, eventually allowing them to produce and sell more than 100,000 plants per year. They developed methods for harvesting and drying seed, planting the fresh seed out in large woodland seed beds, and shipping plants tipped out of their pots with some soil removed to cut the weight. The Piccadilly Farm "chicken boxes," a special type of heavy-duty waxed cardboard box, became a familiar sight at nurseries throughout the United States.

To assure adequate seed production, the Joneses planted a large hillside with hellebores, and this wooded slope is a lovely sight in late winter. These open-pollinated plants produce flowers that reflect a wide variety of shapes, and the colors range from white—both spotted and unspotted—through all shades of pink, rose, and plum. They both stress the variability of the *Helleborus* hybrids and the need to recognize this trait. Their garden is often photographed for magazines, books, and television programs, which bring new customers to the nursery each year.

Piccadilly Farm was one of the first nurseries to open early in the season for special Hellebore Days, a practice that is now common at other nurseries. The road leading to the nursery is packed with vehicles, and happy customers fill their wagons with plants. Rain or shine, Hellebore Days at Piccadilly is an event not to be missed.

GLENN WITHEY AND CHARLES PRICE

Seattle's Glenn Withey and Charles Price have raised many thousands of seedlings from open and controlled crosses, and they have reserved the very best color and flower forms for their controlled-cross seed strains. They offer many clear, reliable color lines including white, yellow, clear pink, smoky purple, dark purple, and the elusive black flowers. Withey and Price's work predates that of most Americans.

Gossler Farms Nursery, the Gossler family's operation in Springfield, Oregon, was the original nursery to carry selections made by Withey and Price in the early 1990s. Their stunning seed strains rivaled the best-named cultivars available in Europe at the time. They continue their breeding work today and their plants are excellent.

DICK AND JUDITH TYLER OF PINE KNOT FARMS

Pine Knot Farms in southern Virginia imports seeds and new stock plants from many sources around the world to add to their collection. The nursery selects superior color, floral, and foliage forms for introduction to the nursery trade. Pine Knot's breeding program is based on both named cultivars as well as exceptional seed-grown plants that are hand-pollinated. Their mission is to provide high-quality, affordable seed strains in a good range of colors, rather than expensive and slow-to-propagate named selections. Seedlings are available from hand-pollinated color strains as well as the less expensive open-pollinated plants.

Pine Knot focuses on developing vigorous, healthy plants that combine good foliar shapes and flowers with long-lasting colors. A wide range of leaf shapes and sizes are selected, including serrate margins, narrow leaflets, and heavy substance for weather resistance. Blooming-sized plants are offered in stable, rich colors from Ashwood seed as well as from their own crosses. The hand-pollinated 'Pine Knot Select' strain offers

Dick and Judith Tyler

152

outward-facing, usually single flowers with full, round petals and rich, heat-resistant colors, as well as interesting foliage. The 'Southern Belle' strain consists of double and semi-double or anemone-centered blooms in all available hellebore colors.

ERNIE AND MARIETTA O'BYRNE OF NORTHWEST GARDEN NURSERY

The O'Byrnes opened Northwest Garden Nursery in Eugene, Oregon, in 1992, after some 17 years in the landscaping business. When the O'Byrnes' clients began requesting plants that were not available commercially, they opened their nursery to meet the demand for unusual plants. They also hoped to be able to stay at home, and once the nursery took off, they gave up landscaping and opened their garden and nursery for business. The garden is open free to the public during regular nursery hours. Shoppers are tempted by the lavish plantings and are able to see plants in mature form. (For more on the O'Byrnes, see "The Garden at Northwest Garden Nursery" in Chapter 9.)

Today, the O'Byrnes' line of hellebores is among the best. Marietta handles the breeding work. She has a great eye for color and seems to have a sixth sense that governs her choices of both seed and pollen parents. Reds from their lines are the best in America. Marietta started with five seeds from 'John Burbeck' after she saw the cultivar featured in the book *Helen Ballard: The Hellebore Queen* and wrote to Gisela Schmiemann asking if she might acquire some seed. The five seeds she received launched an exceptional line. Four of the five seeds germinated: three were deep red, and one was a vibrant purple-red. The foliage on all plants was exceptional, and all plants were resistant to black spot. Through thoughtful and judicious selection, Marietta produced excellent lines of reds, purples, and slates that come fairly true. Doubles are also favored. She combines Party Dress Hybrids and larger *H. ×hybridus* doubles to create elegant flowers that age gracefully on short pedicels.

The current line has been augmented with plants from England and Holland. Strangman, Ashwood, and Kramer plants have expanded the breadth of colors available. The benign Northwest climate enables the nursery to produce blooming plants the second spring, which are sold in gallon-sized containers. Shoppers can take potluck and purchase unflowered seedlings of singles in tall band pots, which establish quickly and bloom the following spring. We have purchased many plants this way, and all are exceptional when they bloom. Doubles are sold only in flower.

The nursery introduced an exceptional *H. foetidus* called 'Red Silver' strain from a chance cross between 'Wester Flisk' and 'Sopron'. The gunmetal foliage and red stems are extraordinary. Plants bloom the second spring from self-sown seedlings, but they decline after flowering. Marietta notes that although this is a short-lived species, 'Red Silver' will seed true if isolated, and self-sown seedlings perpetuate the planting.

The O'Byrnes are also interested in species. They import seeds from Phedar Nursery and other sources and sell species from time to time. Species' slow growth means flowering-size plants are expensive, and many shoppers still prefer the garden hybrids. Marietta developed a line of *H. torquatus* hybrids with red or purple flowers and artfully dissected foliage to bridge the gap, and these plants attract enthusiastic collectors. The flowers are small and colorful, and the summer foliage display is fantastic. Current breeding lines involve other species with good foliage such as the ferny *H. multifidus* subsp. *hercegovinus*, which she now crosses with her *H. torquatus* hybrids.

Marietta told us that "even, wide, and overlapping sepals; short pedicels to hold the flowers outfacing; and rich, pure colors" is hellebore perfection. She would love to develop a line with deep purple foliage that holds its color all season. The Holy Grail for Marietta is a double with entirely different colors on the inner and outer segments. No doubt she will find it somewhere, either in her newly blooming seedlings or in one of the world's other great hellebore nurseries.

David Culp

The best of England's hellebores formed the basis for David Culp's 'Brandywine' strain. When you visit his Exton, Pennsylvania, garden, you can see them by the hundreds adorning his famous "hellebore hillside" in every shade from pure white to the deepest slaty black. Culp first traveled to England in 1983 to secure the best plants for his garden and his dream of making high-quality, richly colored plants more widely available to American gardeners. Other hellebore breeders contributed to his D.L.C. Hybrids, which started from open-pollinated seed collected from the hillside where they grow together. Originally, his seed was distributed through the Hardy Plant Society's Mid-Atlantic Group seed exchange. Sunny Border Nurseries, a wholesale distributor in Connecticut, is the outlet for Culp's plants. The new 'Brandywine' strain is now produced from controlled crosses and features outstanding single and double plants in a full range of colors.

Culp's greatest contribution to the American hellebore scene is his tireless promotion of his favorite plants. Through lectures and tours of his incredible hillside garden, he has introduced countless gardeners to the new wave of hellebores. On his shaded half-acre, hundreds of hellebores thrive beside a wealth of winter-blooming bulbs and perennials.

John Elsley

John Elsley is known for his *H.* ×*hybridus* 'Royal Heritage' strain, which has evolved since the mid-1980s. A former director of horticulture at Wayside Gardens, a large mail-order nursery, Elsley traveled extensively for his job. As he visited nurseries all over the world, he picked up plants for his personal garden. One early interest was hellebores, and he visited Ballard's nursery to shop for plants a number of times. These plants, combined with others from breeders in the U.K. and Europe, became the seed stock for the 'Royal Heritage' strain.

In his South Carolina garden, Elsley had a large bed planted with some of his finest seedlings. When his interest in hellebores outgrew the perimeters of his personal garden, he began a partnership with a large commercial nursery. The facilities and climate were amenable to commercial hellebore production, and in a short period of time, huge numbers of *H. ×hybridus* plants began to appear in nurseries all over the United States. Color strains like 'Royal Heritage Purple' are now available and brighten the winter gardens at thousands of homes.

DAN HINKLEY AND ROBERT JONES AT HERONSWOOD

Heronswood Nursery in Kingston, Washington, is a destination for plant lovers from all over the world, perhaps somewhat unusual since it is a mail-order nursery that supplies plants without the customer having to leave the comfort of home. Founders Dan Hinkley and Robert Jones were among the first nurserymen to offer species plants from wild-collected seed. Hinkley travels extensively and has collected hellebores from across the globe that are displayed

The display gardens at Heronswood Nursery feature a collection of exquisite hellebores that delight visitors and serve as the basis for plants used in Heronswood's breeding program.

in the exquisite garden. These provided the stock for their color strains that are some of the best in the United States.

Although the hellebore breeding program at Heronswood is relatively young, progress has been made in developing well-shaped flowers in a wide range of stable color lines. Integration of 'Betty Ranicar' into Robin White's Party Dress Hybrids series has created vigorous doubles that have proven exceptional. Emphasis is on integrating color into hybrids based on *H. multifidus* subsp. *hercegovinus* for its handsome, deeply divided foliage. Vigor and hardiness of good-foliaged forms of *H. ×sternii* are also being developed. Heronswood is also developing clonal selections of single and double forms from tissue culture.

More American enthusiasts

Enthusiasts abound across America, and their ranks are swelling. One long-time devotee is Charles Cresson, who has been growing hellebores since the mid 1970s. He grows plants in his Swarthmore, Pennsylvania, garden that were given to him by Gertrude Wister. The Wister garden, on the Swarthmore College campus, was a paradise for more than half a century. Cresson favors *H. niger*, but he also grows a number of *H. ×hybridus* selections.

Dixie Hougen gardens with hellebores and a myriad other woodland plants on two acres in northern Virginia. Her fascination with the genus began around 1970 when she moved to a garden containing *H. niger*. The plant persisted for years before it ultimately died. By that time, she had discovered *H. ×hybridus* and was pleased as punch with green-centered, poorly formed mauve blooms. She traveled to England in February 1998, and that trip changed everything for her. She currently collects a full range of rich colors and is the American distributor for plants grown in England by Graham Birkin.

Nurseries that are marketing superior introductions of garden hybrids as well as other hard-to-find species include Plant Delights Nursery in Raleigh, North Carolina. Owner Tony Avent has a keen eye for great plants and offers excellent hybrid seed strains as well as a number of species grown from wild-collected seed. Barry Glick of Sunshine Farm and Gardens in Renick, West Virginia, is a tireless promoter. He has a mountainside covered with beautiful plants, and his nursery sells many hellebores through Internet promotions and at plant society sales. Bob and Brigitta Stewart of Arrowhead Alpines in Fowlerville, Michigan, sell many species grown from wild-collected seeds as well as *H. ×hybridus*, intersectional hybrids, and a large-flowered *H. niger* descended from 'Potters Wheel'.

Russ Graham has a passion for most plants, especially wildflowers and woodland treasures. Hellebores vie with trillium and cyclamen for favored status. Graham grows hellebores acquired from breeders and hobbyists around the world in his Salem, Oregon, garden. He is particularly fond of *H. niger* and grows dozens of forms, especially early-blooming ones. He collects early forms from all corners and has plants that consistently bloom for the Christmas holiday. The catalog of his nursery, Russell Graham: Purveyor of Fine Plants, lists a number of seed strains and species, which are grown in beds and dug in spring and fall for shipping.

Kelly Dodson was introduced to hellebores by friend and mentor Ken Gambrill. In the 1970s, they worked together at the Rhododendron Species Foundation in Seattle, Washington. As curator, Gambrill traveled around the world collecting seeds and plants to build the garden's collections. Among the rhododendrons, species peonies, and other treasures brought back to Dodson, who served as horticulturist, were species and hybrid hellebores. The hybrids, while not a direct part of the garden's mission, caught Gambrill's eye as he visited the great hybridizers of the day, including Eric Smith of the Plantsman Nursery and Helen Ballard. Ballard's plants and their progeny were distributed by Dodson and Gambrill to many local gardeners, who in turn passed them on.

Dodson opened Reflective Gardens nursery in Poulsbo, Washington, in the early 1990s. The nursery sold a variety of uncommon plants, including species peonies and a variety of species and hybrid hellebores. Among the favored *H. ×hybridus* plants were excellent yellows bred from "Ballard's Yellow #1" and seedlings from Ballard's "Red Select", which are noted for their richly colored, outfacing flowers. Though Reflective Gardens is now closed, Dodson sells a limited number of hellebores through his new nursery, Far Reaches Farm, in Port Townsend, Washington.

The plants introduced by Gambrill live on in gardens and nurseries through the region. Pete Ray at Black Dog Nursery (formerly Puget Garden Resources) on Washington's Vashon Island still sells a variety of hellebores, some descended from the original plants as well as many others, such as *H. lividus* from Crûg Farm Plants.

THE FUTURE OF *HELLEBORUS ×HYBRIDUS*

Selected hellebores are not cheap, but they are worth every penny to enthusiasts. Flowered seedlings or divisions from selected superior forms usually sell for three to four times the price of an unselected form. Doubles go for as much as twice the price of bloomed singles. Demand for good plants often outstrips supply, especially for doubles, but this is changing. Hellebores are so high on the crest of the popularity wave that the Perennial Plant Association voted *H. ×hybridus* the Perennial Plant of the Year for 2005. High praise, indeed.

Dozens of new seed strains are being introduced as breeders and nurseries rush to capitalize on the popularity of hellebores. Some of these strains are excellent, based on years of careful selection and controlled pollination. Others are simply names given to open-pollinated plants; this is a shame. Open pollination does turn out some nice plants but usually produces more ugly ducklings than swans. Open-pollinated strains offer a mélange of results. No doubt if a breeder starts with good plants, he or she will produce good plants, but variation will be the rule. When buying unflowered plants, it is potluck as far as color and form go.

We believe that the proliferation of seed strains may ultimately do little to improve the quality of available hellebores. Though we have long been proponents of seed strains versus named selections, the advent of successful tissue-culture techniques will no doubt encourage naming of many selections. The good news is that buyers can select unflowered, and presumably less expensive, plants of a chosen color with assurance that they will get the specified color. The downside is that we will be back to the point of people asking for plants by name without realizing or acknowledging that many unnamed plants are of equal, or better, quality. The crucial step will be self-policing by the nursery industry to assure that only exceptional plants are named and tissue cultured. Just because we can provide it by tissue culture doesn't mean we should name it and sell it. We must never go back to the days when every slight variation was given a cultivar name.

What's to come from the breeding programs? What new traits will nurseries be selecting? David Culp strives to produce true blue and pure red flowers. Tony

Avent of Plant Delights Nursery is thrilled with the successes in the tissue culture of hellebores, particularly as superior forms of *H. ×hybridus* are introduced. He believes that by the second decade of the 21st century, hundreds of named selections will be available in nurseries and garden centers. While thousands of hellebores with identical flowers do not interest collectors, garden designers who want to install a sweep of 50 to 200 pure white or deep purple hellebores may be thrilled. It's an exciting time to be a hellebore enthusiast. Stay tuned!

JAPANESE AND SOUTHERN HEMISPHERE BREEDERS

Any plant that can so completely captivate gardeners in the United States and Europe is undoubtedly popular in other parts of the world. Since the 1980s, species hellebores have proliferated among specialist plant aficionados. Other groups of plants have fan clubs, societies, groups, and online e-lists, but none rival the passion of hellebore groups. Perform a Internet search using the keyword *Helleborus* or *hellebore*, and you will see multitudes of listings.

In Japan, the group Nihon Kurisumasu Roozu Kyookai (Japan Christmas Rose Society, or *Helleborus* Society of Japan) provides a web site with links to a dozen others dedicated primarily to hellebores. A number of Japanese nurserymen devote the time, energy, and expense needed to start their own strains of *H. ×hybridus*. Like others worldwide, they journey to Europe and the U.K. each winter to collect the newest hybrids and species plants from specialist growers.

In both Australia and New Zealand, breeders are producing some wonderful plants. Although the importation of plants was once permitted, in recent years both countries implemented very strict importation policies. Ian Collier from the Canberra area of Australia grows double and single garden hybrids as well as a number of species. He has created a double-flowering strain called Insomnia Hybrids. Ted West of Ornamental Plant Conservation Association of Australia holds the national collection of hellebores in Upper Ferntree Gully in the Australian state of Victoria. Peter Leigh at Post Office Farm Nursery produces hybrids as well as a number of interesting selections of hellebore species originally grown from wild-collected seed.

From Tasmania comes 'Betty Ranicar' (the "Tassie" double), a double-flowering strain that produces up to 95 percent double white flowers from seed. The plant, named for the owner of the garden where the original was found, has spread around the world. John Dudley of Elizabeth Town Hellebores is among those who sells seeds and plants of this strain. The "Tassie" double, with white flowers with varying numbers of petaloid segments and often a green center, occasionally produces offspring that may be pollen or seed sterile. In addition to Dudley, others such as Marcus Harvey and Sue Wallbank of Hill View Rare Plants have been crossing 'Betty Ranicar' with other doubles to produce flowers in different colors.

Barbara Jennings, a breeder in Hobart, Tasmania, is working on *H.* ×*hybridus* in hopes of broadening the scope of available flower colors and shapes. Jennings also works with doubles derived from three different groups—'Günther Jürgl' strain, 'Betty Ranicar' strain, and *H. torquatus* 'Dido'. The universal popularity of hellebores is illustrated by the fact that a plant from Tasmania may be added to the German double-hellebore hybrids and the Bosnian *torquatus* cultivars found by Strangman as progenitors of many double-flowering plants.

In New Zealand, Pat Stuart was given seedlings that included a particularly vigorous form of *H. niger* that was christened 'White Magic'. Stuart's daughter and son-in-law, Ken and Kate Telford, at Clifton Homestead Nursery, produce 'White Magic' and breed hellebores. The Dunedin Botanic Garden has a collection of hellebores. Nearby, Peter Cook breeds hellebores at Hereweka Garden and Nursery. Joy Plants is run by Terry, Pam, and Lindsey Hatch; the strain known as 'Winter Joy Bouquet' exhibits a nice mix of colors.

Hellebore propagation in the Southern Hemisphere goes by a schedule that, while variable according to area and temperature, is approximately as follows: seed germination occurs typically during the months of May to July; plants flower during the months of June to September, with peak season in July to August; seed ripens and is ready for sowing during the months of October and November.

New Zealand Gardens Online lists a dozen or more mail-order companies that specialize in hellebores, while Australian Nurseries Online lists a dozen mail-order nurseries that sell hellebores. Hundreds of retail outlets offer blooming plants during the season, and a number of nurseries specialize in hellebore seed.

6

GROWING HELLEBORES

What mysterious flowers these are, coming into bloom in the nadir of gloomy
days, providing great patches of subdued color with their creamy petals,
freckled with crimson and lime green.

Mirabel Osler in *A Gentle Plea for Chaos* (1989)

Hellebores are the perfect antidote to winter. They begin to bloom when few other plants are stirring and
continue to add color right through spring.

Freezing and thawing do not usually damage flowering hellebores. In the wild, hellebores like this *Helleborus viridis* are often blanketed with snow while they are in flower.

HELLEBORES ARE BEAUTIFUL and durable garden plants. They are easy to grow in the garden, and most species are extremely long-lived. This combination of traits, along with their abundant, early flowers, makes them indispensable for winter and spring gardens. The season-long foliar display of hybrids and a few of the persistent species make them all the more valuable in the shaded garden, where so many plants are summer dormant.

All plants accept a range of conditions under which they perform best. Hellebores are no exception. Within that range, however, gardeners have latitude. Hellebores grow in shade or sun. In warmer zones, plants need protection from scalding afternoon rays. They tolerate drought once established but may succumb to waterlogged soils. Lush growth and dense flowers are produced on rich, loamy soil, yet plants perform well in sandy and silty soils with fertilization.

The following comments are guidelines; don't be afraid to experiment. Some species have exacting requirements. For specifics, see the individual species entries in Chapter 3.

EXPOSURE

Hellebores grow wild in open woodlands, clearings, meadows, and on rocky mountainsides. Often found in *ecotones*, such as transitional bands between woodlands and open grasslands or scrub, they are amazingly adaptable. Though not strictly woodland plants, all thrive with some degree of summer shade. Many of their haunts are sunny in winter and spring but overgrown by scrub or bracken in summer. This overgrowth provides some protection from the full summer sun.

In the garden, the more sun hellebores receive, especially in spring while the foliage is expanding, the fuller the plants grow and the more prolifically they bloom. Light to partial shade is best for most species and hybrids. Full sun tends to burn the leaves, and flowering is poor in full shade. The stemmed species such as Corsican hellebore are likely to flop in shade, and they tolerate full sun except in the American Deep South.

In gardens, plants perform admirably under deciduous trees. Bare winter branches allow ample sunshine to reach the evergreen foliage. The flowering stems bear leafy, photosynthetic bracts that help fuel their growth and replenish reserves depleted by flowering before the fresh leaves emerge. The foliage is often fully expanded before the tree canopy is in full leaf, and the abundant broad leaflets catch sun even after the canopy has closed above them. In autumn, as the trees are shedding their leaves, *H. orientalis* and its hybrids produce a fresh crop of new foliage to take advantage of the warm sun. Several species are fully deciduous in winter, and *H. vesicarius* and *H. thibetanus* are summer dormant, so they demand a sunnier spring position for best growth and flowering.

SOIL AND MOISTURE

Ample moisture is mandatory while plants are flowering and hardening fresh growth. Hellebores should be planted in humus-rich, evenly moist loam or clay soil. Most species are widely tolerant of soil pH but benefit from the addition of ground limestone where the soils are highly acidic. Research by Kraus and Warren (see Appendix C) shows that plants perform best in the range of pH 7 to 6.

Under ideal conditions, you can get a hellebore to bloom the second year from seed. That said, most plants bloom in the third year, which is when most flowering-size plants are sold in the nursery trade. Small plants that are not root-bound recover from transplanting fairly rapidly. Once planted, sparse to moderate blooming occurs the following season. It takes two to three years for plants to reach full steam. Once they are cruising, the plants increase in size and number of flowering stems with each season. Mature plants of *H. ×hybridus* can measure several feet across and produce hundreds of flowers.

SOIL PREPARATION

Preparing a bed for hellebores is really no different from preparing a bed for any long-lived perennial; all perennials perform best in soil that is tilled or otherwise worked, with competing roots removed and any amendments added before planting. Some hellebore species are shallow rooted, as described in Chapter 3. These species grow well in soil prepared to a depth of 6 in. (15 cm), while others require soil prepared to a depth of 12 to 16 in. (30 to 40 cm).

Once you determine the required depth of your planting bed, clear the soil of any existing turf or other ground cover by spraying with a glyphosate-based herbicide or mechanically stripping the turf. If working with heavy clay, it is often advisable to add a "clay buster" material such as composted pine bark, pelletized gypsum, composted seaweed, expanded slate, or any other organic material at hand. This improves drainage and tilth, conditions the soil, and gives your new plants a head start toward long lives in your garden.

A soil test is always advisable before adding any fertilizer or amendment to alter the pH, but you can usually add compost without a test. If you live in an area where voles and moles are common, it is advisable to incorporate one of the expanded slate products sold to help prevent these creatures from devouring the roots of your carefully chosen plants. Hellebore roots are not usually eaten, but the little devils tunnel under the plants, leaving their exposed roots waving about underground.

Once the beds are thoroughly turned, large roots and rocks removed, and any additives tilled in, regrade your soil to follow the contours of the surrounding terrain. Hellebores prefer growing on slopes in areas with heavy soil. The most effective time to create a slope is when you are fine-grading; a few pulls of the rake can create the desired contour.

HARDINESS

Hellebores are tough, adaptable, and usually long lived. The vast majority of acaulescent species are native to mountainous regions of Central and Eastern Europe (see individual species accounts in Chapter 3). Snowfall is usually persistent in these areas, and winter temperatures can fall well below 0° F (−18° C). Origins in mountainous regions bestow great hardiness, and in our experience, all acaulescent species except *H. thibetanus* and *H. vesicarius* are hardy to USDA Zone 4 (−20 to −30° F or −30 to −35° C) with winter protection and may survive well into Zone 3.

Cole grew several species in his Zone 4 garden with a winter mulch of marsh hay. If you mulch, check plants in early spring and lighten the mulch as the flower buds emerge. *Helleborus thibetanus* grows successfully in Zones 6 to 8, but even experienced gardeners find *H. vesicarius* a challenge. It needs dry summer dormancy and moderate winter moisture. Slugs love them, and most people fail to raise them to flowering size. English gardeners fare better, especially in alpine houses. Plants in the open garden are dicey.

The caulescent species are exceptions to the rule of longevity and superior hardiness. *Helleborus argutifolius* and its hybrids are bud hardy in Zone 7, but the foliage and stems are damaged if daytime temperatures remain below freezing for long. *Helleborus lividus* is the least hardy and needs protection in Zone 7. Plants of *H. lividus* with remarkable hardiness may actually be *H. ×sternii* rather than the true species. Stinking hellebore (*H. foetidus*) is reported hardy to Zone 5 and sometimes Zone 4. Most American gardeners north of Zone 6 enjoy little success, however.

Caulescent species often decline after a few years. Cut old stems to the ground before they get truly ragged, but wait until new growth is emerging. Tattered plants spoil the garden and can promote disease.

Hellebore flowers seem indifferent to cold. Heavy frost bends the bloom stalks, and flowers often end up face down on the frozen soil; they pop back into position as the air warms. Repeated bitter cold may compromise or obliterate the flower display, but this is rare. When flowering stems endure protracted cold, they rise only partially, causing a crimp in the stem. These swan's neck stems continue blooming and get more fanciful with each cold spell.

BUYING HELLEBORES

There are no ugly hellebore flowers. Well, maybe a few are, but most, however subtle or muddy, are still attractive. Some are just more richly colored or aesthetically shaped than others. The perfection of a flower's form and color is subjective, though most enthusiasts agree on what is beautiful. We realize that we have high standards for the hellebores we grow, but not everyone wants to spend the extra money required to buy exceptional flowering-sized plants. The good news is that you do not need to spend a fortune to get a good plant.

Buying unbloomed seedlings of species or hybrids is certainly more economical than waiting for flowering-sized plants. Each year a plant is held in the nursery it gets more expensive, so young plants are the most affordable. The downside of buying unflowered plants is that you are gambling on flower form and color. A degree of unreliability is present in even the best seed strains. Even if you get the color you hoped for, the intensity of that color may be disappointing. The form of the flower is also quite variable.

Buy the best plants you can afford. If you want a collection of exceptional flowers, you must be ruthless with inferior plants. Rogue out all mediocre plants at the start. They are desirable castoffs, so you'll have no problem adopting them out to other gardeners with criteria less stringent than your own.

RETAIL NURSERIES AND GARDEN CENTERS

Hellebores are available as bare-root stock, plugs, or containerized plants from nurseries. Containerized plants dominate the market. Look for them at your local garden centers and nurseries. They are neat, well established, and easy to carry away. They are also perfect targets for impulse shoppers—so easy to snatch up. Containers allow roots to develop and become established before the plant is sold. Too long in a container, and the plant becomes pot-bound.

When kept too long in an undersize container, prolific hellebore roots become densely matted and are difficult to plant without major disturbance.

AMERICAN MAIL-ORDER NURSERIES

Ordering plants through the mail is fun. Browsing catalogs keeps winter-weary gardeners from going mad, and the anticipation of opening a box of treasures spurs enthusiastic shopping. Mail order is also the only way to get certain hellebores. Many people are reluctant to order by mail, however, because they fear the plants won't survive if they are not grown locally. Not so. A few simple rules help assure that all goes well.

Order early to assure the best selection, because hellebore species and choice seed strains sell out quickly. Remember that you cannot control aesthetics when you order plants by mail, so order from a nursery with a good track record. Specify a ship date appropriate to your area. For example, plants shipped from the southern United States should not be sent north until danger of hard frost is past. These plants arrive in full growth when northern treasures are just emerging. Gardeners in the U.S. South will not be able to get plants from the North until late in the spring. If heat and drought are factors, consider a fall shipment. Likewise, if you live in the northern part of the country, specify early fall shipment to give plants ample time to become established before winter.

Unpack plants as soon as the box arrives. Water the plants well, and get them in the ground as soon as possible.

PLANTING TECHNIQUES

We should tell you not to buy a single plant until you know where you are going to plant it and the bed is ready to receive it. If we stuck to that advice, however, we would have purchased very few hellebores! We believe that you must get good plants whenever and wherever you can. If that means condemning a plant to a year in a pot, well, hellebores are tough. One rule that we do adhere to is this: Before you plant a hellebore, make certain that the soil in the bed where you wish to place it is properly prepared.

Plants recover faster, grow to blooming size more quickly, and bloom more profusely if transplanted when young. We have set out blooming-sized plants from 2-gallon pots alongside two-year-old seedlings, and in two years, the seedlings are more lush and floriferous than the larger plants. No matter the size, try to minimize root disturbance. That said, if containerized plants are root-bound, you must disentangle the roots before you place the plant in the soil. Hellebore roots grow down as well as laterally. Keep this in mind when planting, and never shove a large plant in a small hole.

CONTAINERIZED PLANTS

Most hellebores sold today are containerized. The ease of planting depends on how long the plant has been in the container. Remove the root ball by inverting the container with your hand cupped around the crown of the plant. Shake the container or rap the rim on a solid surface to dislodge the plant. Right the plant once it falls into your hand. Examine the roots to see how pot-bound it is. A healthy plant fills the container with roots, and extremely vigorous plants are often pot-bound. Before planting it, you must break up the root ball. At the very least, you want to slice or score the roots so that you can break the root ball apart. Better yet, disentangle the mass and shake the excess potting medium from the root ball.

Most media used in pots is light and dries quickly. These media are almost always quite different from your garden soil, as most garden soils are far denser than commercial potting mixes. If you plunge the plant into the ground as is, the soils will be incompatible, and soil incompatibility results in different rates of drying and slows plant establishment. Therefore, it is best to remove the excess soil mix so there is maximum contact between the root ball and the existing garden soil. The process seems brutal, but after a brief setback, the plant ultimately performs better.

An extremely pot-bound plant with loads of circling roots at the bottom of the pot calls for different treatment. You must disentangle the roots if you want the plant to establish well. This step requires a bit of fortitude. Using your fingers, a sharp knife, or clippers, you must attack the roots and free them from bondage. Tease the roots apart with your fingers or cut them where they bend at the bottom of the pot. If a root is badly twisted or bent, cut it above where it bends. This may seem brutal, but the results are worth it; plants establish much more quickly. The danger of containers, especially cell packs, is that plants can stay in them too long. Once the roots are prepared, treat the plant like it is bare-root and get it in the ground.

When setting the plant in the garden, make sure it is at the same level at which it was growing in the container. Hellebores buried with their crowns in the soil exhibit inferior flowering, if they bloom at all, though they continue to produce foliage. The crowns produce short vegetative stems that raise the leaf buds up to the soil surface, but in our experience, when buried alive they seldom flower.

BARE-ROOT PLANTS

Bare-root plants are just that—plants without soil on their roots. Though most hellebores are sold in containers, a few mail-order nurseries send plants without soil. (It's cheaper than sending heavy soil through the mail.) Nurseries grow bare-root plants either in the field or in pots. When it comes time to ship them, they are carefully dug from the ground or knocked out of their pots. The roots are shaken or washed clean and wrapped in moss or another material to keep them moist. They arrive at your door ready to plant.

Unpack your plants immediately and inspect the roots for signs of damage. If roots are dry, soak them in warm water for several hours before you plant. If they are

Healthy hellebore roots (right) are of several types—black older roots seem to help hold the plant in the soil and newer paler brown, beige, or white roots are the actively growing ones. Unhealthy or diseased roots (left) are flattened and pasty brown.

rotted, cut off the affected portions. If the plant is done for, make a claim with the nursery. Most nurseries require immediate claims for loss or damage.

Note that if you buy hellebores abroad and plan to bring them home to the States, you must bare-root them to get them into the country. See "Preparing Plants for International Shipping" a little later in the chapter.

Planting bare-root plants is a much easier task if the soil is well prepared. Dig a hole twice as wide as the longest roots. If this is unreasonable, trim broken or excessively long roots to a manageable length. The hole needs to be about 8 to 10 in. (20 to 25 cm) deep, depending on the size of the plant. Make a cone of soil in the center of the hole tall enough to bring the crown of the plant level with the soil surface. Spread the roots evenly around the slope of the mound. Holding the crown in place, fill in with soil to bring the hole up to grade. Firm around the crown and refill. It is imperative that the soil be in contact with the point at which the roots radiate from the rhizome. Plants may rot or fail to thrive if you leave an air pocket under the crown. Water plants well. Keep a check on the soil moisture for the first growing season and never let the soil become dry.

TRANSPLANTING

Sooner or later, your plants are going to spread. You'll find seedlings popping up in the oddest places. Some seedlings germinate where they contribute to the overall design of the garden, and some conflict with it. Many fall within or adjacent to the crown of the parent plant. We recommend culling or transplanting these seedlings so they do not compete with the parent for water and nutrition. Other seedlings may arise where there is no room to grow. These hapless wanderers are perfect candidates for transplanting.

The goal of transplanting is to move the plant without disturbing it. To this end, you must endeavor to dig up the entire root system with the soil intact. This requires some knowledge of the plant's root system (see Chapter 1). Seedlings are easiest to move when they are small. Insert a trowel all around the plant and lift out the freed root ball. Replant it in a hole of the same proportions. Move the excess soil to the original hole from which the seedling was lifted.

To transplant a mature hellebore, you must use a sturdy garden spade to dig an ample root ball. All but seedlings are too large to lift with a trowel. Cut into the soil 12 in. (30 cm) or so from the outer edge of the crown. Hold the spade upright, so that the blade goes into the ground at greater than a 45-degree angle. Circle the root ball entirely to make sure it is free. Cut any tree roots that are growing through the root ball. Then, holding the spade at a 45-degree angle, free the root ball at the base, just below the depth of the cuts you made encircling the root ball. Once severed below, the root ball should pop out of the ground. Lift the plant and move it to the new location. Replant in the new hole at the same depth at which it grew before. Remember: do not plant too deeply or the plant won't flower.

MULCHING AND SOIL CONDITIONING

Mulch holds moisture in the soil by providing a barrier to heat and wind and keeps the soil from getting too warm. A good blanket of mulch also helps keep weeds down; weed seeds need light to germinate, and the mulch keeps seeds in the dark. Apply mulch to all newly planted beds and around transplants. Replace mulch annually.

The best mulches are fine textured, such as chopped leaves, coarse compost, well-rotted manure, well-rotted sawdust, or shredded weed-free straw. Apply the mulch evenly over the bed 1 to 2 in. (3 to 5 cm) deep. Avoid putting the mulch against hellebore crowns, as they may rot, especially when freezing and thawing in late winter. The mulch settles and knits together, which helps keep it from washing away.

Straw mulch is most useful for winter protection. Place a fluffy layer over the crown after the ground is frozen. Mulch keeps the ground at an even temperature and keeps the frost from penetrating. Loosen or remove the mulch before buds break in late winter.

PREPARING PLANTS FOR INTERNATIONAL SHIPPING

We acquire many of our best plants abroad. The sobering reality of bringing plants back, however, is that they must be entirely bare-rooted. This arduous task is enough to discourage all but the most ardent collectors. We usually travel in winter so we can see the plants in bloom before we buy them, and cold temperatures and numb fingers can make the bare-rooting work exceptionally tedious, dirty, and time-consuming.

Begin by tamping or beating as much of the medium off the root ball as you can. No need to be delicate. After you shake the soil from the roots, methodically use a dibble or chopstick to untangle the root ball. Remember that every bit of soil has to go; if you are too timid, you'll never get the job done. As the roots come apart, shake the plant frequently to dislodge soil. Your task is complete when you can run the dibble through the root ball without meeting the resistance of any tangled roots. By the time you finish, you'll be certain that the plant is doomed from being so totally ravaged, but it is amazing how tough they are; they do recover. The mass of soil and broken roots you leave in your wake is disturbing, but don't think about it.

Once the root ball is totally free, wash the roots thoroughly and pull off any clumps of peat or other remnants of the potting mix that still cling to the roots. (When the U.S. Customs people say "bare-root," they mean it.) Wrap the root ball in paper towels. If you wrap the roots just after you finish washing them, the towels retain sufficient moisture. If the roots are too wet, the plant can rot, so do not soak the towels; you can always add more water later if necessary. Slip the clean, wrapped plant into a plastic bag, covering only the roots.

All soil must be removed from plants before importation into the United States. Start by combing the soil from the root ball with a dibble.

Gradually work with the root ball until the major roots are disentangled.

Wash the roots thoroughly to remove all traces of soil.

Wrap plants and carry them to the inspection station in a suitcase or other protective container.

BRINGING PLANTS INTO THE UNITED STATES

The United States Department of Agriculture, Animal and Plant Health Inspection Service (APHIS), Plant Protection and Quarantine, governs importation of plants. As of this writing, U.S. airport inspectors operate under the auspices of the Department of Homeland Security.

You are allowed to hand-carry up to 12 hellebore or other approved plants without an import permit. If you enter the United States through a port that has an agricultural inspection station (most major airports have one, but a plant inspector is not always on duty), your plants get inspected upon arrival. When in doubt, check in advance—they may take your plants and hold them for later inspection. Make an appointment with the inspector if possible. Without your presence to ensure a timely inspection, plants can languish before they are inspected and mailed on.

New regulations as of 2003 require that a phytosanitary certificate be issued in the country of origin. This means that before you leave for home, an agricultural inspector in the country of origin has to inspect your plants to make sure they are free from pests and diseases. The certificate also requires a soil test to certify that the medium is free of root nematodes. If plants are deemed healthy, you are issued a certificate that you must show when you enter the United States. Without a phytosanitary certificate, your plants are likely to be confiscated and destroyed. The certificate also indicates the total number of plants being imported. If the number on the certificate exceeds 12, the plants will likely be sent to an inspection station.

Arranging to have your plants inspected is a nuisance. You can do it at the agricultural inspection station at your departing airport, but the process is very time-consuming, and if you wait until the last minute, you may miss your flight. It is best to go to the station the day before your scheduled departure. Be sure to check the hours of operation well in advance, and make an appointment if possible. You'll find regional agricultural offices located throughout most countries, and you may choose to take your plants to an office for inspection. With a little planning, you might get an appointment with the inspector at your hotel.

Rules vary by country and region, and as with all things bureaucratic, the rules seem to change daily. Often, you get different information from each person to whom you speak or each office that you call. One person (in the U.S. or another country) may even tell you two different things on two different days. The moral of the story is to check twice and be prepared for disappointment. Don't wait until the last minute or you could lose the plants that you worked so hard to clean.

If you wish to bring back more than 12 plants, you are required to have an import permit. The import permit allows you to bring an unlimited number of approved plants into the United States. Even with an import permit, a phytosanitary certificate is required for all the plants you are carrying. The first time you shop overseas, you are sure to be greedy and buy too many plants. But before you get too euphoric at the thought of carting home hundreds of plants, read on.

Most folks at agricultural inspection stations at airports are too busy or just plain unwilling to inspect large numbers of plants. You will usually have to ship them or leave them at the airport when you arrive to be sent to a regional office for inspection. Any time you relinquish your plants, you run the risk of eventually receiving them damaged, desiccated, or even dead. In some cases, you may never see them again: if a problem is found, the plants are destroyed.

Many people use brokers to get their plants back. A broker receives your plants by mail (or other shipment), walks them to the inspection station, makes sure that they are examined in a timely fashion, repacks them properly, and mails them to you while they are still fresh. This is a great way to go in theory, and it works most of the time, but no system is foolproof. Some brokers are a bit slow carrying out their duties, and plants can suffer if not attended to in a timely fashion. Brokers are also expensive, so unless you are sending a huge number of plants, the unit cost is high.

To move plants quickly through the system without a broker, establish an account with an international courier service. It is possible to send properly inspected plants directly from the country of origin to the agricultural station specified on your import permit. Check with your courier well in advance. Another option is to carry plants on the plane and deliver them to the agricultural station at the airport when you arrive. Prelabel the package with a contact name and address at the regional station indicated on your permit. Inside the box, include a fully filled out return slip for delivery from the station to your address. Include a copy of your import permit and a copy of the phytosanitary certificate. Carry a copy of your permit and phytosanitary certificate with you to show to the inspector at the airport. Ask him or her to arrange a pick-up for you. If possible, call the inspector at the receiving station to make sure the package arrived and to see when it is scheduled to be inspected and sent on.

For more information, you can log onto the USDA's APHIS web site on the Internet or call the USDA.

MAINTENANCE AND MANAGEMENT

Thriving hellebores are robust and fecund. They form very stout crowns with multiple eyes and dense, tangled masses of roots. Under garden conditions, most hellebores remain green and actively growing through the summer. Species that are summer dormant in the wild often retain their foliage, due no doubt to the rich, moist environment of the garden, free from competition for light, moisture, and nutrition. *Helleborus thibetanus* and *H. vesicarius* are the sole exceptions. In spite of the best conditions, they are fully dormant by summer.

Many species and all the hybrids maintain their foliage not only through summer, but throughout all or part of the winter as well. Hellebore foliage is a valuable asset in the winter garden, but it can also create some problems. Flowers of acaulescent species and hybrids emerge from the center of the clump and often become entangled with the old foliage. Winter foliage is subject to attack by aphids, which not only drain energy from the plant but can transmit diseases (see "Pests and Diseases," the next section in this chapter).

Old foliage often obscures the emerging flower scapes.

Plants look tidy and display flowers to best advantage when old foliage is removed.

Flowers are not the only charms of hellebores. Their richly textured leaves add structure to the summer and winter garden. In mild winters, they come through midwinter unblemished. In severe weather, they are easily crisped by cold, dry winds. Where snowfall is consistent, the leaves lie hidden all season but emerge unscathed in spring. In any case, as the flower buds begin to stir in the center of the rosettes, it's best to remove all the foliage to make way for the flowers. Nothing spoils the garden display like a tangle of flowers wrestling with winter-burned leaves. The juice is caustic and sometimes causes a rash, so take care when removing the old leaves.

Hellebores seem to produce more offspring than rabbits. Seedlings appear all around the parents, and often at a distance. Ants, rodents, and even water move the seeds. Unless you are trying to build up huge numbers of plants with no regard for color, it is best to remove the old flowers before the seed is released. Rogueing out seedlings from the crowns of established plants is also advisable. One puzzles over the notion that hybrid hellebores might become invasive exotics due to their free-seeding nature.

PESTS AND DISEASES

Hellebores are by and large pest-free—good news for lazy gardeners like us. A few diseases bother hellebores, but often their severity varies greatly from region to region or country to country. Viral diseases are the worst, and all gardeners live in fear of these infections with no cure. The remainder of pests and problems are bothersome but unlikely to cause permanent damage or death. When the environment of the garden is in balance, beneficial and predatory insects and animals control pest species. Prevention is easier than control. Clean up debris as eggs overwinter on old leaves and stems. Occasionally, things get out of balance or an outbreak occurs that needs treatment. Some of the more common pests are described here.

INSECTS

Insects are the most common animals on Earth. It often seems that with such odds, we can never outsmart or eliminate them. This is, in fact, the case. So, if you can't beat 'em, join 'em, right? To a greater or lesser extent, this is the best strategy. Plants evolved with insects, and they depend on one another for survival. Too much insect control and you can eliminate butterflies, bees, and other beneficial insects; the environment suffers as a result of our intolerance. In a well-balanced organic garden, predators help you with control: birds eat many insects, and some insects eagerly devour others. Most gardeners hardly miss the bits and pieces of plants that are consumed by insects when the garden is in balance with the environment.

This said, at times the balance tips, and an attack ensues that demands action from the gardener. When pests do occur, treat them immediately before a full-blown epidemic develops. Use a control that is labeled for the pest, and apply only as much as is necessary to achieve control. Most hellebore pests are easily subdued with organic insecticides.

Aphids are extremely destructive, especially if their populations explode. The soft-bodied insects come in a rainbow of colors depending on the species. Most hellebore aphids are fat and green, though pink and black species occur. The host-specific hellebore aphid is *Macrosiphum hellebori*.

Aphids attack succulent leaves, stems, and flowers. A telltale sign of an aphid epidemic is a glossy coating on the foliage; this honeydew is excreted as the aphids grow. They also shed their skins as they become ever more corpulent. The cast-off, translucent exoskeletons fall onto the leaves below. Aphids are more than an aesthetic nightmare, however. They multiply like lightning and can coat the undersides of leaves. In our gardens, temperatures close to 0° F (−18° C) do not harm the insects, so they feed all through the winter. As the buds emerge, the aphids transfer to the succulent growth and quickly deform the flowering stems and shrivel the flowers.

Cut old foliage before the new growth starts. Running your fingers up the stem easily squashes the soft bodies. The easiest control is a stiff spray with the hose to knock them off. If this fails, spray with insecticidal soap or horticultural oil every three to five days for two weeks. Pyrethrum sprays also offer excellent control.

Aphids are insidious pests that attack flowers as well as new and old foliage.

Aphids and other sucking insects easily spread viral and some bacterial diseases, so try to keep populations under control.

Spider mites are tiny arachnids, not actually insects. Though rare on hellebores, they can appear during hot, dry spells. They feed on the undersides and occasionally the surfaces of hellebore leaves. They suck the juices from leaf tissue, causing a slight mottling visible on the surface. As populations build, thin, silvery webbing appears on the leaves, making control more difficult. Severe infestations damage the leaves. The simplest control is to remove infected leaves. If broader control is necessary, spray with soapy water or horticultural oil.

Weevils chew foliage, making irregular patterns on the edges of the leaves. This cosmetic damage is annoying but not debilitating. More dangerous are the larvae, which feed underground on roots. In severe cases, they consume the entire root system of a plant. Though hellebores are not a favored food, weevils feed on what is available. Predatory nematodes are an excellent control, but you must apply them when the grubs are active. Consult an organic gardening supplier for the correct timing in your area. The nematodes come suspended in a cake or sponge that is dissolved in water and sprinkled on affected areas. Adult vine weevils feed at night, and you can hunt them down on early summer evenings and squash them by hand or drop them in a tin of soapy water.

SLUGS AND SNAILS

Everyone knows these slimy critters; they chew holes in the leaves of your favorite foliage plants. What is worse, they leave mucus trails all over the garden. In a woodland garden, slugs find endless places to hide. If the garden is small, you can use barriers around susceptible plants. A barrier excludes the slugs from getting to the plants they love best. One such barrier, diatomaceous earth, is made up of millions of tiny exoskeletons from deceased sea creatures. The sharp shells cut the slugs that encounter them. Encircle each plant or group of plants with a ring of diatomaceous earth, and reapply after heavy rains. A more practical method for larger gardens is to set traps, and some of the most effective traps are shallow pans filled with beer. The smell attracts the slugs and snails, and they fall in and drown. Disposing of the carcasses is a bit hard on the stomach, but this method is extremely effective. Where rainfall is high, these methods are not effective. Baits are often recommended, but many are toxic to non-target organisms such as pets and birds. However, you can buy an organic bait safe for animals but deadly for slugs.

Mammal pests

As much as we love animals in our gardens, sometimes they become pests. They eat shoots, dig up plants, chomp, trample, and wreak wholesale havoc. Tolerance is the best remedy, but there is a limit to what even the most tolerant gardener can endure. Mice, voles, squirrels, rabbits, woodchucks, and deer (and other ungulates) are the main pests, in order of magnitude.

Mice sometimes nibble hellebore buds or young shoots. If the garden is heavily mulched in winter, they sometimes nest in the crowns. They can also bother seedlings, but in general, damage is minimal. If mice cause a problem, set snap traps baited with peanut butter. Be sure to hide them under heavy pots so birds are not inadvertently killed.

Voles are mouse relatives that resemble dark brown to grayish hamsters. They eat the roots, crowns, and young shoots of plants, though hellebores are not a favored food. They are insidious pests because they work underground. If an otherwise healthy plant suddenly wilts and collapses, give it a tug. If it comes up freely and rootless, you've got voles. They also work under the snow in winter, eating the dormant crowns till spring. The best way to control voles is to make it difficult for them to feed. Excess mulch and debris in the garden give voles a place to hide and munch. If you can locate the burrows or the runs under mulch or snow, place rat traps baited with an apple or carrot where they are likely to encounter it. Cats and dogs are also good deterrents.

Squirrels and woodchucks nibble, trample, dig, and eat most plants and plant parts. Rabbits do everything but dig plants up. Though they don't generally eat entire plants, they often chew off leaves and flower stems, only to discard them when the sensation of the bitter taste reaches their pea-sized brains. The best control is live trapping. You must be diligent. Another method is to spray plants with a repellant, but this requires regular application. Hot pepper soaked in water is a good organic choice. Generally, the damage they do to hellebores is negligible.

Deer are a real problem in many areas. They eat all the choice plants, including hellebores. Don't believe the literature that says hellebores are totally deer-proof; hungry deer disregard the books. They eat the foliage in winter and devour the flowers in early spring when little else is green and growing. Though hellebores are not preferred, deer seem to tolerate the bitter sap. You can spray with repellents as you do for smaller animals, but if your garden is large, this is impractical. Fencing your property is expensive but is the best long-term solution.

Brown or discolored foliage is not always a sign of disease. The *H. niger* leaf on the left has black spot, while the one on the right is simply going dormant.

DISEASES

Diseases of hellebores are frustrating for both gardeners and professional growers. Environmental conditions and individual susceptibility determine which plants are affected by disease and how badly. Humid, wet weather is most favorable to the growth of bacteria and fungi. Good air circulation is mandatory; don't crowd plants together, but space them properly so air can move around them. Early detection is important and immediate control is more successful than last-ditch efforts. Clean up affected debris from the garden and remove and dispose of infected stalks in the autumn so spores do not overwinter.

Rots are caused by a variety of different organisms and can affect foliage, stems, or roots. The key to prevention is siting the plants carefully. Protracted wet and/or humid weather can pose problems. Pick off and dispose of affected leaves and flowers. Prune affected stems and sterilize clippers afterward with alcohol or bleach. Clean up decaying debris from around the crowns of affected plants for long-term control.

To date, little research has been published on hellebore diseases, and very few pesticides list hellebores on their labels. If your plant is not listed, what do you do? We are presented with a catch-22, and only experience can guide us in these situations—and experience is gained only by action. One option is to make a test

Spots pepper the flowers and stems of *H. dumetorum*. Black spot is a common disease of hellebores that is most often problematic in areas with abundant winter rainfall.

application with a product you know is successful for treating the problem on other plants.

Common symptoms of many hellebore ills are spotting, browning, or yellowing of the leaves. This is sometimes confusing, since some leaf damage is mechanical, not physiological. Species hellebores often retain their leaves longer in the garden than in their native habitats. These deciduous species are often ragged by autumn. Garden plants sometimes accumulate a few horrid age spots, perhaps caused by an earlier chance encounter with a rake. Plants may also lose one or two leaves during the season; the leaves gradually yellow and turn brown. This is normal and not due to disease. If more than one or two leaves are affected or you notice symptoms on more than one plant, the situation requires investigation.

The most common disease encountered by gardeners is black spot, which disfigures flowers and fresh vegetative growth. *Coniothyrium hellebori* is often the responsible organism, but a number of other fungi also cause spotting and rotting of leaves. Black spot itself may not kill the plant, but a weakened plant is susceptible to other problems. The cycle begins as spores that overwinter in the soil or on old foliage. The warmth and moisture of spring brings them to life, just in time to attack the fragile new growth of your hellebore. Small dots the size of pinheads enlarge and become irregular black or brown spots that often display a central tan zone. Symptoms often occur on both sides of the leaf. In advanced cases, the spots merge to cover the majority of the leaf, eventually spreading onto the stem and flowers. Leaves and stems yellow and eventually weaken and fall over. Infected flower buds

Botrytis attacks the stems of hellebores, often causing them to keel over and rot off at soil level. This fungus also attacks foliage.

wilt and the stems weaken and collapse. Black spot attacks the caulescent group in a different manner, often striking at soil level, lurking unobserved until the stem topples over. Cutting the stems eliminates the floral display but usually saves the plant.

Fungicidal sprays or drenches, including copper-based preparations, control the problem if it is caught early; however, the easiest option is prevention. Remove foliage from acaulescent plants during the autumn or winter to prevent fungi overwintering and to keep the crowns dry. For *H. niger*, which needs its winter foliage, the best preventive method is to site the plant in a location where moisture does not accumulate around the crown and keep mulch well away from the stems.

Compost teas are another good preventive measure. Aerated compost tea is the most biologically active. Ions in the tea bind to receptor sites on the leaves that are often the routes of infection for pathogens. With receptor sites occupied, the disease organisms can't get in, and plants stay healthy. Tea treatments are particularly effective in preventing foliar diseases. You will find more information on the Internet at sites such as www.soilfoodweb.com.

When growing hellebores in containers in a greenhouse or nursery situation, a regular fungicide spray program is necessary to prevent and contain fungal attacks. Alternating fungicides is important to prevent the organisms from building resistance to any one preparation. Choose fungicides registered for use on hellebores. Venting

Crown rot quickly destroys seemingly healthy plants.

with fans is crucial, and keeping foliage as clean and as dry as possible helps prevent the onset of spotting and other foliar problems in production. Standard horticultural sanitation and cleanliness practices are an important element in the fight to control fungal problems. Keep debris from gathering under plants and on benches, since it harbors the spores. Remove infected flowers, leaves, or plants and discard or burn them. Never compost diseased plants.

Botrytis cinerea and several other species are responsible for a distinctive fuzzy gray mold that can infest plants. A string of three or four cool, gray, rainy, or drizzly days in a row in any season with temperatures hovering around 60 to 70° F (15 to 20° C) can promote the development of *Botrytis* infection. The spores reside in soil or in debris from the previous year's growth and come to life when conditions are right. *Botrytis* does not usually occur on healthy plants, but it can set up a secondary infection on any plant that is wounded, weak, or under stress. In production greenhouses, the fallen stamens and nectaries are prime candidates for infection. In a matter of days, these once lovely plant parts become covered with the gray fuzz that signifies *Botrytis*. Take care to avoid handling the infected parts as the spores are easily dislodged.

Control is similar to that used for black spot, often involving a spray or drench with a fungicide registered for *Botrytis* on herbaceous perennials. Alternating the chemicals used helps prevent the fungi from becoming resistant. Cleanliness is again of vital importance. Remove any infected plant parts as soon as possible. Dip your shears in disinfectant such as alcohol or bleach between each cut. Keep foliage as dry as possible, especially during an outbreak of *Botrytis*, and avoid contamination by splashing the spores to other plants.

The one disease that affects hellebores most drastically is rot, a perplexing and often fatal problem. The most common root and crown rot fungi are *Rhizoctonia*, *Pythium*, *Phytophthora*, *Cylindrocladium*, and *Fusarium*, pathogens that are present in soils worldwide. They are responsible for spreading the rotting diseases that kill both hellebores grown in gardens and those growing in containers. *Rhizoctonia* spends the winter in soil as sclerotia, while *Fusarium* lives on dead plant tissue and in soil. *Pythium* and *Phytophthora* are introduced through contaminated soil or water. The spores move easily from one area to another in irrigation water. Hoses and hose ends can also carry the tiny spores about, and this is one of the reasons we never drop our watering wands onto the floor of a greenhouse or on the ground in the garden.

Symptoms include wilting and dark, dead patches of tissue on the petioles at the crown. As the disease advances, the whole plant may collapse. Infection often begins underground as dark patches on the roots. These patches often grow together and cover the entire root system. The problem can also start at the crown and move down into the roots. There is a visible difference between infected roots and those that are not involved. Healthy roots are tan or brown with white growing tips, while infected roots are rotten and brown to black. Crown rotting begins with leaves wilting and tearing away from the crown. As the disease progresses, the entire crown disintegrates. Fine feeder roots can appear white and healthy even though the crown has rotted away. The reverse is true with root rot; the crown appears healthy, but no living roots are attached.

Rot is very difficult to cure; good horticultural hygiene in both garden and greenhouse is of paramount importance. Prevent these diseases by maintaining good drainage and providing the best possible growing conditions. Minimize overhead irrigation and avoid splatter from puddles of water. If plants are growing outdoors or in holding beds, mound the bed so the crowns are high and drainage is improved. Place containerized plants on gravel or a porous ground cloth, not on plastic or soil.

Good air circulation and adequate light promote strong growth rather than weak, etiolated stems. Protect young plants from high temperatures and drying winds. When potting, use clean, new, or sanitized pots and sterile potting media. Take care not to contaminate the media with infected media from other containers, workbenches, tools, or wheelbarrows.

Fungicide drenches are used to manage root and crown rot diseases in containers and in garden soil. Try to get a diagnosis from a local university's plant pathology department or the county extension service to determine the specific cause of the rot. Many fungicides that are listed for *Rhizoctonia*, *Fusarium*, and *Cylindrocladium* do not control *Pythium* and *Phytophthora*, so you must know your target organism. Alternating fungicides is the best bet to achieve broad-spectrum control. Remove any remaining infected plants from gardens in autumn to prevent fungal bodies overwintering in the foliage and reinfecting plants the next season. Treat the soil

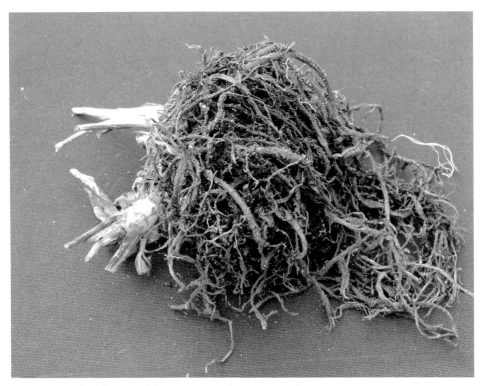

Root rots are insidious and destroy plants that are waterlogged or in heavy, compacted soils.

with fungicidal copper sulphate, Bordeaux mixture, or household bleach applied at a ratio of 10 parts water to 1 part bleach or fungicide.

It is sometimes possible to salvage a special plant with root rot by removing the soil, cleaning the roots, and cutting away any affected parts. A soak in fungicide before repotting in clean, light medium should help. Maintain soil moisture at a moderate level—not too wet and not too dry—and repeat drenches as prescribed. Often, plants that survive root or crown rot develop a distinctive condition, in which many small leaf clusters are produced instead of the normal sized stems. The plants eventually outgrow this condition, providing many divisions in the process.

Hellebores are occasionally overcome by another soil-borne fungus, *Sclerotium rolfsii*, commonly known as southern blight, although it is sometimes found as far north as Minnesota. We do not see evidence of this problem in the garden until after the arrival of hot, humid weather. Symptoms include wilting or total collapse of all or part of the clump. On close inspection, we notice the telltale burnt umber to tan sclerotia that account for another common name, mustard seed fungus. Petioles often look moldy at the base, and the whole plant is often loose and easily pulled from the soil. Southern blight rots the crown at the soil line. Dormant buds on the rhizome often resprout after the fungus is killed or goes dormant. Plants affected by this disease do not necessarily die, but they need several years to recover. Soil infested with fungal bodies usually responds to a drench with a 10 percent bleach solution.

Damping-off is caused by any number of soil-borne fungi that cause crown and root rots. Infected seedlings are killed at the soil line. Infection usually starts in a small spot, with just two or three plants, which appear wilted. If you lift a seedling for examination, you will see few, if any, roots left intact. The problem spreads quickly, usually in a circular pattern, until the whole sowing is affected. If not caught in time, all the seedlings will be lost. In preemergent damping-off, the radicle emerges and then the seed rots. Damping-off is also seen in new transplants. A slight injury to the stem while transplanting exposes the plant to infection. *Pythium*, *Sclerotinia*, and *Phytophthora* are more prevalent in cool, damp soils, while *Rhizoctonia* and *Fusarium* are active in warmer and drier conditions, so problems are possible year-round. *Pythium* causes roots to rot below the soil level.

Prevent damping-off by using fresh medium and clean flats for each new sowing, as previously used media and containers are often infected. Sow the seed as thinly as possible; crowded plants are much more likely to contract fungal problems. Apply water gently with a mister or fine nozzle. Compacted, waterlogged soil and poor drainage contribute to the problem. Let the soil dry slightly between waterings. Give seedlings as much light as you can; sunlight is a good sanitizer. Keep air circulating with fans; plants develop husky, more resistant stems in areas with greater air movement. Drier soil, brighter light, and better circulation lessens the danger of continued damping-off. Remember, though, that the medium cannot completely dry or the seedlings will die.

If infection does occur, drench with a fungicide registered for damping-off. Organic growers may want to treat the infected soil with a tea brewed from chamomile. Brew the tea as for a bedtime drink and then cool, strain, and pour over the affected area. It is advisable to remove the infected plants and the healthy-looking neighboring plants for an inch or two (3 to 5 cm) around the afflicted area, since they are probably contaminated as well. After treatment, move the flat to a location where air circulation is greatest.

Smut fungus on hellebores is rare in the United States, but this disease is reported in Europe. It is probably only a matter of time until Americans see smut on their hellebores. *Urocystis floccosa* is the smut that affects hellebores. It causes swelling and cracking of the petioles and flowering scapes. Infected parts crack open vertically to reveal dark spores. Remove and destroy affected plant parts. As with other fungi, the spores of smut survive in soil or dried plant material, waiting for the next warm, moist day to begin the cycle again.

Viral diseases are difficult to detect and impossible to cure. Symptoms include, but are not restricted to, mottling or streaking of foliage, and foliage that is twisted or misshapen, elongated, dwarfed, or discolored. Blotches or streaks of green or yellow or ring-spots can indicate a virus. Viruses cause a mosaiclike symptom on plants. Mosaics are characterized by intermixed patches of spots or small blotches of the normal green and light green or yellowish on the leaves.

Tobacco mosaic virus (TMV) is one of the most frequently seen viral diseases on ornamental plants. Viruses, unlike fungi, do not produce spores and must enter the plant through a wound. The most common method of transmitting TMV is by smokers working with the plants. Smoking cigars, cigarettes, and pipe tobacco contaminates the hands, and working with plants results in transmission of the virus. Do not smoke while transplanting or cutting back plants. Tools touched by smokers or used to cut out infected plants can carry the virus as well, and dipping in laundry bleach does not banish the virus. To sterilize tools, place them in boiling water for 5 minutes and then wash with a detergent or strong soap.

Viruses do not usually kill plants, but sometimes they are severely weakened. Viruses can cause variegations, some of which are attractive and have horticultural merit. Plants like Rembrandt tulips display colorful flames in the tepals due to viral infections. We do not, however, want to spread pathogenic viruses to our plants. As with fungal and bacterial infections, sanitation is imperative. Do not discard plants infected with virus on the compost heap or leave them in the

Black death travels through the veins of hellebore leaves and stems, often producing streaking on petioles and flowers.

greenhouse. Insects easily spread viruses, and weeds are often hosts, making weed control an important element in preventing viral problems.

The mention of black death puts the fear of God in hellebore enthusiasts. This disease, likely a form of *Carlavirus*, is usually fatal and so far there is no cure. Plants in the U.K. and Europe, where the problem is common, exhibit symptoms similar to several other rotting diseases. The main symptoms are streaks of black between the veins and black lines that extend down the petioles. (This streaking is reminiscent of the experiment we did in kindergarten or first grade when we put a flower in dark dye or ink and watched the darkness spread up the stem and all through the flower.) Two aphids, *Macrosiphum hellebori* and *Aulacorthum circumflexum*, are often involved in the transmission of this disease. Research is under way in Europe, the U.K., and in the United States at Washington State University. For more information see Appendix B.

7
PROPAGATING HELLEBORES

Hellebores cannot be grown from cuttings, tissue culture techniques have not yet succeeded, clumps may be slow to reach dividable size, seed may fail to germinate unless freshly collected, and seedlings from hybrids cannot be guaranteed to replicate the parent plant. Therefore, choice forms remain scarce, expensive, and so eagerly sought that American enthusiasts chase off to England in winter to hunt them down. Don't feel deprived if you're not up to this search—
there are no worthless hellebores.

Pamela J. Harper in *Time-Tested Plants* (2000)

Despite advances in tissue culture, seed is still the best way for both nurseries and home gardeners to produce hellebores such as Ashwood's stunning "Neon".

HELLEBORES CAN BE INCREASED only by one of three methods: seed, division, or micropropagation. Since most people don't have the sterile laboratory facility for micropropagation by tissue culture, the only truly practical ways to get more plants are by seed and division. Hellebores are one of the easiest plants to produce from seed if the gardener adopts the cycle the plant follows in nature.

If you grow *Helleborus* ×*hybridus* in your garden, you have no doubt noticed the annual crop of seedlings that ring almost any plant, like chickabiddies around a mother hen. Seeds ripen on the plant in late spring or early summer and fall to the soil, where they lie unnoticed. The seeds of hellebores have a fleshy aril along one side known as an *elaiosome*. Ants or other small insects move them about, as they find the small, white elaiosome tasty. The "ant express" offers a possible answer to one mystifying question—why plants are found growing uphill from their source. Wherever the seeds end up, they usually begin to germinate around the winter solstice. It is easy to lift these little plants and either move them to a new location or pot them up individually. In fact, if the small plants are not moved, the skirts of expanding foliage smother them before midsummer.

Though it is possible for beautiful, healthy plants to arise from open pollination in the garden, most enthusiasts and breeders make hand-pollinated crosses from selected parents. As the seeds ripen, they are collected and stored under controlled conditions. The seeds are sown in flats or other containers to assure the best germination, maximum seedling survival, and fastest growth.

GROWING HELLEBORES FROM SEED

Most hellebores produce abundant seed. A single *H.* ×*hybridus* flower can easily produce between 25 and 50 seeds, while some of the Balkan species rarely produce more than a dozen per plant. The seed of each species is slightly different in size and shape, but the color is similar in most of them. The newly forming seeds are

Each hellebore seed
has an elaiosome
along one side.

green, and then creamy white. As they ripen, the color darkens to café au lait, then to a darker wheat-toast brown, changing finally to the lovely black of patent leather Mary Jane shoes. When fresh, seeds of most species, especially those of *H. foetidus*, feature a white, fleshy elaiosome attached to the seed case like an umbilical cord. The ⅛ in. (3 mm) seeds are ovoid, and as they dry they shrivel and lose their gloss. The elaiosome dries and seems to disappear with ripening.

Seeds of other species, while similar, present a few differences. *Helleborus ×hybridus* produces larger seed that is approximately 3/16 in. (5 mm) long and ⅛ in. (3 mm) in diameter, slightly flattened, with the dried elaiosome forming a ridge on one side rather than disappearing. Seeds of *H. niger* are just a tiny bit longer than and not quite as rounded as those of *H. ×hybridus* and have a well-developed elaiosome. *Helleborus argutifolius* and *H. lividus* and their hybrid *H. ×sternii* often have seeds that are smaller than those of the acaulescent species; *H. lividus* seeds are only 1/16 in. (2 mm) long. *Helleborus vesicarius* seeds are larger, ⅛ in. (3 mm), round, brown, and as different from the other hellebore seed as the parent plants are from other hellebore species. The seeds of this species are enclosed in inflated seed cases. *Helleborus thibetanus* usually produces only two carpels, and the number of small seeds in those two carpels is always disappointingly low. The seeds of *H. thibetanus*, at 1/16 in. (2 mm), are not as large and round as those of *H. vesicarius* and are closer in color to the shiny black of the acaulescent group when the pods are first opened.

Though traditionally considered sterile, *H. ×ericsmithii*, *H. ×nigercors*, and *H. ×ballardiae* sometimes seem to produce viable seed. Several times we were sure that we had discovered something new, a fertile strain of an intersectional hybrid. The seed in each case aborted before maturing or never ripened correctly. Backcrossing by placing fertile *H. niger* pollen onto the stigma of the intersectional hybrids produces seeds, but in most cases they are not viable, though occasionally fertile clones are reported. Perhaps micropropagation, insertion of cell-altering phytohormones, or embryo rescue will eventually produce fertile seeds in laboratories.

Old seed is often difficult to germinate due to complex dormancy and lowered viability. A few species seem to germinate readily from old seed, however. *Helleborus lividus*, *H. ×sternii*, and *H. vesicarius* all germinate from seed stored for several years, indicating longer viability in these species. Perhaps the drier climate where these species naturally occur has influenced the germination patterns. The seeds of *H. niger*, *H. foetidus*, and *H. argutifolius* may require an extra year, or even two in some cases, to germinate if the seed is not absolutely fresh. With the exception of *H. ×hybridus*, we find that acaulescent species are rather slow from seed, even fresh seed. On several occasions, we kept seed flats for five years before we saw any germination, while at other times, seedlings planted in early summer popped up around the first of the new year.

COLLECTING SEEDS

By collecting from your own plants, you are guaranteed fresh seed. Hellebore flowers contain two to eight follicles that begin to swell soon after pollination and continue to enlarge as the flower ages. The lower flowers, which are the first to open, are usually the first to ripen. When the seeds are close to ripening, the flowers are dry and papery and the pods usually produce a rattling sound when they are shaken. As follicles mature, they begin to split, opening along the center and rolling back to allow the seed to escape. While it is usually better to collect seed when it is fully ripe, immature seed seems to germinate quite well.

On the plants that we hand-pollinate, we tie up the flowers in small muslin bags known as "parts bags," which are available from mail-order companies that specialize in selling all things automotive or mechanical. These bags are easy to apply, reusable, and invaluable for capturing the seeds of special plants that invariably seem to ripen and spill to the ground. The bags are available in a wide range of sizes, from 3 by 4 in. (8 by 10 cm) to 12 by 16 in. (30 by 40 cm). The smaller bags are perfect for enclosing one special flower, while the larger bags can capture seed from an entire plant of *H. foetidus*. Sacks for capturing seeds are also easily made from nylon tulle fabric with small-diameter holes or from a pair of stockings or pantyhose cut into appropriately sized pieces. In fact, a square of tulle or similar fabric fastened around the ripening seed pod with a bit of string makes an excellent and inexpensive receptacle. The mesh bags in which daffodils and crocus bulbs arrive also make wonderful receptacles for the large panicles of *H. foetidus* if the diameter of the mesh is not too large. Before we began to use bags, we frequently found ourselves on our knees in the garden trying to pick out the escaped seeds of special plants. More often than not, we had as many sticks and gravelly bits jammed into our knees as we had seeds in our palms.

For many gardeners, catching every seed is not a matter of great importance, and it is quite simple to watch and wait until the first follicles split. Collect the seeds by cutting off the flower stalk or just the individual flower heads. Place them in a container; a brown paper bag is a good choice. We use a shallow cardboard box lined with newspaper or a paper shopping bag, depending on the number of plants from which we are collecting. Placed in a warm, dry area, the remaining follicles should open and release the seeds.

The temperatures in the area where plants are growing determine ripening times of hellebore seeds. Since this differs vastly region by region, make appropriate adjustments to any ripening times presented. In our southern Virginia

To assure no seeds are lost, bag flowers in net or muslin after pollination.

garden, the first species to ripen, often by late April or early May, is *H. niger*, followed by *H. purpurascens*, *H. atrorubens*, and the other Balkan hellebores. *Helleborus thibetanus* and *H. lividus* ripen quite soon after, and *H.* ×*hybridus* can begin to ripen anywhere from mid- to late April on into late May or early June, depending on the temperature outside. *Helleborus foetidus*, *H. argutifolius*, and *H.* ×*sternii* are usually the last to ripen in our gardens, following *H.* ×*hybridus* into May or June. If the weather is unusually warm, it is amazing just how rapidly the seedpods can ripen. Take care to check the maturing pods every few days during the ripening times. Once the first two or three pods on a plant open, we cut all the stems and allow the remaining seeds to ripen in a well-ventilated place.

We write labels as we cut the stems. We never trust our memory, even for the distance between the garden and the drying area. If the seeds come from a special cross, a tie-on tag is already attached to each flower head. You may say to yourself, "Certainly I will know the difference between these *H. niger* flowers and the flowers of *H. foetidus*, as the *H. niger* flowers are white and these *H. foetidus* blooms are green." We know all too well from personal experience that after a week or two in the drying area, it is almost impossible to tell one flower from another; the colors of the blooms all fade to brown.

At Pine Knot, we want to capture as many seeds as possible. We detach the flower heads from the stems and spread them to dry on paper-lined tables in a well-ventilated building. Most of the seed pops out of the flower heads as they dry. We remove the fully dry flowers, leaving the clean seed on the paper. To capture any retained seed, we place the flowers on newspaper and roll back and forth over them with a wooden rolling pin. This usually releases any seeds that are hiding in the corners. We then tip the seed into a sieve and shake it in front of a box fan until most of the detritus blows away. Once the seeds are reasonably clean, we sow them as quickly as we can, optimally within a few days to two weeks. Even a month or two of refrigerated storage lessens the germination rate.

A WORD OF CAUTION ABOUT SAP

Some people are sensitive to hellebore sap and develop contact dermatitis when working with seeds and plants. We occasionally experience a rash on our arms after cutting back hellebore foliage. Since the foliage of some species is both leathery and heavily toothed, it is often difficult to determine whether a reaction is from sensitivity to the sap or whether the skin has simply been pricked or scratched. On occasion, our fingertips tingled or burned after cleaning a great deal of seed. The sensation is similar to the irritation felt after cutting up hot peppers. If the follicles are still fresh and juicy, contact with the sap is implicated. Symptoms are usually unpleasant for only a short time and do not require treatment other than applying skin cream. We suggest wearing protective gloves and a long-sleeved shirt when working with seeds or large amounts of foliage, especially if your skin is sensitive, until you determine your personal susceptibility.

TIMING THE SOWING OF HELLEBORE SEED

If hellebore seed is sown soon after harvesting in midsummer, precocious species should begin germinating around the time of the winter holidays in North America. What a wonderful gift! No matter how old we grow, or how many millions of seeds we sow, the first uncurling radicle (seedling root) followed by the new shoots of tender seedlings gives a thrill. With most seeds, we can peek under the covering grit and find the radicle uncurling several long weeks before we see the first emerging shoot poking up through the medium. This preview of the beginnings of life is often enough to brighten the dullest day.

The key to germinating hellebore seed in containers or nursery beds is to duplicate nature as closely as possible, beginning with fresh seed. While old seed usually germinates, this is not a speedy process, perhaps taking an extra year or even two. Finding nothing in the seed flat day after day is a great disappointment. We have had great success increasing germination of purchased and old seed by soaking it overnight in warm water. We have never done a replicated study to determine whether the seed-soaking process actually increases the rate of germination, but we think it helps, especially with old or dry seed. Containers of seeds that were soaked had noticeably better germination than the containers with seed that were simply sown without soaking.

Our method is to pour the seeds into a clean glass container and cover them with warm water, allowing several inches of water over the top of the seeds, since the soaking process utilizes water. We keep the label with the container. Adding a drop of washing-up liquid helps break the surface tension of the water, which we find helps the seeds to sink after stirring. We then leave the container several hours or overnight in a safe place away from small hands and curious kitties. After soaking, the water smells a bit foul. This usually attracts our cats, which always prefer to drink the smelly water from an old flower arrangement rather than the clean, fresh liquid in their bowls.

After soaking and draining, we rinse the seeds under running water and then dry them with a bit of toweling to make sowing easier. We mix our seeds with equal parts of washed, coarse builder's sand. This permits even scattering of the seeds over the medium and results in properly spaced, more vigorous seedlings.

Where then to find fresh hellebore seed if no hellebore plants are growing in your own garden? Plant societies often host seed exchanges that send out fresh seed in small numbers. Some nurseries offer fresh seed from hellebore plants listed either as a mixed lot or by the color of the parent plant. Some seed companies sell fresh seed, and a few specialist nurseries offer wild-collected seed. Unfortunately, there is usually little choice for commercial growers wanting to build a collection of hellebores except to purchase seed. Before investing, contact the seed source to determine the age and condition of the seeds. (See "Sources" at the end of the book.)

SOWING HELLEBORES

The methods for sowing seeds are probably as varied as the number of gardeners doing the sowing; every individual has a favorite or best method. Conventional wisdom says to sow seeds and keep the containers in a warm, moist environment for six to twelve weeks. Follow this with another eight to twelve weeks of cold storage—in a refrigerator, not a freezer. Next, remove seed from the fridge, and after six to twelve weeks of warmth, you can expect germination. This method, a form of stratification, duplicates the seeds' natural progression from ripening to germination. When we tested this elaborate process at Pine Knot, it produced no faster germination and no more seedlings than the simple method of sowing the seeds in containers placed outside or in a cold poly house for natural chilling.

Elizabeth Strangman of Washfield Nursery once showed us her method, which involved dividing the top of a filled pot into quadrants and sowing each of the quadrants. This wonderfully exact method produced seedlings that were an inch (3 cm) or so from their neighbors; each plant grew well and was easy to transplant. Strangman also fitted the top of each seed pot with circles of asbestos so that marauding vermin would be kept away from the precious seed. While we truly admire her precision, we do not have the perseverance to duplicate it, so we developed methods that suit our needs.

At Pine Knot, we find that a deep flat or tray is best for sowing hellebore seed. A depth of 3 in. (8 cm) is good and 4 to 6 in. (10 to 15 cm) is even better, since hellebore roots go straight down. Deep flats are easily ordered from companies that specialize in greenhouse and nursery supplies. The flats are filled with commercial sterile medium. You should choose your brand carefully and make sure it is reliably consistent from bag to bag. Any good-quality sterile soilless medium should suffice as long as it is well drained. We prefer a medium that has little or no added vermiculite, which seems to develop a very slippery layer on the top of the flat. We sow seeds sparingly; it is far better to end up with too few seedlings in a flat than too many. We must remind ourselves each year that if seeds are sown too heavily, the insufficient air circulation around the new plants makes them much more susceptible to damping-off and other problems. Each of our 12 by 16 by 3 in. (30 by 40 by 8 cm) flats hold approximately 200 seedlings. As long as the seedlings are moved on before they begin to crowd one another, we are successful using this method.

We use much more conservative techniques for special plants, such as the double hybrids or hand-pollinated interspecies and intersectional crosses. We do not want to run the risk of losing a potential double dark purple or another treasure in a flat, so they are sown in small lots in square 6 in. (15 cm) pots.

After sowing, the seeds are covered with a light dusting of potting medium, topped off with an expanded slate product that resembles very small gravel. Coarse builder's sand works in a pinch. Total depth over the seeds is approximately ⅓ to ½ in. (6 to 12 mm). A covering of grit is not strictly necessary, but we find that the top dressing helps prevent damping-off and reduces the growth of algae and mosses. We usually hold on to a container that includes seed of special crosses or rarities for at least three years before we toss it (and when we do dispose of the container, we dump the contents somewhere in the garden, just in case).

Once seeds are sown, we water them thoroughly and put the well-labeled flats in an out-of-the-way spot in the garden, a propagation house, or a cold frame. A propagation house or frame is ideal since the care of the seedlings after germination is much easier if they are protected from the elements—the first seedlings usually appear around the new year. If a cold frame is not available, a spot under a deciduous shrub is a suitable place if the shrub is limbed up enough to permit easy access. We recommend covering any flats growing outside with a bit of screening or hardware cloth. Having tucked the container safely in bed, all that remains is the long wait until wintertime germination. The seeded flats, pots, or cells can dry out slightly, but they should never become completely dry. We irrigate at least once every week, or as needed. In cooler areas of the country, the interval between water applications is greater. In the best scenario, nature should provide enough water.

Germination and early growth

The first seedlings to appear at Pine Knot are always those of *H. lividus*, with *H. ×sternii* popping up just behind, often in late October or early November. The radicle of *H. vesicarius* often begins to emerge in October, but usually nothing is visible above soil level until December or January. *Helleborus argutifolius* and *H. foetidus* are next to emerge for us, coming up in late November and early December. Older or dried seed of *H. foetidus* usually takes an extra year to germinate. Seedlings of *H. ×hybridus* can

begin to germinate in December and continue popping up well into spring, especially if seed is not fresh. After the first of the year, we usually see *H. purpurascens*, *H. croaticus*, and *H. atrorubens* emerge. The last to come up is invariably *H. niger* or intersectional crosses with a high percentage of *H. niger* blood.

In the coldest areas, seeds wait until later in the season to begin their journey into planthood. The Balkan species, such as *H. torquatus*, are more reluctant to reproduce.

As a hellebore seed germinates, the radicle emerges first, and then the young shoot follows. The cotyledons unfold quickly, and then the first true leaves emerge.

In our experience, it seems the species with the most extremely divided leaves seem to produce fewer flowers and fewer viable seeds.

During the germination period, keep the medium moist, but not waterlogged. This is always a delicate balance. If the newly developing radicle dries out too much, germination aborts and no plants are produced. If the medium is kept soggy, the seeds rot. Feel the surface of the media or stick a finger into the flat to determine the moisture level. We water our seed trays with a medium-density spray nozzle. Media absorb water from a medium spray readily. Take care not to use high-pressure spray that can compact the soil and cause rotting problems.

A FEW CHALLENGES

Though not common, seedling death is caused by easily identifiable factors—damping-off and pests. Damping-off principally affects seedlings that are grown in overcrowded, damp conditions or those that have sustained a minute injury to the stem. It is possible for seeds to damp-off before or just at the point of germination. Pre-emergence damping-off is usually the result of keeping the medium too wet, especially in cold or very warm soil. Post-emergence losses can occur in the seed flat or after the seedlings are transplanted. The early symptoms often appear as wilting or leaning of a seedling or two, and then the wilting spreads out in a circular area. (See Chapter 6 for more information.)

Mice are annoying in almost any situation, with the possible exception of characters in children's books. The creature that nibbled the tops off our double hellebore seedlings one winter rates a place on our Ten Most Wanted List to this day. Be forewarned, and use whatever methods your conscience permits to protect your seedlings.

Insects are not usually a problem on seedlings early in the year, but aphids seem to find hellebores from any distance in any weather. These voracious beasts are usually found on tender new growth, such as in the juncture of cotyledons or on the undersides of newly expanding leaves. Fungus gnats are often found in warmer growing areas; watch for those that fly about and take measures to destroy the larvae that inhabit warm, moist soil, feeding on decomposing plant matter. Spray with a pesticide if you must, but only as a last resort, and read any labels carefully, since harsh chemical sprays easily burn tender new growth. The ever-present slug or snail also enjoy your tender green babies, so observe your plants carefully to prevent these hungry pests from invading your trays or flats. We do not use pelletized slug bait in seed flats as they promote fungal growth, which transfers easily to seedlings.

TRANSPLANTING SEEDLINGS

Transplanting is just that, transferring the plant from one place to another place. Bringing the seed flats inside makes transplanting your seedlings much more pleasant. Several conflicting theories regard the best time to transplant hellebore seedlings. The traditional view is that plants need at least one true leaf before being transplanted.

To transplant seedlings, prick them out individually and insert them into cell packs.

Where we garden, this is often as late as April for some species that germinate in January. Pine Knot plants respond much better if we get them out of the seed flat as soon as we can, preferably in the cotyledon stage. We generally transplant as soon as a week or 10 days after germination. If we wait, they are much more likely to suffer from transplant shock or damping-off. If the plants are moved when still very small and before the roots begin to go down, they do not seem to notice the transition. No matter when the seedlings are transplanted, take particular care always to handle the plantlet by its cotyledon, never the stem. The plant can grow a new leaf, but if you damage the stem you may as well throw the plant away.

We transplant most of our seedlings directly into black plastic containers called cell packs that are sold in sheets with varying diameter openings. Try to find the cells with the greatest depth; what is called (in the United States) a "deep 36" is good, although the deepest cell you can find is best. A deep 36–size cell translates into a sheet of plastic with 36 openings, each roughly 3¼ in. (9 cm) deep by 1 ½ in. (4 cm) wide, placed in a carrying flat. For convenience, these plastic items are unbeatable—inexpensive and readily available. Paper or styrofoam drinking cups, peat pots, or even containers made from compressed newspaper can work as well if you are growing small numbers of plants. Use a sterile, well-drained, soilless potting medium for your seedlings. Do not compromise on this step. Soil from the garden does not give satisfactory results and reusing media from previous plantings can risk exposing your seedlings to disease. The medium need not be peat based, but it must be sterile.

After filling the container, firm the fluffy medium by pressing to allow for a greater volume. It is very important to pack the medium firmly into the containers.

Water the medium well, for it is exceedingly difficult to get it thoroughly moistened after transplanting, especially when using cell flats. Equally moisten all cells. Dig down into a few of the cells and check to see that the moisture has penetrated equally well into each cell. With some media, you must allow the newly watered cells to "rest"; then rewater them to achieve a proper moisture level.

If you have never transplanted before, moving a tiny new seedling can be like holding a newborn baby; both are fragile and hold the promise of a beautiful life ahead. Grasp the little plant by a cotyledon and fiddle the roots out of the seeding medium with a transplanting stick, pencil, chopstick, or similar pointy tool. Holding the plantlet, place your stick under the root of the seedling and lift the stick and the plant simultaneously. Gently move the plant into a hole that you made in the medium with your stick, being careful not to fold the roots. Very gently firm the moist medium around the stem and continue with the next plant until the flat is full.

Carefully and thoroughly water the plants with a gentle stream or spray of water. Keep the seedlings moist, but not wet, and protect them from strong sunlight for a few days after transplanting. We recommend watering as needed with a dilute mixture of all-purpose fertilizer, since most soilless media provide only a starter charge of fertilizer and hellebores are hungry plants.

Although it appears simple, the skill of watering is a difficult one to acquire, and unfortunately we all seem to lose more than a few valuable plants as we learn. Take your time, and pay attention to what you are doing. When using a breaker that spreads the water out over 6 to 8 in. (15 to 20 cm), the plants in the center of the spray zone receive a greater amount of water than those on the outside edges. When watering a flat of deep 36 cells, we move slowly up and down each side of the flat twice. This usually provides enough water for each cell to absorb what it needs to become properly moistened. Moist medium is dark while drying medium is somewhat pale to ashen. Feel and appearance together are the best indicators of proper moisture levels.

Once plants are fully rooted, go back and pull a cell out after watering to determine that the water has percolated evenly throughout. In our opinion, practical hands-on experience is greatly preferred over any gauges and meters used to evaluate the moisture levels in soil.

Transplanted seedlings are best protected from very harsh winter weather, although they do not need to be stored in temperatures above freezing. A frame or other sheltered place helps protect the new babies from drying winds. *Helleborus ×hybridus*, *H. foetidus*, *H. argutifolius*, *H. ×sternii*, and *H. lividus* grow faster than other species and usually need potting on by mid- or late summer. In cooler areas, plant the well-rooted transplants directly into the garden in early to midsummer (June or July in the U.S.), but in the "fry-eggs-on-sidewalk zones," it is better to wait until cooler autumn temperatures prevail. By early autumn, the seedlings should be large enough to survive the rigors of garden life. Getting the hellebores into the garden relieves the grower of the chore of watering small pots. Soil temperatures in black plastic pots can reach very unpleasant levels during hot weather, and keeping the pots watered becomes a drudgery that is eliminated by putting plants out into the garden.

COMMERCIAL GROWING

It has taken us a number of years to develop a successful program at Pine Knot, since *H. ×hybridus* are not the easiest plants to produce under usual nursery conditions. Hellebores are slow to mature compared to most herbaceous perennials and are not at their best when growing in containers. In commercial production, we find it is advantageous to keep the seedlings growing at a steady pace all through the year. Hellebores are heavy feeders; we give the young plants a low dose of a balanced water-soluble fertilizer with each irrigation cycle. We transplant as soon as possible after germination, taking appropriate care not to damage roots or stems.

Seedlings we transplant into cells during the months of January through March are usually ready to step up to 1-quart pots in August or September. These are sold green in late fall or overwintered. Most bloom the second year after germination, so seedlings are grown on for another full year to produce a blooming-size plant.

Helleborus ×hybridus plants produce three or four growth flushes each year. In our nursery, new foliage is produced in late summer (August); another flush occurs in October to November, then again just before bloom in December to January, and a flush of foliage just after bloom in April to May.

The exact timing of growth flushes and blooming varies, depending on climate. Wherever the plants are growing, it is advisable to make sure they are well fed during these times.

A very well-drained pine bark–based medium is the best substrate for use in containers. Even in well-drained media, container-grown hellebores are quite susceptible to rotting diseases such as *Fusarium* crown and root rot and *Rhizoctonia* crown and stem rot, especially if grown outside in regions with high temperatures and humidity. Since many outdoor holding areas are not shielded from rain or thunderstorms, irrigation cycles need careful monitoring during the summer to prevent overwatering. A preventive program of fungicide application with a product labeled for these fungi is advisable in areas with high summer temperatures and high humidity.

The cycle for producing hellebores from seed at Pine Knot in southern Virginia is as follows:

Year 1	January–March: Pollinate June–July: Collect and sow seed December: Germination begins
Year 2	January: Germination continues February–April: Transplant to plugs June–August: Transplant plugs into quarts
Year 3	January–February: Some plants will flower (1 year after germination) May–June: Step up into gallons
Year 4	January–February: More plants begin to bloom (2 years after germination) June–July: Move plants from gallons to 6 qt. or 2 gallons
Year 5	January–February: Slower colors begin to flower (3 years after germination)

Our friends Ernie and Marietta O'Byrne at Northwest Garden Nursery in Eugene, Oregon, are able to produce blooming-sized plants faster than we can, probably because of their cooler summer temperatures. Here is their schedule:

Year 1	February–March: Pollinate May–June: Collect and sow seed December: Germination begins
Year 2	January: Germination continues February–March: Transplant directly into 4 by 4 by 6 in. cross-bottom band pots (quarts) July–August: Step up into gallons
Year 3	February–March: About 50 percent or more flower in the gallons; doubles a bit slower to bloom April–May: Move plants from gallon to 2-gallon pots
Year 4	January–February: 2 gallons flower, with very few exceptions

DIVIDING HELLEBORES

Traditionally, division is the only way to acquire clones or named cultivars. Consequently, dividing hellebores is the subject of much discussion. At one point in time, the conventional wisdom was circulated that hellebores should not be divided. This is not the case.

Helleborus ×*hybridus* plants are the optimal candidates for division, since they make more rapid growth and seasonally produce multiple stems once established. These hybrids are primogenitors of many fine forms that produce identical offspring only when divided to preserve their unique characteristics. It is possible to divide

H. niger, but plants often suffer a setback, refusing to bloom for several years after division. The Balkan species, such as *H. torquatus*, *H. multifidus*, *H. croaticus*, and *H. atrorubens*, grow much more slowly, taking quite a number of years before they are large enough to divide.

Division of the caulescent, or stemmed, species—*H. argutifolius*, *H. lividus*, and *H. foetidus*—is perhaps not impossible but is decidedly difficult, and only large plants provide enough material with which to work. These three species produce abundant seedlings that, with careful selection, can resemble the parents.

SELECTING THE CANDIDATES

Select plants for division carefully since dividing mature hellebores is time-consuming and a bit troublesome. Your best plants are always good choices for propagation, no matter which method is used. Choose a plant with special historical or sentimental associations, such as Strangman's *H. torquatus* 'Dido'. A plant whose variegated foliage is truly spectacular is also a candidate for division, since this characteristic does not pass on to seedlings. An especially dark-flowering double or a plant with particularly attractive foliage is also a good prospect. A weak or pest-infested plant is not strong enough to recover from division, so select only healthy stock. The plant must have multiple, well-defined crowns. Size depends on species; a five-year-old plant of *H. ×hybridus* produces quite a few divisions, while a five-year-old plant of *H. torquatus* may not be large enough to divide. Make an extra label for the plant you are going to divide before you begin the process, and make certain that this label follows the plant wherever it goes.

TIMING DIVISIONS

When asked what was the best time to divide a plant, Judith's grandmother always answered, "When someone offers you a piece of it." The sage advice of doing divisions on a cool, damp day in autumn is, of course, like most clichés, partially true. Considering the busy, complicated lives we lead today, one usually has to accomplish such chores when there is time to do them, which is not necessarily on an ideal day.

The best time to divide hellebores depends on both the species and the environmental conditions in which they are growing. In general, the ideal period is just before the new foliage begins to emerge so that new divisions produce fresh foliage shortly after dividing. Dividing before flowering in late winter or just after flowering in early to midspring works well in areas with a long spring. This gives the new plants plenty of time to settle in and begin growing before the hot summer temperatures arrive. Early to midautumn also works well. In either case, it is always best to avoid dividing during periods of hot, dry weather or when freezing winter temperatures are just around the corner.

Some species from the Balkans are very slow to bulk up compared to the hybrids. These species seem to respond best to division just before they begin to grow in late winter or early spring, when the foliage is still in leaf bud stage. Dividing as plants go dormant is also successful in areas where long autumns allow plants to settle in before winter arrives. Don't worry if your newly divided species go dormant early or even remain dormant for a year. This very frightening process occurs fairly often when plants are disturbed, but in time they emerge and settle in.

Helleborus niger also seems to respond best to division in late winter or early spring, although it is always a pity to remove the flowers that brighten the dark days of winter. If you divide *H. niger* shortly before the new foliage begins to emerge, remove any old or broken leaves. The intersectional hybrids *H. ×ericsmithii* and *H. ×nigercors* perform quite well when divided in late summer. It is preferable not to cut off the old stems of these two hybrids until new growth begins to break from below soil level. *Helleborus thibetanus* also seems to respond well to being divided while dormant, but our experience with this plant is limited.

LIFTING THE PLANTS

Whether you choose a cool, cloudy spring day or a crisp autumn morning on which to lift a mature plant, the job is easier if the plant is well-watered. The soil should not be sticky and wet, but just moist enough so the roots lift easily without tearing. For a mature clump of *H. ×hybridus*, dig a circle 8 to 10 in. (20 to 25 cm) outside the ring of foliage, going down 12 to 18 in. (30 to 45 cm). Use the spade to lift from under the center of the crown, which pries the plant from the soil. Work your way around the circumference. This produces a very large ball of soil. Knock some soil off the root ball to refill the hole.

To divide a plant properly, you must be able to see all its parts. Shake off as much loose soil as possible (much easier said than done). On very large plants, this can require another person to assist with the initial effort. If no one is available, loosen the large ball of soil by beating along the outside with a wooden mallet, the flat side of a hammer, or the back of a spade. You need to use something flat that does not cut the roots but provides enough force to loosen the soil. Work around the outside of the plant, striking the soil with your chosen instrument. After a few bashes, the soil should begin to fall away. Give the plant a quarter turn and continue soil bashing until you reach the place where you began. Lift the plant and give it a shake, or bounce it up and down if you cannot lift the whole thing at once. If the roots are not yet visible, work your way around the plant again, banging and shaking to remove more soil. When you can see the crowns, use your fingers, a dibble, or a chopstick to work excess soil from around the roots.

WASHING UP AND MAKING CUTS

Washing the roots removes the remaining soil and exposes the rhizome and crowns. A high-pressure nozzle makes this job easy. Place the clean plant to be divided on a potting bench or other stable work area. Carefully examine the crowns to see where any natural breaks or separations occur. Each portion should consist of a leaf or three, a piece of the rhizome, and fresh beige or white roots. The thickened rhizome

Individual crowns of a garden hybrid hellebore are easily divided with a sharp knife.

resembles a segmented centipede. Depending on the number of divisions you want to make and the species, a five-year-old plant yields from two to ten new plants. The larger the division, the sooner the plant regains the strength to bloom.

You need a sharp knife or pointed shears to cut apart the crowns. Dip the blade in alcohol or a 10 percent bleach solution to prevent the introduction of diseases. Select the piece to remove and use the knife to cut the rhizome; then carefully tease apart the tangled roots. Continue around the plant, selecting pieces with good growing points. Discard any old woody pieces and old black roots as they will not resprout. Trim off any broken leaves and roots to avoid leaving injured tissue to discourage the entry of disease. We feel better if we give the plants a dip in a good all-purpose fungicide, following label directions.

If you possess strong wrists and forearms, you can actually make the divisions by grasping the plant in both hands and twisting the crowns apart. Continue twisting and teasing the roots apart until the plantlet is easily separated. Most of the divisions done this way seem to naturally fall apart at the proper place. As ever, roots of newly divided hellebores must not dry out.

DIVISION FOR PROPAGATION

In our experience, hellebores that are divided into small pieces to produce the maximum number of plants suffer less shock if they are first heeled in to allow a bit of respite before being planted or potted up. We accomplish this by creating a bed of soft, sterile bagged medium for the newly divided plants and nestling them in with their crowns just at soil level and the roots spread out but not touching another plant. Some breeders use well-rotted sawdust or peat moss for heeling in, but we find that the availability of good quality, sterile bagged medium eliminates the necessity of using any other material. We leave the heeled-in plants in this bed for a few weeks to a couple of months, depending on the time of year and the species we are dividing. The plants must be kept evenly moist, but do not let them get too wet or too dry.

If you hold plants for several months, use a dilute fertilizer application weekly or as part of a continuously applied irrigation program. Watch for the appearance of new white or beige feeder roots, which signify a successful division. Bare-root plants will also sprout fresh roots when handled in this way. Healthy roots, not necessarily lush foliage, signify healthy growth.

POTTING UP OR PLANTING OUT

No matter when you divide, make sure you provide new plants with a sheltered environment for a few weeks until they settle in. If you make many small divisions, pot the new plants into containers or heel them in, as described, so you can monitor them more easily. Once they recover and form new growth, they are ready for the garden.

If you are planting directly into the garden, prepare the spot well. We usually try to incorporate some amendment to improve drainage for our heavy soil. Well-rotted pine bark, small gravelly bits, or an expanded slate soil conditioning product work well. When planting, keep the crown of the plant just below soil level, and do not allow soil to pile up to the bases of the petioles. Build a mound of soil in the prepared hole to support the crown. This keeps the crown at the proper level and allows the roots to spread out around the mound without being twisted. Firm the soil around the plants to avoid air pockets, but do not overly compact the soil. Continue to pay special attention to watering. Do not let the plants dry out during the season following division. Plants begin growth quickly but usually take a year to resume flowering.

MICROPROPAGATION BY TISSUE CULTURE

Since the latter part of the 20th century, many advances have been made in growing hellebores via tissue culture. In-vitro (flask or test tube) propagation produces thousands of identical plants in a relatively short period of time. Division, on the other hand, produces a very limited number of plants from each parent.

Micropropagation by tissue culture is a clonal method of production that uses a small piece of tissue without destroying the mother plant. Micropropagation requires special facilities where sterility is assured. The process entails four stages: preparation of plant material and insertion into sterile medium, establishment of material in medium, multiplication and rooting of plantlets, and growing the resulting small plantlets outside the protected environment. Very small pieces of the parent plant are cleaned thoroughly and grown in-vitro under sterile conditions using gel media until they form shoots. After shoots are initiated, the plants are transferred into a medium containing hormones that stimulate root formation. When sufficient roots have formed, the plants are transferred to soil and treated like any other small plants.

Tissue-cultured hellebores such as *H. niger* 'Double Fantasy' are becoming more common, but seed-grown plants still dominate the market.

Certain hellebore plants are produced by micropropagation with a minimum degree of difficulty, while the key to other species is yet to be discovered. *Helleborus* ×*nigercors* and *H.* ×*ericsmithii* are successfully produced by a number of companies that specialize in commercial micropropagation. Plants of a double-flowering selection of *H. niger* have become more commonly available from at least one major supplier. *Helleborus* ×*hybridus* plants are a bit more challenging, and the large numbers needed for commercial profitability have not been successfully produced as of this writing. Several companies have had success working with a few clones. In time, if a gardener desires a hillside planted with identical double white-flowering hellebores, they will be available.

Stage 1

During stage 1, the growth medium and plant tissue are prepared and sterilized. Work areas must be scrupulously clean and located in an area with minimal air flow to prevent contamination from mold spores or bacteria. Equipment ranges from commercial- or university-grade laminar flow hoods to transfer boxes made from a home aquarium turned on its side and fitted with a plastic or acrylic cover. The air inside the transfer chamber must be filtered to remove contaminants. All utensils, media, containers, and toweling must be sterilized in an autoclave or pressure cooker prior to use. Medium is mixed and inserted into the culture vessels and sterilized before being inserted into the sterile transfer box or cabinet.

Explant is the term used for the fragments of plant or propagules that are inserted into the sterile medium. Different parts of plants can be used to create the explants—buds, seeds, leaves, root, stem, petiole, meristem, or flower—depending on the genus and species being cultured. Cells from one tissue source may respond favorably to propagation, while cells from another area of the plant do not proliferate. Soaking them in a solution of chlorine bleach, ethanol, or other agents cleans the selected plant parts. This is a tricky bit, since the aim is to kill any pathogens on the plant but not the plant itself.

After sterilization and thorough rinsing, the explants are cut into small pieces and inserted onto the medium. Different media are designed for different genera and have different components—agar (gel), water, fertilizers, sugars, vitamins, and whatever chemicals or other ingredients the researcher chooses. The containers, usually test tubes or flasks, are placed in environments where light and temperature are monitored and controlled to initiate the culture. The containers are watched daily and contaminated vessels are discarded. If successful, the explants should begin to multiply, forming masses of undifferentiated cells that ultimately create new plants.

STAGE 2

The proliferated cell masses are placed into culture vessels on media containing growth regulators—auxins and cytokinins or other phytohormones. The proportions of ingredients in the media are critical to the development of tissue. A lower auxin level and the culture may not produce shoots or roots, while if the level is too high an overproduction of roots can occur. Cytokinin levels control the development of roots and the degree of tissue formation. If the correct balance is achieved, the plant hormones initiate the formation of *callus tissue*, which is composed of cells that have different characteristics than other plant cells. These bits of callus tissue split and grow into a collection of pale beige cells that have the ability to develop into other cell types as the plant grows.

Depending on the plant, shoot multiplication to form plantlets can take days or weeks. In some instances, no multiplication occurs. After successful multiplication, the cell masses may be transferred into containers to produce roots, of they may be cut up and used to multiply the number of plants. If further shoot multiplication is to be attempted, the cut-up plant pieces are returned to a sterile medium to begin another multiplication cycle. With each cycle, the number of potential plants increases dramatically. The exact medium components and the conditions that are necessary to initiate and maintain plantlet growth are often different for each genus and sometimes for each species within a genus. The particular conditions for each species are discovered only through time-consuming experimentation.

STAGE 3

In stage 3, the plantlets are transferred into another medium containing higher concentrations of root-inducing and lower concentrations of shoot-inducing phytohormones. As with each stage, utmost care must be taken so the medium does not become contaminated. If and when rooting begins, light levels are increased and plants are allowed to continue root growth.

STAGE 4

After roots are formed, the plants begin the fourth stage, the establishment or ex-vitro stage. Plantlets are removed from the gel medium and washed thoroughly, removing all traces of the chemicals that nourished them during their development. This adjustment is similar to the hardening-off process cuttings must undergo as they are removed from mist or seedlings experience as they are gradually exposed to more light and different temperatures in garden conditions.

In the culture environment, the high humidity and perfectly balanced nutrients allowed the plantlets to mature quickly with little stress. Life outside the test tube is decidedly different, with dry air and bright light; the plantlets must make their adjustments to these factors gradually. The small plantlets are moved into cells containing a sterile soilless medium and grown under mist until the new foliage is able to withstand the desiccation experienced outside a test tube environment. As the plants become established in the outside world, they are treated in a similar manner to newly transplanted seedlings.

The hellebore growth cycle from this stage is identical to that of seed-grown plants. Cultured material seems to establish and bloom at the same rate as seed-grown plants.

These young hellebores are just out of the flask and ready to be potted up.

ADVANTAGES AND DISADVANTAGES OF MICROPROPAGATION

Plants produced via micropropagation are clonal duplicates of the parent, theoretically allowing production of potentially millions of identical hellebores. Plants are uniform and crop numbers can be predicted in advance. Particularly choice or unusual forms may be produced in numbers unattainable by traditional methods. Because the entire crop is produced under sterile conditions, the plants are free from any diseases that may be latent or undiagnosed in plants produced by seed or division. Plants resulting from difficult interspecies and intersectional crosses are produced with confidence by using micropropagation techniques.

On the down side, the replication of the clone is not always exact. *Sports*, mutated plants with different characteristics, sometimes result from slight chromosomal alterations during culture. Sports are often seen in *Hosta* and some other species, producing variants in foliage and flower form. Certain double-flowering hostas may develop triple or quadruple flowers during the process. The double-flowering form of *H. niger* produced by micropropagation shows similar variation. Flowers produced on these plants can be double, semidouble, or single, although the basic shape and growth habits of the plant remain the same.

8

BREEDING HELLEBORES

I am often asked of a plant, by people who are wondering whether it might be
worth getting for their own gardens, "How long does it flower?" If I say, "For a
good month," in a tone of warm encouragement, they feel all right; but if I say,
"Perhaps three weeks," in a noncommittal sort of voice, they look dubious.
Yet the truth about the majority of spring-flowering trees and shrubs is
that they last in beauty for one week only.

Christopher Lloyd in *The Well-Tempered Garden* (1970)

Protruding pistils and rings of frothy stamens add to the beauty and allure of hellebore
flowers at the time of pollination.

GROWING HELLEBORES often instills in us the desire to create new plants. Perhaps it is the time of the year they are in flower, when little else is happening in the garden. Since we are not busy weeding, watering, and performing the numerous chores associated with garden upkeep, we have more of that precious element, time. Or it could be simply one more example of mankind's never-ending efforts to alter our natural world. Whatever the reason, once bitten by the hybridizing bug, hellebore fever unquestionably makes its symptoms known and a new obsession is born.

Propagating and growing *Helleborus* ×*hybridus* from seed is a rewarding pastime, and breeders can potentially produce exciting plants. These seedlings are each different from the parent plants and are not permitted to carry any name of the parent plant. At Pine Knot Farms, we are asked many, many times if we sell named hellebores, such as 'Ballard's Black'. Our answer is invariably "no." 'Ballard's Black' must be clonally produced by division or micropropagation. While named plants are part of hellebore history, they are almost certainly no longer commercially available. Many beautiful, well-rounded, dark-flowering *H.* ×*hybridus* plants are grown from seed and appear identical to 'Ballard's Black', but they cannot bear that name.

GOALS OF A BREEDING PROGRAM

Every person who breeds plants has different methods and different reasons for pursuing the task. Some are very scientific, documenting each plant and each cross using an elaborate numbering system. Others simply run about with no more logic to their progress than a butterfly, putting pollen from any plant in flower onto any other plant with a bud.

To establish a successful breeding program, certain defined criteria must be met and certain procedures must be followed. While the criteria vary among hybridizers, the essential elements remain the same. If the process is taken step by step, it is fascinating and quite attainable to breed, select, and actualize an exciting new hellebore. Plants chosen for breeding purposes must be disease-free, healthy, and vigorous. They must be proven pollen or seed producers. Take care to establish that the cross is free from outside influences, properly labeled, and the resulting seeds gathered. You must keep records to determine the results of the crosses. Selections must be evaluated and failures discarded.

DETERMINE AND WRITE DOWN YOUR GOALS

Before the first bit of pollen is collected, the beginning breeder must go through a number of steps. The first step is to determine your objectives. Are you attempting to create a color strain of *H.* ×*hybridus*? Perhaps you are trying to produce taller or shorter plants. Do you want plants with different foliage, shape, or number of flowers per stem? Whatever your goals, writing them down helps to solidify the idea in your mind and gives you the conviction to keep going when failure threatens. You don't need a thesis statement; usually a few simple lines suffice to remind you what and why you began your experiment and perhaps give a prod toward completion.

Having determined your goals, you are ready to begin considering the selection of potential candidates for breeding. You need a plant to serve as seed parent and at least pollen from a male parent. If you do not have a plant of the desired pollen parent, a friend may supply a flower or even a few pollen-bearing stamens. Some plants set seed more easily than others, and this is an important criterion when selecting the seed parent. It is interesting to work the cross both ways; this is especially valuable if you are trying to incorporate a particular asset from the chosen mother plant. Doing this improves your chances of producing the desired seedlings.

Hybridizers must remember that modern *H. ×hybridus*, with the delightfully broad range of colors that we enjoy, contains the blood of as many as 10 different species. The species potentially involved are *H. atrorubens*, *H. croaticus*, *H. cyclophyllus*, *H. dumetorum*, *H. multifidus*, *H. occidentalis*, *H. odorus*, *H. torquatus*, *H. viridis*, and *H. orientalis*, plus *H. orientalis* subsp. *abchasicus* and *H. orientalis* subsp. *guttatus*.

From these species, modern hybrids acquire a wide range of flower colors and shapes, as well as leaf shapes and sizes. These characteristics may or may not transfer to the offspring, since plants with complicated parentage seldom breed true. For example, if you select two dark purple–flowering plants as parents for your cross, their progeny may produce flowers in colors that range from dark purple to white. Breeders must wait until the seedlings from their crosses flower, a period that can seem interminable, to determine whether the results of their work are anywhere near the objective with which they began.

The time between making the first cross and seeing the results of that cross varies depending on location, climate, and the color of the plant with which you are working. Plants growing in very hot climates usually take longer to flower than plants growing in cooler zones. Hellebores seem to grow at a steadier and therefore more rapid rate in areas where the air and soil temperatures do not fluctuate dramatically.

BASIC PLANT SEX

To produce seed, a plant must be pollinated. *Pollination* is the transfer of pollen from the anther to the stigma. The male part of the flower, the stamen, consists of the anther and the filament. The filament is the stalk of the stamen, with the anther at its head. The pollen-bearing anther resembles a flattened Parker House roll—a softly rounded, cream-colored oval that appears creased in the center lengthwise. As the pollen ripens, the stamen takes on the appearance of a tiny dandelion, a slender stem with a bouffant hairstyle. A hellebore is constructed so that the outside rings of stamens loosen and uncurl before the adjoining bands mature. As the stamens age, the filament begins to rise up toward the stigma and eventually curves out toward the sides in some species.

The female part of a hellebore flower, the pistil, is composed of the stigma, style, and ovary. The stigma lies at the very tip of the style that is the narrow, gracefully curved tube that leads down to the ovary. When receptive, the stigma has a viscous coating, which helps pollen adhere while it germinates. The stigma of an individual flower is usually receptive before the stamens develop. After the pollen grains land on the stigma, they germinate and grow down through the style and enter the ovary. When sperm and egg meet, fertilization occurs. After fertilization, the carpels containing the ovules begin to swell and eventually contain the treasure we are hunting for—seeds.

MAKING A CONTROLLED CROSS, STEP BY STEP

Cross-pollination is the transfer of pollen from the anther of a flower to the stigma of the flower of another plant. You can use plants in the open garden or in containers when breeding. Having plants in pots in a cozy, warm environment is a decided advantage; not only does the pollen flow more freely in warmth, but one's arthritic knees are protected from the indignity of being pressed into cold, wet soil.

Self-pollination is the transference of pollen from the anther of a flower to the stigma of the same flower or any flower on the same plant. Insects, the wind, or passing animals (or coattails) can all accomplish this. Plants habitually take care of this matter themselves. Manual self-pollinating is usually necessary only if no insects are about due to extremely cold weather or if plants are growing inside an insect-free, screened poly house.

Backcrossing is the method of crossing a plant with one of the plant's progenitors to intensify a particular color or whatever aspect the breeder is trying to establish.

MATERIALS AND METHODS

A minimum of supplies is required to begin, along with the obvious and most important—the plants. The basics include a notebook, a No. 2 pencil, a pair of tweezers, very good eyesight or a magnifying apparatus such as a jeweler's loupe or hand lens, and something with which you mark your crosses. A simple composition type notebook is perhaps the most indispensable tool. The more information you write down, the more you learn, since memory is often selective. Keeping records not only helps you repeat successes, but it also helps you learn from failures.

In the notebook, write the details of each cross, including the date the cross is made, the number of the cross, and the information on both seed and pollen parents. A typical entry might read like so: "14 Feb. 2005 #26 *H. niger* 'Nell Lewis' strain (emasculated) × *H. argutifolius* Large Flowered Form." At Pine Knot Farms, I label each bud I cross. If I make the same cross using several buds on a scape or on the same plant, each bud is labeled with the number of that cross. If I make several different crosses on one scape or plant, each bud bears a different number. The cross number follows any seeds that result throughout the path to planthood. When the seeds are sewn, the flat carries a label that gives the source of the seed (*PKF* for Pine Knot Farms seed), the year, and the number of the cross. Any seedlings that germinate carry this information on their nursery labels. Using this method, we can track any individual plant back to its parents and the date the cross was made, and we know whether the seed parent was emasculated, important information if working with two different species.

Each hybridizer has favorite implements, accessories, and methods for working with plants. At Pine Knot, I keep my notebook in a flat, split white oak basket of tools I carry when I go out to do the breeding. Inside this basket, I've placed a plastic silverware organizer, and into the sections meant to hold knives, forks, and spoons I put my pencils and pens, tweezers, forceps, labels, tissues, and all of the other implements I use when working with my stock plants. With my loupe on a string around my neck and a foam kneeling pad under my arm, I am prepared to head out into the garden or stock house and make like a bee.

When moving stamens from one plant to the next during breeding, I prefer to use tweezers or forceps with flat ends. I find that the locking type forceps allow me to carry two or three small pollen-filled stamens from one side of the nursery to the other without losing the valuable cargo. For emasculation, I prefer free-moving tweezers or forceps with narrow and very pointed ends, which make it much easier to remove a stamen without damaging the style or nectaries.

For some breeding work, I use a small artist's paintbrush; for other work, a black, fuzzy pipe cleaner does the trick. While working within one color group of an established color strain, I use the same brush for all the plants within that group. For example, if I am pollinating several dozen *H. ×hybridus* 'White' strain each day, I use the same brush for all of the plants, picking up pollen as I go from flower to flower and plant to plant. Since the aim is to produce seed from white-flowering *H. ×hybridus* to grow more white-flowering plants, it does not matter whether the pollen from one white-flowering plant becomes mixed with the pollen of another white-flowering plant once the strains are established.

If working with hybrids of several colors, I use a different brush for each plant to ensure that my cross is not contaminated by pollen from a different-colored flower. To remove pollen from my brushes, I dip them in rubbing alcohol and let them dry thoroughly before I reuse them. Some breeders use the cap of a ballpoint pen to transfer pollen, while others use the pointed end of a plastic plant label. The tip of your finger works in a pinch. Anything that moves a few grains of pollen without losing them or causing damage to the bud when they are being deposited works.

Timing pollination

Tradition advises making the cross in the middle of the day, to give the temperature time to rise and the pollen time to flow. We usually work during the hours of 10 a.m. until 2 or 3 p.m. Because the stigma is receptive before pollen is mature, we have several days in which to make the cross without fear of self-pollination (the plant fertilizing itself). Emasculating the flower of the seed parent assures that a cross remains uncontaminated. We do this while the flower is still in bud, before insects visit it or the plant's own pollen ripens. This rather painful-sounding process is achieved by removing the stamens from the selected flower. It is wise to practice this procedure on some less-valuable plant before attempting to emasculate the bud on your choice and probably expensive plant. Once you have gained skill on some less precious flowers, you should feel brave enough to begin with your special plants.

EXECUTING THE CROSS

To make the cross, choose a bud that is unopened but advanced enough so that the stigma is receptive. It takes a bit of investigation before you are able to recognize which buds are closest to being at the perfect stage. Gently peel back the outer parts of the flower and check the stigma with your lens. A nicely ripened stigma stands unfurled and upright with a bit of sheen on the tip. Use your lens to make sure the stamens have not begun to unfurl. Do this very carefully to avoid damaging the style or the carpels that are very tender and easily bruised or broken. Take care not to spread pollen from another flower onto your chosen bud.

Using a small, sharp knife, scissors, tweezers, or forceps, gently pinch, cut, or tear out the stamens. Begin at one side of the flower, resting the edge of your tool at the base of the stigma, and slowly work your way around the center, cutting away the filaments as you go. You can see the bases of the carpels quite clearly once the stamens are removed. The result is a somewhat urn-shaped vessel, with the styles extending up from the carpels, receptive stigmas waiting at the top. Hellebores have anywhere from one to more than a dozen styles, depending on the particular plant. Each style leads down to a carpel that eventually contains the seeds.

Once the emasculation is accomplished, the application of pollen is quite easy, especially if pollen is plentiful. If the pollen-bearing plant has only one flower, gently remove a few stamens with ripe pollen and carry them to your selected seed parent with tweezers or locking forceps. If flowers are plentiful, pick a bloom with ripe pollen and carry it to the designated seed parent.

To work ahead, collect blooms and ready the pollen by floating them in a saucer of water inside a warm house. This allows the pollen to ripen for use the next day. Apply the pollen to the tip of the receptive stigma with your brush, fingertip, or other tool. It is necessary to apply pollen to the tip of each stigma; if no pollen is applied, that particular style withers away and no seed is produced. The pollen grains stick to the viscous coating of the stigma, which you can see clearly with a magnifying glass.

After pollinating, gently close the bud so there is no danger of insects visiting before your pollination rounds are complete. Further protect the flower by bagging it. An alternative method we chanced upon when we ran out of bags is to tape the flower closed with clear cellulose tape. We have used this method for the last several years with success. On some plants, it is necessary to remove the sepals as the carpels begin to swell, but by then we do not fear insect invaders. Although fertilization and the resulting seed production are possible with one application of pollen, tradition

Controlled crossing requires the transfer of pollen to the stigma of the mother plant.

To prevent self-pollination when making a cross, emasculate the flowers by removing all the stamens that surround the pistils.

After pollination, bag the flowers to prevent the addition of pollen from other flowers.

dictates repeating the cross for several days in a row.

After executing the cross, it is important to mark the bud you pollinated. After a few days, all of the flowers begin to look the same, and you may not remember which one you pollinated. Some hybridizers mark their crosses with different colors of yarn, using a key for each color. This method of marking gives the garden a rather festive appearance in the gray winter landscape. Some breeders use flexible plastic plant labels looped around the flower stem without breaking the flower. Many sizes of paper and plastic labels are easily available at any large office supply store. The labels used to mark prices work quite nicely and are not too obtrusive in the garden. The paper labels hold up fairly well outside if really harsh weather is not a factor, but too much snow and ice turns them to paper mâché. Plastic-coated labels are a definite plus for outdoor plant marking in moist areas.

For labeling, long-lasting and weatherproof markers are critical. Few things are more frustrating than gathering seeds of a cross and spreading the seed capsules out to dry, then turning to look at the label and seeing nothing at all. No matter how many times one turns the label over, the writing is gone, faded away with one's dreams. Because of this, we write our labels with several utensils—a No. 2 pencil, a permanent marker, or a paint pen—hoping that at least one of these remains legible until after the seeds are collected and sorted.

PROCURING POLLEN

The pollen-bearing parent for a cross provides a vital contribution. A single flower is easily carried across the garden, across town, or even across the sea to provide the pollen necessary to make a special cross. If ample flowers are available, the process is simply a matter of transferring the pollen from one flower onto the waiting stigma of the other flower.

Ripened pollen is fluffy and stands out around the anther. In cool temperatures, hellebore pollen ripens gradually over a period of days, with the pollen of the outside ring of stamens ripening before the inside circles of stamens begin to unfurl. Later in the season, high temperatures seem to hasten the process, and the anthers of some blooms are full of ripe pollen before the flower bud has completely opened.

The easiest way to determine whether pollen is ripe is to examine it closely, which usually requires a lens. Another way is to hold a dark piece of paper under the center boss of the flower from which you hope to gather pollen. Tap the flower gently but firmly, and if the pollen is ready, it will fall onto the paper. Hellebore pollen is golden yellow and shows up well on a dark background. Pollen grains are small and very lightweight. If you are working outside, it is prudent to use a windscreen such as an umbrella around the chosen plant to prevent a sudden breeze from carrying away the golden dust.

Stored pollen is handy for crossing hellebores that come into flower at different times. When collecting pollen, choose a day when the temperature is warm enough for the pollen to dehisce, or flow freely. Place the container under the boss of stamens and tap the back side of the flower several times. Usually the ripe pollen falls into the container. Another method is to scrape the pollen gently from the anthers into the container using a card, knife blade, or other flat item. A third way to collect is to cut the fully ripened pollen-bearing anthers from the stamens. This method usually requires a period of drying before a lid is placed on the container to prevent the pollen from becoming moldy.

Storing pollen is a fairly simple procedure. We find that we are able to see the pollen more easily if we place it in a dark, shallow container with a lid. Film canisters seem ideal, but they are too deep for pollen storage in their unaltered state. This is easily rectified with a hacksaw or chop saw. We cut the canister about an inch (3 cm) above the bottom. The altered tube is perfect and free. Stored pollen lasts at least one year if kept in a cool, dry place, such as a refrigerator.

ROBIN AND SUE WHITE OF BLACKTHORN NURSERY

Robin and Sue White of Blackthorn Nursery pause on a cold day.

Blackthorn Nursery in Kilmeston, Alresford, Hampshire, U.K., is located down a narrow country road that is packed end to end with cars on the Hellebore Open Days—so packed, in fact, that the local villagers are a bit put off by the traffic. British understatement aside, Blackthorn is *the* place to be if you are interested in hellebores, and the genteel-looking lady standing so discreetly beside your group of plants may just take one of them for herself. There are even rumors of fights breaking out over the last plant in a particularly delicious color. Customers flock from all around the country, snatching up the plants as fast as the staff can restock the tables. In the center of the display area is a bench full of the Blackthorn-bred Party Dress Hybrid hellebores, a lovely double-flowering selection that rivals a troupe of ballerinas for daintiness and charm; the bench is surrounded by customers.

The Whites have been breeding hellebores since the 1970s, when they began their nursery. Although Robin admits that daphnes are his favorite, his breeding skill has created a place for the Blackthorn plants in any hellebore lover's garden. He bred his Party Dress Hybrids from Strangman's double-flowering plant, *H. torquatus* 'Dido', incorporating some *H. ×hybridus* blood for improved vigor. Party Dress plants feature attractive foliage, often flushed with crimson or bronze when young. Mature foliage is often very finely divided, reminiscent of their *H. torquatus* heritage. When in bloom, they display many petite flowers on well-branched stems, each plant having several stems at maturity. Robin has also bred a complete range of colors of *H. ×hybridus*, as well as 'Blackthorn' strains of *H. ×sternii* and *H. ×ericsmithii,* and a lovely double-flowering red-spotted primrose strain named *H.* 'Marion White', for Robin's mother. Their *H. niger* 'Blackthorn' strain, which was created using blood from *H. niger* 'Louis Cobbett', is a particularly beautiful selection with dark red stems, each bearing two white flowers heavily blushed pink and centered with rose-pink styles.

This pair has carved a pleasant niche for themselves at Blackthorn: a garden for all seasons, a nursery full of interesting plants, and the enduring pleasures of the companionship of one another, working together for many years to make beautiful things to fill their world. Who could ask for more?

ESTABLISHING YOUR OWN LINE

Establishing your own line of *H. ×hybridus* is easy now because of the availability of quality plants and seeds from many sources. Whether you are a home gardener with a taste for experimentation or a nursery seeking to establish your own line, the basic approach is the same—only the numbers are different.

To create a new line of *H. ×hybridus*, select parents that are vigorous and proven breeders. When presented with a choice of stock plants, choose the best, just as one would if breeding race horses. Having established the ability to produce viable seed, the next thing to look for in the seed parent is flower shape or form. *Helleborus ×hybridus* flowers range from star to cup or bowl shaped. There are surely as many hellebore flower shapes as there are hellebore fanciers; since taste is so very personal, the choice is up to the individual. Interesting foliage and vigorous growth are additional assets to consider when choosing breeding stock.

Choose the pollen parent for color first, since this is what attracts most people. This plant could compliment the seed parent to produce a deeper shade of the same color or something unexpected. If you are lucky, the cross will produce a completely new color. Along with color, it is also a good idea to reinforce the same characteristics you used in selecting the seed parent. If you wish to incorporate markings such as red nectaries, stars, veining, or spots, it is helpful to use the plant with the attractive markings that you are trying to incorporate into your line as both seed and pollen plant.

After proven seed production, shape, and flower form, the next item in the selection process is foliage shape. Wild hellebore species offer the opportunity to breed some very different and wonderful foliage into your plants. Occasionally, newly emerging foliage has a dark purple or red color produced by the presence of anthocyanins, plant pigments that make blueberries blue and raspberries red. Colorful foliage is seen more often early in the year or in areas that enjoy cooler weather in spring, since warmer temperatures eliminate the coloring. In areas with long, cool springs, this aspect is worth exploring.

CHOOSING TRAITS

What makes perfection? Most breeders select stock for vigor, color, form, and the other more obvious facets. We all want perfection: a healthy, floriferous, disease-resistant plant with bright, long-lasting flower color inside and out. Interesting sepal markings, colorful nectaries, a full boss of stamens, and styles in a contrasting color are all desirable traits. Add foliage with interesting structure and presence, and you approach perfection.

The physical structure of a hellebore is important. Height is important; some stand tall with open inflorescences, while others are more diminutive and compact. Flower size, either large and full or dainty and numerous, more reminiscent of the species ancestors, is a matter of taste. Flower carriage is important. Flowers held on short pedicels tend to look outward at a 45-degree angle and present the interior of the bloom. While most of the newer hybrid strains feature plants with flowers that are outward-facing, one wouldn't want an upward-facing hellebore bloom. It would fill with water and present a messy sight, rather like a bowl of cereal with milk left too long on the kitchen counter.

We are particularly interested in selecting for the color on the reverse of the flower. The lovely insides of hellebore flowers are the reward we get for bending over to turn them up, but the backs of the flowers are what we see most often. We find that the color of the fading blossom is almost as important as the color of the freshest flower. Many parts of North America experience warm or even hot weather during the flowering season, which fades the flowers. If a plant has a pleasing tone as it ages, the period of interest is prolonged.

Contrast also makes flowers distinctive. Stars, rings, blotches, or other center markings are as attractive on faded flowers as on fresh ones. Dark nectaries and even dark styles stand out against pale sepals. A white-flowering plant with red nectaries and styles is beautiful when freshly opened. When the nectaries fall after pollination and the colored carpels begin to swell with seeds, the darker tones of the carpels are very appealing.

Some consider foliage the most important trait when choosing hellebores, since foliage is present in the garden year-round. Foliage of the hybrids can vary greatly in size and shape, offering another path on the numerous avenues available for the hellebore breeder to explore.

NAMING STRAINS

Plants or seeds from Ashwood Nurseries carry the Ashwood line or trade name, perhaps something like *H. ×hybridus* Ashwood Garden Hybrids, which is given to a strain to identify the nursery where it was created. When you cross two plants purchased as Ashwood Garden Hybrids, your seedlings should not bear the name "Ashwood Garden Hybrids," as the Ashwood breeder did not do the cross. Once you are two or three generations on in your breeding program, the seedlings are most definitely no longer Ashwood Garden Hybrids, even if they are bred from 100 percent Ashwood Garden Hybrids blood. Each hybridizer approaches the task in a different manner, and therefore the seedlings produced are different. Your crosses can carry any strain or line name that you choose, providing the name is not already being used.

SEED STRAINS

Opinions differ on the advisability of selling seeds or unbloomed plants of *H. ×hybridus*. The purest seed strains can be up to 95 percent true to color, but there will always be that 5 percent that is markedly different. If a customer purchases an unflowered plant of a pink strain that turns out to have white flowers, that customer is bound to be disappointed. Seed-grown plants are much less expensive, since the

Pure colors in green, pink, plum and purple are the result of annual reevaluation, removing any plants that produce inferior offspring.

customer spends the years growing the plants instead of the nurseryman. Perhaps the disappointment would be even greater if the same customer had sown seeds of the same pink strain and waited several years until the plants bloomed, only to find a mix of different colors. If the chance of variability is carefully explained before purchase, and the plants are labeled accordingly, the nurseryman has a clear conscience and hopefully the customer will not be disappointed.

ESTABLISHING A COLOR LINE

To begin a line, select stock from blooming plants with the purest colors, especially those with few or no overtones of another color. Choose the best you can find for stock even if the price is a bit high. Your investment pays for itself by cutting out years of producing mediocre plants. Select plants in a color range similar to the color of the offspring you are imagining. It is possible to begin with only one plant, self-pollinating the flowers for the first generation, but this adds several years to the project.

Color lines like these in pink and white are attainable only with time and patience.

Cross the two selected plants with each other using each for both sides of the cross, at least until you know whether one plant is a better seed producer. Keep records of which plant produces the most seed, the temperature at the time you made the crosses, and how many flowers you pollinated. It is wise to make as many notes as possible, especially at the beginning of the project.

Be patient. It can take a period of two or three years until you begin to see the results of your work. At Pine Knot, two seasons after germination are usually required for the majority of plants to flower. Hellebore breeders who work in climates with moderate temperatures, especially the U.K. and the U.S. Pacific Northwest, are often able to produce blooms the first season after germination. These breeders see early bloom on enough seedlings from each cross to get an indication of the direction their work is going.

Flower color of the plants with which you are working also influences the amount of time between germination and first flowering. Flowers from light-colored, white, or cream-colored plants bloom earlier than those of other colors; dark purple and slate-blue plants often take an extra year to flower. The most recalcitrant plants wait until the fourth year after germination to bloom.

Selecting the next generation

Eventually, the first seedlings from your crosses begin to flower, and all at once you have hundreds, if not thousands, of plants. The hardest part is rogueing (eliminating inferior plants); after tending them for several years, you may come to regard them as members of the family. Disposing of them is tantamount to sending puppies to the pound, but rogueing is essential. If the color or shape of the flower is wrong, remove it from the breeding program. Keep only the very best for stock. You can dispose of culls in many ways: you can plant them in other parts of your garden, give them to friends, or donate them to plant sales.

It is not uncommon for the first generation of crosses to produce plants inferior to the parents, especially if the plants with which you began are exceptional. Always remember that these plants are hybrids, and throwbacks occur with some regularity. Even the best breeders achieve only 90 to 95 percent true color and form when working with hellebore hybrids. Many color strains breed only 50 to 75 percent true for color. Do not get discouraged if your first attempts are not what you expected.

Select the very best plants to continue the work. In the second generation, you can make crosses within the group and backcross onto the parent plants. Keep records of everything you do; your future direction depends on the information you manage to accumulate. When the second generation of seedlings begins to bloom, you should see signs of progress. From this time forward, the process becomes easier, although it is still time-consuming. By the time the third generation blooms, the color strain should be fairly stable for the pure color forms. More complicated colors, such as apricot, true yellow, and the picotees, continue to produce a higher percentage of plants that are not true to color.

GLENN WITHEY AND CHARLES PRICE

The dynamic Withey-Price duo is responsible not only for creating exciting gardens in the U.S. Pacific Northwest, but for creating a line of splendid *H.* ×*hybridus*. Partners in life as well as business, Withey and Price began breeding hellebores in the late 1980s and early 1990s. Many of the plants they used when they began their breeding were acquired through an unselfish act of love. One of the country's premier plantsmen, Kevin Nicolay, was critically ill and began taking pieces of his garden apart, giving his plants to friends. Among the many unusual and interesting plants in his garden were divisions of superior plants from Helen Ballard, created when she was at the peak of her prowess, including good darks and what was at the time a good yellow. In 1989 a 'Primrose' strain seedling from Washfield, followed by a picotee from Washfield in 1994, combined with the Nicolay plants to give them a good start on the full range of colors. The line currently incorporates excellent singles in a range of colors from Ashwood as well as doubles from Blackthorn's varied stocks of Party Dress Hybrids and others.

The 'Withey-Price' strain is known for its excellent dark-flowering plants and the depth of the yellows, although they offer a full line of colors. Their focus is good,

The garden of Glenn Withey and Charles Price, who have been breeding hellebores longer than most other American breeders, features Ballard plants as well as some of their many hybrids.

vigorous garden plants available at reasonable prices. The color on the reverse is of particular interest, as it is what most people actually see in the garden and comprises their landscape so far as color goes. The development of comparatively dependable seed strains allows them to offer unbloomed seedlings by color. The currently popular doubles make up a large percentage of their production, with emphasis on the larger flowering hybrid forms. Their plants are distributed wholesale to outlets throughout the western United States by Blooming Nursery in Cornelius, Oregon.

COLOR STRAINS AT PINE KNOT

As we continue to work on color strains at Pine Knot, we find that each generation has a higher percentage of plants that are true to the colors we are attempting to produce, though they are not perfect. When pollinating by color, we use one brush for the pale pinks, another brush for pale pink with spots, another for the dark pinks, and others for the remaining different color strains. We pollinate the flowers within each group, such as pink, by moving from plant to plant, carrying pollen on the brush used only for that strain. It does not matter if pollen is mixed among all the very best plants in each group. What we are doing is open pollinating within a closed group. By selecting the first, second, and third generations of stock plants carefully, we are able to develop seedlings that produce a very large percentage of pink-flowering plants.

Of course, not all colors are as easy to breed as pink. The percentages of apricot- and yellow-flowering plants are not nearly as high. Seedlings of spotted plants bloom reliably around 95 to 98 percent true to color. It is more difficult to produce seedlings continually in these same colors with no spots. Somehow, it is difficult to breed spots out of a line. Special colors such as good true yellows and apricots, reds, picotee, and blotched forms also produce a higher percentage of plants that flower in some different color. Because of this, greens or creams appear in the yellows, pinks or yellows in the apricots, and pinks or purples in the reds. Every year in the seedlings from our apricot crosses we find a few dark purple or slate-colored plants, throwbacks from a dark ancestor somewhere in the bloodline. Picotees can produce both pinks and whites, and blotched forms invariably produce some plain-old spotted blooms. This continuing variability is the reason we must flower plants before we can guarantee their color.

BREEDING HELLEBORES AT NORTHWEST GARDEN NURSERY

Marietta O'Byrne

We keep most of our stock plants under cover in a poly tunnel on tables grouped by color. Singles and doubles are also separated. It takes several hours every second day to keep up with the pollination, and plants rowed out on tables are a great back saver. Pollinating insects are kept at a minimum, and the plants, the person pollinating, and the pollinating brush stay dry in the closed poly tunnel.

I use good quality, soft artist brushes, numbers 5 and 6. They are expensive but long lasting and hold pollen well. You can also see from the yellow powder if any ripe pollen is stuck to the brush. I use a limited number of brushes, so I dip them in a little jar of isopropyl alcohol between attempting different crosses. This will kill any pollen clinging to it. I wait until the brush is dry before reusing it.

I pollinate each blossom before it has opened fully, usually twice. I do not emasculate the flowers since it is very time consuming. It is difficult to brush the stigma of a nonemasculated flower in full bloom without touching the anthers at the same time and inadvertently pollinating it, so I take extra care to brush the stigma when its anthers are still completely curled up and tightly closed. By the time the flower is open and its own pollen is ripe, my work is done. I have achieved consistent results with this method, indicating that no unintended pollination has occurred. If the flower has been emasculated, timing is not too critical, because the stigma is receptive before the bud opens until after its own pollen is ripe.

When I am crossing to produce quantities of seed of a particular color, I will use my very best proven stock plants, gathering pollen from several flowers until my brush is coated and then pollinating several flowers at once. I cross all my plants of each color with other plants of the same color. I do not need to label the crosses, as all yellows are crossed only with yellows, reds with reds, and so on. Special crosses that are experimental and performed on only a few flowers are marked individually. If a cross is new or experimental using only one or a few flowers with the same seed and pollen parent, the first flower pedicel is marked with colored wool and a short plastic tag. The tag is labeled with the numbers of the seed and pollen parent. The pedicels of the flowers of the same cross are tied with the same color woolen thread.

I self-pollinate only if I cannot find a partner for a plant of great merit. I do quite a bit of line breeding (the process whereby relatives are bred to one another) to increase the depth and strength of a particular color or good habit.

Each of my stock plants has a number and two or three letters designating the source of its origin. I keep a reference log in which we can locate ancestry of a plant as far as we know it. I also keep particulars of each plant, including a digital photo, which is a useful memory aid when the plant is not blooming.

A rigorous review is made every spring, and if a plant has been superseded by a superior selection of the same color, it is culled. Since I pollinate every flower on each stock plant two to three times, I must be ruthless in culling any inferior plants from my stock to keep the numbers down to a reasonable level. I have used a few plants over and over through the years if they have proven to be excellent seed parents with various pollen parents, and most of their progeny are superior plants. Other plants, even though beautiful in themselves, are culled if their offspring show latent faults such as tall, floppy flowering scapes; excess foliage; or muddy colors. Record keeping is, therefore, very important for any serious breeder.

These are some shortcuts that make breeding easier for me to accomplish. I achieve good results, but I am always open to new ideas and willing to try new approaches to improve my technique and my results. Each breeder will develop her or his own techniques using those of others as a starting point.

WORKING WITH DOUBLE-FLOWERING HELLEBORES

Variability also holds for doubling. If the pollen from a double-flowering plant is placed on a single-flowering plant, the resulting seedlings produce a few doubles and a few semidoubles, but the majority will be singles. Pollen from a double-flowering plant on a semidouble produces both doubles and semidoubles, as well as some single-flowered seedlings. When two semidoubles are crossed, they produce from 50 to 75 percent semidouble flowering plants, a very small percentage of doubles, and the rest singles. The success rates of producing double-flowering plants using double on double are much higher, usually 90 to 98 percent, especially when using plants that consistently produce double blooms. The remaining plants will be semidoubles.

Some first double hybrids produced double, semidouble, and single blooms on the same plant. This problem was often seen on the earliest dark double-flowering plants. Some strains produce double or semidouble flowers early in the season, while later the flowers are single. If your breeding program is focused on producing double-flowering plants, discard these inferior breeders so their faults don't taint the bloodlines.

If only one double-flowering plant is available, use it as the seed parent. Double-flowering plants produce a higher number of offspring with fertility problems, especially self-sterile plants. This is not something breeders want to incorporate into their lines, so a good seed producer is an asset.

Another trait, which we try to eliminate from Pine Knot stock, is the proclivity of occasional double plants to produce "blind" flowers—very small flowers that never open fully. Other faults we choose to eradicate from our stock are plants with long or weak pedicels. This aspect, which is charming in the smaller flowering species plants, is undesirable in larger flowered *H. ×hybridus*, especially doubles, since it can lead to flowers that flop of even fall over.

KEVIN BELCHER OF ASHWOOD NURSERIES

The hellebore program at Ashwood began in 1989 when owner John Massey wanted good quality plants to offer his customers. When he found few plants comparable to the material produced at Ashwood Nurseries, he decided to breed his own. He began to purchase stock material from all of the top breeders and collectors of the time, including Ballard at Old Country, Strangman at Washfield, the Whites at Blackthorn, and McLewin at Phedar. This was perhaps the first time that some of the best plants from such a diverse group of breeders were assembled as stock in one breeding operation. Many of the plants were carried back to the nursery unpotted in plastic bags, for until Ashwood Nurseries began its breeding program, most of the commercially available *H. ×hybridus* stock was grown in ground rather than in containers.

The plants were potted up and Kevin Belcher began his breeding program the following winter. In an amazingly short time, the Ashwood Garden Hybrids hellebores became known worldwide. By 1995, the nursery was filled with customers not only from the United Kingdom but also from Europe, Japan, Australia, New Zealand, and the United States. Early successes were pure whites with little or no green in the center, primrose yellows, and exceptional dark colors.

The year 1999 became known as "the year of the nectaries" when the first of Belcher's crosses with dark nectaries began to flower. Until this time, few plants were available with pure, single-colored blooms with contrasting dark nectaries in the center, but Ashwood managed to produce a full range of colors, beginning with yellow with dark nectaries and progressing to the other colors.

Belcher and Massey and their stands of Ashwood Garden Hybrids hellebores have won numerous gold medals for excellence in the RHS winter shows. Each year, the beauty of their displays astounds the horticultural elite, as they marvel at new introductions. In 2003, the sensation of the winter show was an exceptionally beautiful selection of deep yellow with orange nectaries, yellow petioles, and yellow-green foliage. Then to outdo themselves, in 2004 Ashwood showed off the magnificent "Neon", a yellow picotee with yellow-orange nectaries and a crimson star.

The Ashwood hellebore team features, left to right, Kevin Belcher, Jill Pearce, and John Massey.

Intersectional hybrids always attract attention on the Ashwood stands at London shows. *Helleborus* 'Pink Ice', introduced in 1999, produces outward-facing silvery pink flowers with a delicate texture. The new hybrids' interesting foliage is similar to that of *H. niger* in appearance, and like that species, the new hybrids do not go dormant. Young foliage features an overlay of silver marbling, which gradually matures to the dark green leather look of the more familiar *H. niger*.

Like its cousin 'Pink Ice', 'Briar Rose' is another first from the Ashwood Nurseries hellebore specialist. Ashwood's stand at the RHS winter show in 2003, which highlighted 'Briar Rose', was another gold-medal winner. So named because the flower resembles the British native wild rose, 'Briar Rose' is creamy white with a wide rose rim around the outside of the flower. We expect more of these two beauties from the West Midlands in years to come, since they are not only interesting garden plants but also unusual container plants and potential cut flowers for the high-end designer flower markets.

Belcher, assistant Jill Pearce, and Massey—in company with other hellebore enthusiasts around the world—eagerly await the flowering of the newest interspecies crosses in the Ashwood stock house. When asked what's next on his list of triumphs, Belcher's reply was "Watch this space." Most certainly, hellebore lovers from all over the world will do just that.

9

HELLEBORES IN THE GARDEN

Most people, early in November, take last looks at their gardens, and are then
prepared to ignore them until the spring. I am quite sure that a garden
doesn't like to be ignored like this. It doesn't like to be covered in dust sheets, as
though it were an old room which you had shut up during the winter. Especially
since a garden knows how gay and delightful it can be, even in the very
frozen heart of the winter, if you only give it a chance.

Beverley Nichols in *How Does Your Garden Grow* (1935)

Hellebores in the O'Byrne garden near Eugene, Oregon—a hotbed of excitement for hellebore enthusiasts.

The garden of Veronica and Giles Cross at Lower Hopton Farm, U.K., features snowdrops with single and double hellebore hybrids.

DON'T GO OUT MUCH IN THE WINTER? If frosty nights and brisk days bring an end to your enjoyment of the garden, you are depriving yourself of the pleasures of the unsung season. Winter flowers are among the most precious, and hellebores are the most beautiful winter flowers. You may be missing winter because your garden is missing hellebores. They bloom when few other plants dare to face the chilly air. It is time to add hellebores to the garden and to orchestrate a planting scheme that enhances them.

Winter strips away the garden's veneer, leaving an austere but hauntingly beautiful canvas ripe with promise. Divested of summer's greenery, each plant's architecture is open to scrutiny. As deciduous leaves fall, the branching structure of trees and shrubs emerges against a backdrop of bark, berries, seedheads, and evergreen foliage. Gardens designed to accentuate winter's beauty depend on this simple, changeable framework. A well-planned winter garden captivates us throughout the many moods of the season.

The winter display changes daily as birds feast on berries and wind sets grass seed aloft from its plumes. An early tracery of snow accentuates a branch's quiet beauty, while the heart of winter may temporarily lock the garden in a smothering blanket of ice and snow. In colder climes, flowers wait for snowmelt, but winter pleasures still abound. Virginia is blessed with a moderate winter climate. The worst of winter's cold generally arrives just after the winter solstice. By February, our gardens are once again adorned with flowers. First among them are the hellebores.

Light is a provocative ingredient in the alchemy of a great winter garden. Plants and light conspire in a subtle interplay unique to the season. Consider the soft quality of light during the winter. Place your plants to take full advantage of the low sun angles of winter days. An orange witch hazel bursts into flames when illuminated from the side by the warm glow of the rising or setting sun. Grass plumes seem to glisten from within with backlighting. Hellebore flowers glow like lanterns with the sun behind them.

DESIGNING THE WINTER LANDSCAPE

Thoughtful plant choice and placement are the keys to creating an evocative winter garden. Rather than designate a specific area for winter bloomers, think of your entire yard as a winter canvas. Place key elements throughout the landscape to provide structure, interest, and flowers. Start with the views from your windows. Next, think about the routes along regularly traveled walkways, where interesting plants always make an impression. Expand your scope beyond the safe reaches of the eager eye, and move out into the landscape.

WINTER DELIGHTS

Sometimes we don't want to stir far from our warm couch in winter, so place small, early-blooming bulbs and fragrant plants near the house. Start by working with the view you enjoy most in winter, perhaps the one you see from your sunroom or kitchen window. Beds adjacent to the house should feature small shrubs mixed with evergreen ground covers, small bulbs, and early perennials. Avoid placing large shrubs and full-crowned trees too close, as they can crowd the space and make the garden seem small and cramped.

Hellebores tolerate plunging temperatures with aplomb. They greet a frosty morning with their heads face down, but the flowers rise with the mercury and are fully recovered by 40° F (4° C). Not only do they flower in winter, but their elegant, umbrella-like leaves grace the garden through the seasons. For variety, mix in species with your hybrids. Try *Helleborus odorus*, which sports sweet-scented green flowers and silky, bright green leaves. The spidery black-green leaves of stinking hellebore (*H. foetidus*) are elegant intermingled with ferns or in mass plantings. The chartreuse flower buds begin developing in early winter (December in warmer American gardens), and plants are usually in full bloom by late winter (February).

When you don your coat and venture outdoors, you must find plenty of detail throughout the garden. Winter's flowers should delight you on your journey. Carpets of bulbs mixed with well-placed hellebores are a classic but never stale partnership. Snowdrops hang their first flowers as the hellebores emerge. Free-seeding crocus are a good choice for beds or in the lawn.

Fragrance is a great motivator to entice us outside. For all their attributes, however, few hellebores are fragrant. You need to choose companion plants with strong scents to perfume the air. The subtle scents of witch hazel and flowering apricot are heightened on warm days. Dwarf box, wintersweet, and winter honeysuckle are aromatic enough for the dreary days and indifferent noses.

At Wave Hill in the Bronx, New York, *H. orientalis* ssp. *abchasicus* 'Early Purple' Group graces a spring bed, separated from an open lawn by an elegant, hand-made fence.

CREATING A FRAMEWORK

Trees, shrubs, perennials, and bulbs combine to make the winter garden complete. Woody plants and constructed elements such as fences and walls create the permanent framework, or bones, of the garden. Winter is the time when these bones are most evident. Larger shrubs and small trees define the midground or background of the garden, depending on its size and the degree to which enclosure and intimacy are desired. Mass plantings of grasses, berried branches, and colored twigs accented by drifts of hellebores can divide spaces or mark property lines. Fragrant shrubs can be planted throughout the garden.

Enclosure is the key to creating intimacy in any garden, no matter the scale. *Enclosed* does not necessarily mean walled off, however. Different circumstances require different degrees of enclosure. Let your needs as well as your context determine the degree of enclosure and the opacity or translucency of the screen.

Some parts of the yard need total screening. A single ugly view spoils even the most beautifully planned winter garden. Compost bins, garbage cans, and other utilitarian items detract from the visual appeal of the garden. You might even wish to screen air-conditioning units or other utilities. Use hedges, fences, or deep borders of mixed plantings to block unattractive views. These screens provide a perfect backdrop for flower borders filled to overflowing with hellebores and bulbs. Fences are also good supports for flowering vines such as winter jasmine and espaliered flowering quince (*Chaenomeles*).

If you don't want to use a built structure, use plants. Low hedges define space without blocking views. Along a path, a low hedge or border helps direct traffic and can partially screen a destination to create a sense of mystery. Internal hedges also create transitions from one space to the next. Openings in hedges allow views in without providing physical access. Place a low wall around a space and you define the borders, make it comfortable and intimate, and provide a place to sit as well, where you can enjoy your bulbs and hellebores.

The most distant plantings in the garden should meld almost imperceptibly with the background. If your lot is small, perhaps a hedge or wall separates your property from your neighbor. Use a fine-textured vine on the fence, or plant a hedge such as yew or boxwood, whose small leaves accentuate the feeling of depth. In larger gardens, the view beyond the garden is often impressive. To keep the relationship between this borrowed scenery and the inner sanctum of the garden, leave a gap in the plantings along the sight line that carries your eye beyond the garden's borders. Use lush plantings to frame the view and to delineate the garden's edge if necessary for privacy or to keep pets in.

Whether you are composing a vignette or orchestrating a larger scene, layer your plantings for maximum drama. Layered plantings are more interesting as well as more wildlife friendly. Set a flowering tree against a rich evergreen backdrop for contrast, and then lay a flowering carpet of snowdrops and winter aconite among your hellebores, along with evergreen wild ginger (*Asarum europaeum*) and sword

Shrubs add an internal framework
to orchestrate movement through
a garden and divide spaces. Here a
hedge is accented by *H. foetidus*.

ferns (*Polystichum*). Deep green
hellebore leaves against a bed of
mixed heaths (*Erica*) and heathers
(*Calluna*) offers colorful foliage
and early flowers. Red-twig
dogwood (*Cornus sericea* or *C.
alba*) and paper birch (*Betula
papyrifera*) with an underplanting
of hellebores and bulbs elicit more
emotion than a single dogwood
with no context. That is not to
say that a single specimen cannot
make a powerful statement. The
eccentrically twisted branches of
a moss-covered Harry Lauder's
walking stick (*Corylus avellana*

In the O'Byrnes' garden, Harry Lauder's walking stick (*Corylus avellana* 'Contorta') creates a
veil between two beds containing hellebores, trilliums, and other shade plants.

'Contorta') holds the eye in any context. A lone Japanese apricot (*Prunus mume*) in full bloom against the dreamy haze of wintry branches is riveting. Punch up the show with a carpet of red hybrid hellebores and stand back.

Repetition creates unity and rhythm in a planting. Picture a mountain view, with overlapping ridges as far as the eye can see. Each successive ridge gets paler, until earth and sky meld. Plants farther from the eye should be lighter in color, which accentuates the illusion of depth. Fine texture juxtaposed with bold texture creates the same effect. Choose plants in scale with your space. A small city lot usually has room for only one tree or a cluster of shrubs. Choose a plant with the best combination of branching structure, bark, flower, and fruits. Intermingle shrubs with good winter interest, and lay a carpet of good evergreen leaves mixed with early-blooming plants. In a larger garden, plantings can feature clusters of trees, drifts of shrubs, and sheets of bulbs and perennials.

JUDITH'S WINTER GARDEN FAVORITES

One of the more noticeable symptoms of a hellebore addiction is a garden that has so many hellebores planted that from a distance the soil appears to have a dark green, solid, leafy, 2 ft. (60 cm) ground cover. In an effort to disguise the situation, the gardener may stick in a few Japanese maples, a mahonia or two, perhaps even a camellia; nevertheless, that many hellebores are hard to disguise. Pine Knot has approximately 5 acres of shady gardens, with at least one hellebore featured in almost every square foot; this expresses the depths of our addiction.

Of course, many, many other plants are used in our gardens. Underneath the baking summer soil, the squirrel-resistant *Crocus tommasinianus* and many other species crocus sleep, side by side with a growing collection of galanthus, species narcissus, and many other small bulbs, all waiting to make springtime a delight as they begin their annual cycles. The peak bloom in this area is during the months of March, April, and May, with *Prunus mume*, serviceberry (*Amelanchier*), and other flowering trees. Good early shrubs include *Edgeworthia chrysantha*, *Corylopsis*, and fringe tree (*Chionanthus virginicus*). The woodies are underplanted with *Phlox divaricata* in dozens of shades, trillium, and epimedium, adding their colors to the hellebores and bulbs. In the deciduous forest that surrounds our house, native dogwoods (*Cornus florida*) and redbud (*Cercis canadensis*) bloom as well, adding their colors to the garden's leafy backdrop.

We live in an area with high temperatures and even higher humidity during the summer months. We spend hours each day working outside in the heat. We wanted the gardens around our house to be as cooling as we could make them, choosing to restrict brighter colors to the spring months and keeping the summer garden predominately furnished in shades of green. The house and garden merge into the woodland, and in summer the gardens around the house and those blending into the woods are filled with not only hellebores but with many species of ferns, *Rohdea japonica*, *Selaginella*, and *Aspidistra* in shades of green. Foliage color is added from *Acorus gramineus* 'Minimus Aureus' and 'Ogon', Japanese maple (*Acer palmatum*),

A shaded walk in the Tyler garden in Clarksville, Virginia, features drifts of hellebores along with free-seeding woodland phlox (*Phlox divaricata*), ferns, and shrubs.

fragrant *Daphne odora* 'Aureomarginata', golden *Ceratostigma willmottianum*, and other plants with chartreuse or golden foliage.

In the mountains of Croatia and Slovenia, we saw species hellebores combining perfectly with bulbs, anemones, isopyrum, hepatica, cyclamen, and hacquetia. These plants melded with the hellebores to turn the hills and valleys of the early spring woodland into a haze of soft colors. Many of the species hellebores we saw in the Balkans are perfect plants for our woodland gardens. The delicacy of the species makes them ideal companions for woodland ephemerals. The size and soft colors of the flowers combine nicely with the blues and yellows of springtime. I am particularly fond of our native *Mertensia virginica* with *H. occidentalis*. When both are in flower, the bright green stars of the hellebore and the blue bells of the mertensia present a perfect picture.

In winter, *H. niger* blooms around and under several of the more recent mahonia hybrids, which flower at the same time. We grow a dozen or more selections of this species, some that bloom early enough to justify the common name Christmas Rose, while others bloom later and are long-flowering, still producing fresh flowers when we harvest seed in June. The combination of the hollylike leaves of the mahonia and the white flowers of the hellebores are special favorites for holiday decorations.

If I had to select one vignette to hold in my memory as age and arthritis advance, it would be of the garden in earliest springtime—the species hellebores, hepaticas, species crocus, and other small bulbs; the quiet flowers in quiet colors of blue and yellow, celadon, and dusky plum, invoking in their somber solitude a sense of peace and a feeling of hope for the year ahead.

COLE'S GARDEN AT BIRD HILL

My garden in Virginia is large, covering a gently sloping, wooded hillside that falls away from a terrace and deck at the front of the house. Most winters in this part of the United States are relatively mild. The resultant bloom of shrubs, bulbs, and perennials makes for a colorful as well as architectural winter landscape. There is seldom more than a month after the turning of the year when something is not in bloom. The garden is viewed in all seasons through four large windows that bring the outdoors in and frame a series of dramatic outward views into the garden and to the gently rolling mountains beyond. Key sight lines radiate like spokes from each window. Sitting areas or objects such as water basins are placed to focus each of these views. To accentuate the focal points, each view features a dramatic plant or combination of plants that offers exceptional winter interest. Successive layers carry the eye from beds just outside the windows to the middle ground, the background, and ultimately to the borrowed scenery beyond the confines of the garden.

Beds immediately around the house feature small shrubs mixed with evergreen ground covers, minor bulbs, and early perennials. Though not exclusively a winter garden, these beds are designed for maximum color and fragrance early in the season. The entire garden is easily viewed from inside as well as outside. By early to mid-February, the evergreen variegated winter daphne (*Daphne odora* 'Aureomarginata') is festooned with tight pink flower clusters like miniature nosegays. The fragrance, which has no equal at this time of year, to my nose seems like a perfect mixture of gardenia and lemon. Entering and leaving the house is a treat, and on warm days with the door open, the whole house smells divine. Nurseries also offer *D. odora* f. *alba*, a creamy white-flowered selection, as well as the variegated white-flowered 'Aureomarginata Alba'. Species crocus, cyclamen, species and miniature daffodils, and snowdrops complete the picture. Later in spring, these beds feature trilliums and epimediums, which extend the flowering season. After flowers fade and bulb foliage disappears for the season, ferns contrast with the deep green hellebore foliage. Fall color comes from bugbanes (*Actaea*) and *Tricyrtis*, joined by the floriferous autumn cyclamen (*Cyclamen hederifolium*).

When a warm day draws me outdoors, there are detailed plant combinations to see throughout the garden. Along the species hellebore walk, a carpet of snowdrops (*Galanthus* spp.) alone or mixed with the diminutive lavender chalices of *Crocus tommasinianus* are lovely under a sweep of fragrant, yellow-flowered paperbush (*Edgeworthia chrysantha*). I encourage the crocus to seed into the large, circular lawn. I always keep fragrance in mind and include many scented winter bloomers such as winter honeysuckle (*Lonicera fragrantissima*), a precocious vamp doused head to toe with perfume. The slope below the edgeworthia is planted with red and purple hybrid Lenten roses along with more snowdrops, primroses, and red and purple selections of *Epimedium grandiflorum*.

Larger shrubs and small trees define the midground of the garden. Mass plantings of grasses, berried branches, and colored twigs come into play. I achieve rhythm by repeating a key plant or a key color. Hellebores are the dominant theme, and

The gentle slopes of Bird Hill, in Free Union, Virginia, features hybrid hellebores planted with epimedium, iris, and daffodils

their foliage and flowers unify the garden. One small tree with a vase-shaped form I use repeatedly is witch hazel (*Hamamelis* ×*intermedia*), which is placed layer upon layer in the foreground, midground, and background. The spidery petals unfurl in the strengthening January sun, spreading a delicate perfume. Never mind that night temperatures are still plunging below freezing; the witch hazel simply curls its petals until warmth returns. *Hamamelis* ×*intermedia* 'Diane', with flowers the color of winter fire, is placed close to the house, underplanted with early pink *Helleborus thibetanus*. Her richly colored beauty is most apparent on close inspection. Halfway back, bicolored orange and yellow *H.* ×*intermedia* 'Jelena' and 'Primavera' hold sway with purple single and double hellebores and species daffodils. Golden *H.* ×*intermedia* 'Arnold Promise' is placed at the far reaches of the garden, because its brilliant, rich color reads best from a distance. It is underplanted with white hellebores and a sweep of daffodils that goes from yellow to white at the farthest end of the bed.

Witch hazels are not always the earliest of bloomers. When you can rub two warm days together, the first flowers of winter hazel (*Chimonanthus praecox*) open. The scent of these nodding, waxy yellow flowers, reminiscent of spicy fruit, is as blatant as those of witch hazel are subtle. Flowers seem unperturbed by frost, often emerging unblemished from temperatures in the teens. If flowers are damaged, no fear, because additional buds of this upright shrub to 10 ft. (3 m) tall open when warm weather returns. *Chimonanthus praecox* 'Concolor' has rich golden yellow flowers with red eyes that are larger than those of the species. A dramatic, 30 ft. (9 m) sweep of pure white hellebores forms the backdrop here, along with bicolored yellow and white daffodils such as the sweet-scented heirloom 'W. P. Milner'.

The most distant plantings in the garden meld almost imperceptibly with the wildness beyond. The only boundary is an opaque 8 ft. (3 m) deer fence to protect plants from grazing. I placed a small drift of bronze-leaf sedge (*Carex buchananii*) within the garden's confines to echo the tawny broomsedge (*Andropogon virginicus*) and little bluestem (*Schizachyrium scoparium*) in the meadow beyond. Pale witch hazel (*Hamamelis* ×*intermedia* [also *H. mollis*] 'Pallida') and yellow twig dogwood stand out against the green junipers that punctuate the tawny meadow grasses. Species hellebores, mostly green flowered, occupy the wilder sections at the edges of the garden.

REGIONAL DIFFERENCES

"But," you may say, "my garden is buried in snow all winter! What kind of winter garden can I have?" If you garden where winter is unforgiving, the ground layer of a planting has little impact. You must wait for snowmelt to enjoy your hellebores. You needn't abandon the winter landscape, however. Concentrate on shrubs and trees with exceptional attributes and good winter color. Choose plants with dramatic bark coloration, brilliant berries, and eccentric forms. Shrubby dogwoods are mainstays. Red, orange, and yellow-twigged varieties are available. Willows are another good choice. Flame willow (*Salix* 'Flame') has glowing red-orange stems, while basket willow (*S. purpurea* 'Nana') resembles burnished bronze and makes a natural companion to garden sculpture. Grasses and dried seedheads of tall perennials such as Joe-pye weed (*Eupatorium purpureum*) and cup plant (*Silphium perfoliatum*) protrude elegantly from the deepest snow to ornament the garden.

Elements such as walls, arbors, and benches add their own interest. Free of the greenery that festoons them during the growing season, they take on a new prominence. Plant lots of bulbs such as crocus, daffodils (*Narcissus*), glory of the snow (*Chionodoxa luciliae*), and *Puschkinia* to color the early spring landscape, when it still feels like winter despite the melting of the snow. Hellebores soon join them. In the wild, many species are under snow for six months or more, but they bloom along the snowline as it slowly retreats. The same magical transformation happens in your garden.

In warm-temperate regions (USDA Zones 8 to 9), the winter season is little more than a temporary lull in the usual riot of bloom. Winter gardening is a privilege reserved for those who live in the temperate regions of North America. In the U.S. South, coastal Northern California, and the Pacific Northwest (Zones 7 to 9), winter is relatively mild and short-lived; the worst of winter's cold generally passes with the solstice, and by February gardens are once again coming into flower. Throughout the rest of North America, winter occupies a significant chunk of the gardening year.

If you plan your garden with winter in mind, the end of the growing season needn't bring an end to the garden's beauty. No matter where you live and how severe your winter, you can create an evocative garden that celebrates the sublime beauty of the winter season.

THE GARDEN AT NORTHWEST GARDEN NURSERY

Ernie and Marietta O'Byrne supply exceptional hellebores at their nursery and via wholesale outlets throughout the American West. This photo, taken at Ashwood Nurseries, features (left to right) Dick and Judith Tyler, Marietta and Ernie, and Cole Burrell.

Ernie and Marietta O'Byrne

In the Pacific Northwest we are blessed, or so hellebore lovers believe, with a long, cool spring. This makes a three-month flowering period for most hellebores and affords many design possibilities. Hellebore flowers can outlast three or more flushes of flowering combinations of spring ephemerals, providing a wonderful opportunity for the creative gardener. Of course, black spot and *Botrytis* fungus also relish our moisture-laden spring air, as do slugs, but the former can be checked with a regular spray of compost tea and a good hygiene program. As for slugs, which love to nibble on emerging blooms, any type of warfare is fair: baits, salt, hot-water drownings, clippers, squishing, and squashing. Our relatively mild winters, milder each year it seems, enable us to grow all species outdoors with the exception of *H. vesicarius*. Summers are dry with occasional hot days, but always cool nights, so all gardens are set up for irrigation of some kind.

Our garden is large and densely planted—one could even say packed. Woodland beds abut perennial gardens in full sun, where gravelly alpine beds and conifers are jumbled up with heathers, cannas, grasses, and kniphofias. Hellebores live in every part of this garden, in sun and shade, moist and dry.

I do so love the colors of the hybrids. Every year I see new nuance of color and new streaking, blotching, or spotting in the flowers as a result of our breeding work. More and more, I am enamored of the beauty of structure and leaf form of the species. Under a golden tipped *Cryptomeria japonica* 'Sekkan-Sugi', I planted a mass of *H.* ×*sternii* with sharply toothed silvery foliage. Already in December they push mauve-maroon flower buds at the tips of many sturdy stems. They flower with masses of cream-centered blooms until May or even June, at which time all the old flower stems are cut off. At this time, they are already surrounded by the silvery growth of the newly emerged foliage. What a magnificent ground cover they make, with nary an off season.

Some years ago, a chance crossing of the well-known *H. foetidus* 'Wester Flisk', a cultivar with red stems and petioles, with a silvery cultivar called 'Sopron' from Hungary, resulted in an intensely metallic, silver-leaved plant with red petioles and stems and strong red coloring at the tips of the flowers. It is at its showiest and brightest in fall. This plant, which we named 'Red Silver', comes true from seed, if isolated. We began to find many spots in the garden that could do with a bit of filigreed silver. It shines with blue conifers as background, black mondo grass at its feet, stylishly overhung by a cloud of red berries on the bare branches of a purple-leaved barberry or presiding over a carpet of silver-leaved cyclamens. It stands out behind the rusty, weeping *Carex flagellifera* and pairs admirably with purple-foliaged *Euphorbia amygdaloides* 'Rubra'. Wherever it flings a seedling or two, it looks good. Often plants know how to place themselves to better advantage than when planted by a human hand. All *H. foetidus* are rather short-lived, and 'Red Silver' loses its good looks after a couple of years, but we let just a few flowers go to seed, and, presto, more silver babies.

All the hellebores with a bit of *H. lividus* blood in them love the full sun or just a bit of shade as long as the soil and drainage are good. The foliage of *H. lividus*, *H. ×ericsmithii,* and *H. ×ballardiae* can be beautifully veined with silver, and since they are all relatively compact, we use them to good advantage in containers with exotic neighbors of the half-hardy kind, such as striped agaves, aloes with exotic bloom, and even cacti, where they fit right in. Their creamy-maroon flowers (and they are incredibly floriferous) are of such subtle changing shades that I never tire of looking at them over their three-month flowering time. When they outgrow their containers, off they go into the beds right around the house, where they can stretch their roots in the company of blue *Omphalodes*, creamy yellow and pink trout lilies, yellow *Eranthis*, and the very darkest hybrid hellebores, whose countenance they brighten with their creamy shades.

Helleborus ×nigercors, one of the easiest and most vigorous of the intersectional hybrids, is also one of the hardiest. It inherited the better of its two parents, *H. niger* and *H. argutifolius*, possessing the glossiest dark green, toothed foliage. It absolutely covers itself with cream-white flowers a little smaller than *H. niger,* but still substantial. Sun or shade suits it equally well. It is stunning backed by the delicate, much-divided fronds of ferns with the all-yellow form of *Hakonechloa* toward the front. Add a bit of the early-blooming, dark purple *Lathyrus vernus* and the diminutive, freely seeding blue *Chionodoxa* peeking in between and a beautiful spring picture emerges.

Even though some of the most spectacularly beautiful and varied of hellebore foliage is not always evergreen, that beauty and variation of foliage of the acaulescent species is essential in our woodland garden. Coarser leaved perennials in the shade such as hostas, bergenia, and the larger epimediums need the company of lace and filigree. The complexity of form and shape brings art into the garden of which our eyes never tire, and we find new delights with every garden visit. The finest for foliage is no doubt *H. multifidus* subsp. *hercegovinus*. One wouldn't even guess that it is a hellebore looking at its many divided leaflets overlapping each other. Only coming close in foliage interest are the best forms of *H. torquatus*, emerging through the mulch with leaves of the darkest purple color, paling to green later in spring. Over the years we have collected the best foliage forms, not paying that much attention to the flowers in this case. Yes they are slow, but very long-lived. Their beauty increases each year as they unfold their leaves among creeping evergreen *Vancouveria planipetala* and the April-flowering *Anemone nemorosa*.

A vignette from the O'Byrne garden features red hybrid hellebores with snowdrops, *Primula sieboldii*, and *Corydalis edulis*.

And then there are the hybrids. Everybody loves them. They are as seductive as they are shy. You must lift their heads to get to know them. So you start collecting, and every year the garden fills with just a few more. But they also need companions to take your breath away: purple *Corydalis edulis* or *C. flexuosa* 'Purple Leaf' paired with single- or double-flowered yellow and apricot hellebore; or red *Trillium chloropetalum* mingling with the double-flowered whites and, at their feet, little *Dicentra cucullaria* or green-bracted *Anemone nemorosa* 'Greenfingers', or even an ephemeral mix of the dainty *Anemonella thalictroides*. Though maligned by some hellebore lovers (or, should I say, snobs) as too blowsy, I find the doubles quite graceful and lasting in beauty as their flower color fades to greenish in April. Then they remind me a bit of little faded and old-fashioned roses of yesteryear, keepsakes of an old love. Who would not enjoy a bed of purple-red double-flowered hellebores under an oh-so-fragrant *Daphne mezereum* of the same color, flowering together in February?

The very darkest colors of the hybrids show up much better if interplanted with yellow. It can, of course, be another yellow hellebore next to them, but we particularly like the yellow form of the evergreen woodrush, *Luzula sylvatica* 'Aurea', as a companion. The black-blue flowers of the hellebore nestled in the golden grass are greatly enhanced by the contrast. A carpet of the gold *Lamium maculatum* 'Aureum' would serve the same purpose.

Endless are the combinations. Gardeners are fortunate in that design work need never be finished, unlike with a painting. If another combination pleases us more, there is always next year to begin again. Dig out the old, rearrange, plant the new, and, voila, a brand new painting.

DEFINING SPACE

If perennials such as hellebores form the carpet of the garden, then shrubs and trees are the walls and ceilings. They are essential elements for defining spaces, providing enclosure and privacy, and blocking unattractive views. These vertical elements add beauty and structure to the garden. The naked branches of deciduous shrubs often offer the first sign of spring in the late-winter garden. As flowers unfurl, the season renews itself. Foliage soon follows, providing a myriad of textures to carry through the dog days of summer.

SHRUBS

Deciduous shrubs herald the passing of the season with a blaze of yellow, red, and orange. Their bare branches stand in testimonial to their enduring nature as snow collects along them. Evergreen shrubs impart special interest to the garden during the quiet season. Their foliage adds color to the brown and white landscape. Snow gathers on coniferous boughs, and curled rhododendron leaves tell us when they are suffering in below-freezing temperatures. Emerging spring foliage complements hellebore flowers and completes the cycle of the season.

Shrubs provide the visual and ecological link between the ground layer of perennials and the canopy of trees overhead. The shrub layer in a forest reaches from 3 to 15 ft. (1 to 5 m) tall. Ecologically, shrubs create a smooth transition for animals to move between nesting and feeding sites. They afford cover from predators, pollen and nectar from flowers, and berries for food.

Shrubs offer utilitarian benefits as well. They can screen unattractive views, divide the garden into rooms, create privacy, or provide a backdrop for a flower garden. Whether you plant in a naturalistic pattern or create formal hedges, shrubs add an essential element to the garden picture. Mixed-shrub plantings are natural companions to bulbs, annuals, and perennials in a mixed border. Shrubs are lovely planted under tall canopy trees or in combination with smaller flowering specimens underplanted with ground covers.

The first of winter's flowering shrubs are subtle. What they lack in size and color, they often make up in fragrance. The tantalizing scent of sweet box (*Sarcococca hookeriana* var. *humilis*) mingles with the chilly air. The tiny flowers are easily overlooked as you search for a flamboyant source of the cloying perfume. The glossy evergreen leaves make an excellent ground cover in rich, well-drained soil under berried branches of chokeberry (*Aronia*) or winterberry holly (*Ilex verticillata*) but are equally effective carpeting the ground with mass plantings of hellebores amidst fragrant white forsythia (*Abeliophyllum distichum*), camellias, or witch hazel. Throughout North America, plants are stirring. The catkins on willows and poplars begin to grow, and dogwood stems glow with vibrant color as the sap begins to rise.

Several daphnes scent the late winter and spring air. The undisputed queen of the winter garden is *Daphne odora*, joined in warmer zones by the more upright *D. bholua*. The selection *D. odora* f. *alba* has snowy white flowers. Increased hardiness

A sweep of hybrid hellebores accents the Stair garden in Knoxville, Tennessee.

is the hallmark of the deciduous daphne species. The deep-purple flowers of *D. mezereum* open in late winter and early spring on mounding shrubs to 4 ft. (1 m) tall and wide. Combine them with rich, plum-colored double hellebores for a show-stopping display. Showy but poisonous red fruits follow the flowers. Temperamental but lovely is *D. ×burkwoodii* 'Carol Mackie'. Small, deciduous leaves edged with creamy yellow emerge with the starry, fragrant, pale pink flowers in early spring. The plain green-leaved *D. ×burkwoodii* 'Somerset' flowers equally well. The lovely *D. genkwa* draws you in for a sniff, but the unscented flowers offer no reward. Uniquely colored medium-purple flowers densely clothe the naked stems in early spring, well before the new leaves emerge.

Two Asian natives vie for the floral grand prize in winter. One competes with size, while the other wins your affections with overwhelming numbers. The prize for biggest flower goes to the Japanese camellia (*Camellia japonica*). Huge, saucer-sized flowers in a rainbow of reds, pinks, as well as virginal white open in mid- to late winter, or early spring if temperatures remain cold. The downside to this exotic beauty is that the flowers are frost-tender, and many a winter the shrubs open in full glorious bloom only to fry in a sudden but inevitable cold snap. Evergreen shrubs to 15 ft. (5 m), the flowers are damaged by temperatures near freezing, but in a protected spot they are unequaled. Dozens of selections are available. We like single, red-flowered, cold-hardy 'Paulette Goddard'. As flowers drop, they litter the ground as decoratively as when they graced the branches. Plant hellebores in matching colors for a dramatic early spring display.

Equally impressive, but with large clusters of small flowers, are the viburnums. They scent the air with intoxicating intensity. *Viburnum farreri* and its hybrid

V. ×bodnantense are two of the best and the earliest. Korean spice viburnum (*V. carlesii*) is a old-fashioned favorite with rose-pink buds opening to pompons of white flowers on naked stems in early spring. You can smell the flowers a block away (we're not kidding!). Prague viburnum (*V. ×pragense*) opens its white, less intoxicating flowers a bit later.

TREES

Trees form the ultimate layer in the vertical structure of a garden. A woodland of trees creates its own environment, while a single tree has a profound influence on its immediate surroundings. The smaller, flowering trees form a layer 15 to 30 ft. (5 to 9 m) high, known as the *understory*. Shade trees taller than 30 ft. (9 m) form the highest layer called the *canopy*. Trees influence the environment beneath them in many ways. Most noticeable is the shade that the branches and foliage provide. In spring, before the leaves develop, the trees cast minimal shade. The plants beneath them receive ample sunlight for growth. As spring progresses, the canopy becomes more dense, and light is excluded. The nature of the tree cover dictates which plants can grow beneath it, from the understory to the forest floor. Many hellebores grow wild in woodlands, and many hybrids thrive in deciduous shade, too.

Use trees to manipulate the scale of your space. Intimate spaces employ small understory trees to create a low ceiling that shelters and encloses. Larger spaces are made to feel more expansive by limbing up the canopy trees to create a cathedral-like ceiling.

Through the heart of winter, broadleaf and coniferous evergreen foliage dominates. Evergreens can be a particularly critical element of the winter landscape. They are a reliable source of winter color and provide a backdrop for shrubs and trees with colorful stems or interesting branching patterns. Be sure to include a blend of evergreens with different heights and shapes throughout your garden. Don't confine yourself to conifers; where they are hardy, include broadleaf evergreen shrubs and perennials, too. Larger evergreens are best used as specimen plants or placed near the middle and edges of the garden to serve as backdrops for plantings of shrubs and perennials such as hellebores. Include smaller evergreens in mixed borders or employ them as low hedges.

NANCY GOODWIN AND MONTROSE

It is safe to say that Nancy Goodwin opened our eyes to the breadth of the genus *Helleborus*. Montrose, her lovely garden and historic home in Hillsborough, North Carolina, houses a collection of all of the hellebores that succeed in her climate. Tender *H. lividus* is grown indoors. When Lenten roses were still considered exotic by many, Goodwin was importing seeds of wild-collected plants and slowly building one of the first American collections of species. Like any obsessed gardener, she is still collecting and refining both her plants and her garden. On a recent visit, she took us through a new piece of the garden, not an expanded bed or a new border,

Nancy Goodwin displays one of her beloved hellebores.

but several acres of woodland outfitted with trails and planted with drifts of hellebores.

Goodwin's passion is for good plants in good garden settings. It is not enough simply to possess or grow a certain plant; she wants to display it well, too. Throughout the garden, combinations from subtle to arresting feature winter-blooming and foliage plants with hellebores center stage. Bronze-tinted *H.* ×*sternii* is planted with russet *Carex comans* 'Bronce' above a carpet of black-leaved *Ophiopogon planiscapus* 'Nigrescens'. Christmas roses grow among sheets of cyclamen. New areas of the garden aim for more bang, with monochromatic drifts of hellebores intermingled with sweeps of galanthus, crocus, and other minor bulbs.

Goodwin is selecting hellebores for vigor and gardenworthiness as well as flower color and form. Plants from the Montrose sales yard may be divisions of choice forms or selected seedlings from Goodwin's collection. One gem is a form of *H. orientalis* subsp. *abchasicus* 'Early Purple' Group, with purple and pink flowers tinged with green. A mature group of this form is a splendid example of the charm of hellebores and of Goodwin herself—braving icy winter winds with heads up, ready to greet spring, whenever spring arrives.

Montrose, where Nancy Goodwin grows thousands of hellebores, welcomes gardeners from around the globe.

COMPOSING COMBINATIONS

Creating combinations is like composing garden pictures. When it comes to composing garden pictures with hellebores, you must pair cultural requirements with aesthetics. Think of the gardeners' adage "right plant, right place." If the plants aren't compatible, your combinations won't work. Though hellebores are widely tolerant of sun, soil, and moisture variations, each species and hybrid accepts an optimum range of conditions under which it thrives. (Refer to Chapter 3 for more information on cultural conditions.)

Companion plants

Nature is the most successful designer. Plants grow together in natural associations based on environmental conditions. There is no substitute for seeing a plant in the wild; you quickly learn its native companions. You also begin to understand its cultural requirements. We were fortunate enough to take a trip to the Balkans to see many species hellebores in the wild. The lessons were invaluable. Most species grew in open woods or at the edges of pasture. Some grew out in the open. We found the companions as beautiful and alluring as the hellebores themselves.

The garden plants we grow, native or not, originate in forests, fields, prairies, meadows, and wetlands around the world. These plants are adapted to the conditions in their native environments. Soil and moisture are important influences. Light is also a determining factor. To make the most of light levels throughout the season, plants bloom at specific times of the year. Each plant reaches a specific height at a specific time. They grow and bloom in a continuum from spring through frost. They make the most of the environment by growing together in organized vertical layers.

Another important clue to plant selection lies hidden underground. The size and shape of the crown of a plant are easy to determine visually. Plants also differ in the size and shape of their roots. The size, character, and depth of penetration are important factors to consider. Bulbous plants are different from fibrous-rooted plants like hellebores. This below-ground organization of plants in their environments is referred to as *partitioning*. The position that the root systems occupy as well as the nature of the roots themselves determine which plants can grow together.

Maximizing the bloom season depends on fitting the plants together in compatible ways. Bulbs such as tulips and daffodils are compact and bloom early in the season. Shallow, fibrous-rooted plants such as epimediums can grow over bulbs. Crowns of ferns and late-blooming asters are also free to develop aboveground as the bulb foliage is going dormant. The fibrous roots of hellebores can easily grow adjacent to a group of bulbs without competing for the same soil space. Ideal combinations are created by matching the above- and belowground portions of the plants with their growth and bloom cycles.

Most hellebores are perfect candidates for the shade of deciduous trees and shrubs. Luckily, most early-flowering perennials and bulbs thrive under the same conditions, so combinations are easy. The earliest hellebore to flower throughout most of North

America is the Christmas rose (*H. niger*). Few plants are as precocious, so foliage combinations are most effective at this stage. The elegant straplike leaves of sacred lily (*Rohdea japonica*) are similar in color, but their upright, arching form provides a good foil. Contrasting color is needed to enliven the combination. Consider the delicate, grasslike foliage of *Liriope spicata* 'Gin-ryu' (Silver Dragon) or the silver mottling of *Cyclamen hederifolium*.

Throughout most of North America, hellebores wait out the coldest heart of winter and begin to bloom in February where the ground is free of snow and at the time of snowmelt in colder reaches. Selecting plants to mix with your hellebores is an exciting opportunity. Some plants inherently look good together, while others lend few attributes to a combination. The secret to successful design lies in choosing and combining plants to maximize their individual attributes. Contrast is the secret of an exciting combination. You need to choose plants that provide the color, form, and texture when and where you need it in the garden. Remember that hellebores provide an extended bloom season, so you need a succession of plants to keep the combination going through the entire bloom cycle, as well as when foliage dominates.

Wood anemone (*Anemone nemorosa*), trillium, trout lilies (*Erythronium*), snowdrops, and corydalis are a few favorite bulbs to combine with hellebores. Other spring bloomers that excel in the company of hellebores are primroses, hepaticas, pulmonarias, and epimediums. Foliage from ferns, bleeding hearts, sedges, wild gingers (*Asarum*), and Solomon's seal (*Polygonatum*) carry the summer display. For fall, add bulbs such as cyclamen, colchicums, autumn crocus, *Sternbergia*, and spider lilies (*Lycoris*). Other good associates are *Tricyrtis*, asters, and the fruits of baneberry (*Actaea*) and Solomon's seal. The colorful fruits of deciduous hollies, viburnums, and beauty berries (*Callicarpa*) add light to the autumn landscape along with coloring foliage.

COLOR, TEXTURE, AND FORM

When you compose a combination, start with one or two key plants and build the combination around them. Choose key plants for colorful, long-flowering periods and excellent foliage. The strong anchor plant becomes the basis for adding the rest of the plants, which bloom at the same time. In this case, a hellebore is always center stage. The supporting cast of garden companions usually excels in one or more characteristics but may not provide all the desired characteristics of the anchor plant. Plan your combinations so that many plants come and go while the hellebores are still fresh.

Color is what draws us to the garden and what we respond to when we are choosing plants. Color preferences are as individual as our fingerprints, but color theory dictates a few simple rules worth noting. To help you work with color, try designing combinations with a limited color palette. Too many colors create a muddle. To help you focus the colors, choose a single color scheme or create a color harmony.

Apricot-colored hybrid hellebores echo the tawny stalk of bamboo in the garden of Veronica and Giles Cross in Stoke Lacy, U.K.

Adjacent colors are related to one another by a shared pigment and together form color harmonies. When you combine adjacent colors you get a pleasing composition. An example of this is pairing blue, purple, and red to produce a restful picture. Combine red, orange, and yellow and the colors scream for attention. Opposite colors on the color wheel, called *complementary* colors, make exciting combinations. Combining complementary or contrasting colors creates a bright, dazzling effect. One complementary color makes the other seem brighter, such as yellow with purple or blue with orange. If you can picture a field of bright poppies and bachelor buttons, you get the picture. Remember, color creates memories!

Combinations that use a single color, called *monochromatic* color schemes, create restful and contemplative pictures. Single-color gardens are perfect for people with strong color preferences. Combinations of cool colors are also restful. Visually, cool colors soothe the eye. Warm color gardens are like a sultry breeze on a summer afternoon; they are riveting and sensual.

Color echo is a term coined by noted designer and plantswoman Pamela Harper. Combining two or more plants with the same color creates a color echo. This could entail combining a dark-spotted flower with another that matches the color of the spots of the first flower, or using flowers or foliage with different shades or tints of the same color. The technique is quite sophisticated when foliage, seed pods, and even spots on the flower petals create the echo from plant to plant. Try planting pink, rose, and burgundy hellebores together. They all share the same basic color, pigment-red in this case, but they differ in the amount of white (a tint) or black (a shade) in

246

As the riot of spring color fades, a subtle tapestry of hellebores, ferns, and ground covers ornaments the shade garden at Pine Knot Farms.

each color. Another example is using a rosy picotee-edged flower with a wine-red flower. Add red primroses to spread the effect beyond the hellebore flowers.

Texture and form give added punch to a combination, even when the plants are not in bloom, so they are important considerations for long-season interest. Even when you are choosing plants for their flowers, keep foliage in mind. When the flowers fade, the foliage must carry the combination. Avoid using more than one ephemeral plant, such as a bulb, per combination. Summer combinations are particularly dependent on several different kinds of good foliage, as hellebore foliage is relatively consistent. Use wild ginger, epimediums, ferns, sedges, and grasses to vary the texture and keep things exciting. The colored leaves of lungworts, coral bells, and hostas are particularly useful.

Texture refers to the visual characteristics of both foliage and flowers. Textures are described as fine, medium, or coarse. Ferns are the consummate fine-textured plants, as are ornamental grasses and sedges. Fine textures melt into a dreamy haze at a distance and show their intricacies only on close inspection. Medium textures offer visual detail even at a distance. Good combinations must weigh color and size of the flower, the form of the plant, and the texture of the leaves.

The *form*, or shape, of your plants is another important consideration. Plants add three basic contrasting forms to the garden's profile: spiky or spear shaped, rounded or mounded, and flat or prostrate. Hellebores fall into the category of rounded to

247

mounding, so they need partners with contrasting forms. Spiky plants stand stiffly upright with pointed or conical leaves or flower heads. Flat or ground-hugging plants add an important dimension to beds and borders; they provide visual blank spaces, or gaps, at the front of the garden to enliven the profile. They can set off the dramatic qualities of a single plant, such as a hellebore surrounded by creeping jenny.

Invariably, spring leads to summer, and hellebore flowers fade as seeds ripen. Bulbs and other ephemerals fade and slip into dormancy. Foliage dominates as flowers wane. Ferns unfold their fronds, and the vertical forms lift the gardener's eye skyward. Ground covers lay a rich carpet. Sedges and many choice perennials soon take prominence. Consider foliage as well as flowers when choosing what to buy. Among the garden's summer tapestry, hellebore foliage holds its own. Hybrids and several species posses elegant leaves, deep, lustrous green, and artfully dissected. By autumn, when cyclamen, crocus, and early snowdrops begin to flower, hellebores again stand out among the colorful foliage. They hold sway for another season, until warm winter days coax them out of dormancy for another cycle of bloom and another romp through the winter garden.

ELFI RAHR AND HELLEBORES WOODLAND GARDENS

Elfi Rahr's enthusiasm for hellebores is infectious. Her garden is a canvas painted with subtle pastel-colored flowers that carpet the ground in all directions. During a morning visit, the garden is draped in light fog, and the diffuse light casts magical patterns over the carpets of hellebores. Towering Douglas firs create an other-worldly experience shrouded in the Pacific Northwest mist. As the fog begins to lift, the sun's rays pierce through the dense evergreen canopy, illuminating acres of awakening flowers nestled among moss-covered logs and the native ground cover *Gaultheria shallon*. In the full light of day, the extent of the garden and nursery become apparent. Tucked into a gentle slope above Phantom Lake in Bellevue, Washington, the setting is truly magnificent. It seems impossible to believe that the garden started decades ago with a single plant.

Elfi and Bill Rahr have situated their gardens with such care and consideration for their surroundings that one feels part of a faraway, enchanted place, where the needs of nature have taken precedence over the desires of human inhabitants. There are no cold, antiseptic metal buildings full of plants marshaled in straight lines as soldiers on parade. Elfi displays her selections in color-coordinated clusters. The blossoms she chooses for display are placed face up on a bed of moss, fully arranged in trays, or floating on water in large cut-glass bowls.

Their house is nestled Hansel and Gretel style into the trees, just beyond the nursery. Inside, hellebore memorabilia attests to a lifetime of focused collecting—not just plants, but plant-related books, photos, paintings, and china.

Elfi knows just about everyone who shares her passion. When visitors arrive, she shows off plants given to her as gifts as well as prized new acquisitions from her travels. She turns up favorite hellebore flowers and praises their virtues. They are carefully hybridized for sturdy growth, upright form, and outfacing flowers with rounded sepals sporting evenly distributed spotting on bicolored backgrounds. "Pick a plant to take with you," she urges. These subtle, exquisite beauties are what Elfi values and what reminds us most of her passion for hellebores, as well as her gentle and caring nature. She shares her love for this group of plants with untold numbers of enthusiasts from the Pacific Northwest as well as visitors who flock thousands of miles to visit her. If hellebores have a fairy godmother, her name is, most appropriately, Elfi.

HELLEBORES AS CUT FLOWERS

Combinations aren't limited to the garden. Hellebores are so free-flowering that they always provide blossoms to spare for the vase. Arranged or floated, hellebore flowers make long-lasting cuts. Floating blooms is the current fashion. No wonder; all you need to do is pick the flower and drop it face-up in a bowl. Leave a short stalk on the flower, and it lasts for days—no wilting, no conditioning, pure enjoyment. Enjoy bowls indoors or in an outdoor basin with flowers dancing on the water's surface. This technique is great for an open garden, party, or specialist nursery open house display. Visitors get a quick glance at the full range of colors available without having to turn up each flower until they find perfection.

Floating, though simple, lacks some of the creativity of an arrangement. Cut hellebores require proper conditioning or they wilt. It takes a bit more effort, but the rewards are great if you enjoy the artistic challenges of flower arranging. In their 1948 book, *The Christmas Rose*, the Luedys created stunning arrangements with *H. niger*. Stark simplicity and graceful elegance are the hallmarks of their work.

In Van Pelt Wilson's 1945 book, *Perennials Preferred*, she devotes several pages to cutting techniques and potential uses of hellebore flowers. She notes of the Christmas rose that "When I cut them for bouquets I select both white and pink blooms and, in order not to sacrifice the important evergreen foliage, I select foliage from one of the aralia-like deciduous hellebores. For a special centerpiece Christmas roses with hemlock are unusual and exquisite, and flowers stay fresh for three to four weeks."

To cure stems, many flower arrangers carry a bucket of near-boiling water to the garden and plunge the freshly cut stems directly into the water to sear them. Another method is to stick the freshly cut end into a flame, which accomplishes the same goal.

Frankie Fanelli and John Dole of the Department of Horticultural Science, North Carolina State University, did a comprehensive study to determine the best methods for cutting and displaying hellebores (see Appendix D). Since floating was so easy, they wanted to see whether or not cut stems were viable. It is widely believed that cut hellebores do not last long. Another drawback to cut flowers is the numerous stamens that drop after a few days, creating a heap at the base of the vase. Fanelli and Dole discovered that flowering stems harvested and plunged directly into buckets of water containing a commercial preservative had an average vase life of 17 ½ days!

Floated flowers scarcely last a week. Even better news, there was no difference in staying power between fresh flowers and those that had dropped their stamens. So if debris bothers you, cut the stalks after the stamens drop in the garden, and the mess-free flowers will still last at least two weeks.

An eager gardener will don galoshes and clippers to harvest the early flowers of Christmas rose from a snowy winter garden. (From *Perennials Preferred*, 1945)

PLANTS WITH WINTER INTEREST

Genera marked with an asterisk (★) contain species that may be regionally invasive. Consult your local native plant society or Nature Conservancy chapter for lists of non-native species that are invasive in your area. Invasive exotic species displace native species and may alter plant community structure and ecosystem function. We discourage the use of known or suspected invasive exotic species in gardens and public landscapes.

CONIFERS

Abies spp. (fir) Zones 2 to 7

Cephalotaxus harringtonii 'Duke Garden', 'Prostrata' (Japanese plum yew) Zones 5 (6) to 9

Chamaecyparis spp. (false cypress) Zones 4 to 9

Cryptomeria japonica Araucarioides Group 'Black Dragon' (Japanese cryptomeria) Zones 5 to 9

Juniperus spp. (juniper) Zones 3 to 10

Microbiota decussata (Russian arborvitae) Zones 3 to 8

Pinus mugo (mugo pine) Zones 2 to 7 (8)

Taxus spp. (yew) Zones 4 to 9

Tsuga spp. (hemlock) Zones 4 to 8

BROADLEAF EVERGREEN TREES

Camellia oleifera (tea-oil camellia) Zones (6) 7 to 9

Ilex latifolia (lusterleaf holly) Zones 7 to 9

Ilex opaca (American holly) Zones 5 to 9

Magnolia virginiana (sweet bay magnolia) Zones 5 to 9

Magnolia grandiflora (southern magnolia) Zones (6) 7 to 9

Viburnum awabuki (awabuki viburnum) Zones (7) 8 to 9

DECIDUOUS TREES

★*Acer palmatum* (Japanese maple) Zones 5 to 9

Acer griseum (paperbark maple) Zones 4 to 8

Amelanchier spp. (serviceberry) Zones 3 to 8

Betula spp. (birch) Zones 2 to 7

Carpinus caroliniana (American hornbeam) Zones 3 to 9

★*Cornus kousa* (kousa dogwood) Zones 5 to 8

Cornus officinalis (Japanese cornel dogwood) Zones 5 to 8

Lagerstroemia faurei hybrids (crape myrtle) Zone 6

Ostrya virginiana (American hophornbeam) Zones 3 to 9

Oxydendrum arboreum (sourwood) Zone 5, possibly 4 to 9

Parrotia persica (Persian parrotia) Zones 4 to 8

Prunus ×*subhirtella* 'Autumnalis' (Higan cherry) Zones 4 to 8 (9)

Prunus 'Hally Jolivette' Zones 5 to 7

Prunus mume (Japanese apricot) Zones 6 to 9

Prunus serrula (paperbark cherry) Zones 5 to 6

Stewartia spp. (silky camellia) Zones 5 to 8

Evergreen shrubs

Ardisia japonica (Japanese ardisia) Zones 6 to 9

Aucuba japonica (Japanese acuba) Zones 7 to 10

★*Berberis darwinii* (Darwin barberry) Zones 8 to 9

Buxus microphylla (Korean or little-leaf boxwood) Zones 4 to 8

Buxus sempervirens (boxwood) Zones 6 to 8

Calluna vulgaris (Scots heather) Zones 4 to 6 (7)

Camellia japonica (Japanese camellia) Zones 7 to 9

Camellia sasanqua (sasanqua camellia) Zones 7 to 9

Danaea racemosa (poet's laurel) Zones 6 to 9

Erica carnea (winter heath) Zones 5 to 7

★*Euonymus fortunei* (winter creeper) Zones (4) 5 to 9

Fatsia japonica (Japanese fatsia) Zones 8 to 10

Ilex cassine (dahoon) Zones 7 to 9

Ilex glabra (inkberry holly) Zones 4 to 9

Ilex vomitoria (yaupon) Zones 7 to 10

Illicium floridanum (star anise) Zones 8 to 10

Mahonia ×*media* 'Winter Sun' (winter sun mahonia) Zones 8 to 9

Mahonia repens (creeping mahonia) Zones 4 to 7

Michelia spp. (banana shrub) Zones 8 to 9

★*Nandina domestica* (heavenly bamboo) Zones 6 to 9

Osmanthus spp. (osmanthus) Zones 7 to 9

Paxistima canbyi Zones 3 to 7

Pieris japonica (Japanese pieris) Zones 5 to 8

Rhododendron spp. (rhododendron) Zones 5 to 8

Ruscus aculeatus (butcher's broom) Zones 8 to 9

Sarcococca spp. (sweet box) Zones 7 to 9

Serissa foetida (yellow-rim) Zones (6) 7 to 9

Shepherdia argentea (silver buffaloberry) Zones 2 to 6

Skimmia japonica (Japanese skimmia) Zones (6) 7 to 8 (9)

Ternstroemia gymnanthera (Japanese ternstroemia) Zones 7 to 9

Viburnum davidii (David viburnum) Zones 8 to 9

Viburnum rhytidophyllum (leatherleaf viburnum) Zones 5 to 8

Viburnum tinus (laurustinus) Zones (7) 8 to 10

Deciduous shrubs

Corylus avellana 'Contorta' (European filbert) Zones 4 to 8

Euonymus americanus (American euonymus) Zones 5 (6) to 9

Garrya elliptica (silk tassel tree) Zones (7) 8 to 9

Hamamelis mollis and hybrids (Chinese witchhazel) Zones 5 to 8

Itea virginica (Virginia sweetspire) Zones 5 to 9

Kerria japonica (kerria) Zones 4 to 9

Prunus incisa 'Kojo-no-mail' (Kojo cherry) Zones 5 to 7

Stachyurus praecox Zones 6 to 8

Vaccinium corymbosum (highbush blueberry) Zones 3 to 7 (8)

PLANTS WITH COLORFUL STEMS OR BARK

Acer griseum (paperbark maple) Zones 4 to 8

Acer pensylvanicum (striped maple) Zones 3 to 7

Acer tegmentosum (manchustriped maple) Zones 4 to 7

Betula nigra 'Heritage' (river birch) Zones 4 to 9

Betula papyrifera (paperbark birch) Zones 3 to 7

Betula utilis var. *jacquemontii* (Himalayan birch) Zones 5 to 7

Cornus sericea (red-twig dogwood) and others Zones 3 to 8

Hydrangea quercifolia (oak-leaf hydrangea) Zones 5 to 8

Kerria japonica (kerria) Zones 4 to 9

Lagerstroemia spp. (crape myrtle) Zones (6) 7 to 9

Pinus bungeana (lacebark pine) Zones 4 to 8

Rubus cockburnianus (ghost bramble) Zones 6 to 8

Salix spp. (willow) Zones 2 to 8

EVERGREEN PERENNIALS WITH WINTER INTEREST

★*Arum italicum* (Italian arum) Zones (5) 6 to 9

Asarum spp. (wild ginger) Zones 5 to 8

Asarum shuttleworthii 'Callaway' (hardy ginger) Zones 5 to 8

Aspidistra elatior (cast-iron plant) Zones (7) 8 to 10

Carex spp. (sedge) Zones 4 to 10

Cyrtomium fortunei (holly fern) Zones (7) 8 to 9

Disporopsis pernyi Zones 6 to 8

Epimedium spp. (bishop's hat) Zones 4 to 9

Mitchella repens (partridge berry) Zones 4 to 8

Pachysandra procumbens (Allegheny spurge) Zones 5 to 8

Polystichum acrostichoides (Christmas fern) Zones 4 to 9

Polystichum makinoi (Makinoi's holly fern) Zones 4 to 8

Tiarella cordifolia Zones 3 to 8

BERRY-BEARING PLANTS

★*Cotoneaster* spp. (cotoneaster) Zones 4 to 9

Crataegus spp. (hawthorn) Zones 3 to 8

Ilex decidua (possumhaw holly) Zones 5 to 9

Ilex verticillata (winterberry holly) Zones 3 to 8

Pernettya mucronata [also *Gaultheria mucronata*] (pernettya) Zones 7 to 9

Pyracantha spp. (firethorn) Zones (5) 6 to 9

Rohdea japonica (sacred lily) Zones 6 to 9

Sorbus spp. (mountain ash) Zones 3 to 7

Viburnum opulus var. *americanum* (American cranberrybush) Zones 2 to 7

Viburnum prunifolium (blackhaw viburnum) Zones 3 to 9

★*Viburnum setigerum* (tea viburnum) Zones 5 to 7

WINTER-FLOWERING SHRUBS AND TREES

Abeliophyllum distichum (white forsythia) Zones 5 to 8

Camellia japonica (Japanese camellia) Zones 7 to 9

Chaenomeles speciosa (common flowering quince) Zones 4 to 8 (9)

Chimonanthus praecox (fragrant wntersweet) Zones 7 to 9

Corylopsis pauciflora and others (winterhazel) Zones (5) 6 to 8

Corylopsis spicata (winterhazel) Zones (5) 6 to 8

Daphne mezereum (February daphne) Zones 5 to 9

Daphne odora (fragrant daphne) Zones 7 to 9

Edgeworthia chrysantha (paperbush) Zones 7 to 9

Garrya elliptica (silk tassel tree) Zones 8 to 9

Hamamelis mollis and hybrids (witchhazel) Zones 5 to 9

Jasminum nudiflorum (winter jasmine) Zones 6 to 9

★*Lonicera fragrantissima* (winter honeysuckle) Zones 5 to 8

Rhododendron mucronulatum (Korean rhododendron) Zones 4 to 7

Spiraea thunbergii (Thunberg spirea) Zones 4 to 8

Viburnum carlesii (Koreanspice viburnum) Zones 4 to 8

WINTER-FLOWERING BULBS

Anemone blanda (Grecian windflower) Zones 4 to 8

Anemone nemorosa (European windflower) Zones 4 to 7

Bulbocodium vernum (spring meadow saffron) Zones 3 to 8

Chionodoxa luciliae (glory of the snow) Zones 3 to 8

Corydalis solida (fumeroot) Zones 4 to 8

Crocus chrysanthus (crocus) Zones 3 to 8

Crocus thomasinianus (crocus) Zones 3 to 8

Crocus vernus (crocus) Zones 3 to 8

Cyclamen coum (cyclamen) Zones 6 to 8

Eranthis hyemalis (winter aconite) Zones 4 to 7

Erythronium spp. (fawn lily Zones 3 to 8

Fritillaria spp. (fritillaria) Zones 4 to 8

Galanthus spp. (snowdrop) Zones 4 to 8

Ipheion uniflorum (star flower) Zones 5 to 9

Iris reticulata (reticulated iris) Zones 4 to 9

Leucojum vernum (snowflake) Zones 4 to 8

Muscari spp. (grape hyacinth) Zones 4 to 8

Scilla bifolia (squill) Zones 4 to 8

EARLY-BLOOMING PERENNIALS

Brunnera macrophylla Zones 3 to 8

Cardamine quinquefolia Zones 4 to 8

Dicentra eximia (bleeding heart) Zones 3 to 8

Dicentra formosa (bleeding heart) Zones 3 to 8

Dicentra spectabilis (bleeding heart) Zones 3 to 8

Hepatica spp. Zones 3 to 8

Mertensia virginica Zones 4 to 8

Pachyphragma macrophylla Zones 5 to 8

Polemonium reptans (Jacob's ladder) Zones 4 to 8

Pulmonaria saccharata and hybrids Zones 4 to 7

Sanguinaria canadensis (bloodroot) Zones 3 to 8

GARDENS FEATURING HELLEBORES

NORTH AMERICA

Bellevue Botanical Garden
12001 Main Street
Bellevue, WA 98004
Telephone: (425) 452-2750
Website: www.bellevuebotanical.org

Bird Hill
PO Box 76
Free Union, VA 22940
Telephone: (434) 975-2859
Email: nldr@aol.com
Open by appointment

Bishop's Close at Elk Rock
11800 SW Military Lane
Portland, OR 97219
Telephone: 503-452-2562

Brookside Gardens
1800 Glenallan Ave.
Wheaton, MD 20902
Telephone: 301-962-1400

Dunn Garden
PO Box 77126
Seattle, WA 98177
Telephone: (206) 362-0933
Website: www.dunngardens.org
Email: info@dunngardens.org
Open by appointment

Eco-Gardens
PO Box 1227
Decatur, GA 30031
Telephone: (404) 294 6468
Open by appointment

Hellebores Woodland Garden
Elfi Rahr
Bellevue, WA 98008
Telephone: (425) 746-4803
Open by appointment

Gardenview Horticultural Park
16711 Pearl Road
Strongsville, OH 44136
Telephone: (440) 238-6653
Open by appointment

Gossler Farms
1200 Weaver Road
Springfield, OR 97478
Telephone: (541) 746-3922
Website: www.gosslerfarms.com

Heronswood Nursery
7530 NE 288th Street
Kingston, WA 98346-9502
Telephone: (360) 297 4172
Website: www.heronswood.com
Email: heronswood@silverlink.com
Contact for hellebore open days

J. C. Raulston Arboretum
North Carolina Sate University
Department of Horticultural Science
Telephone: (919) 513-7006
Website: www.ncsu.edu/
    jcraulstonarboretum

Montrose
PO Box 957
Hillsborough, NC 27278
Telephone: (919) 732-7787
Open by appointment

Northwest Garden Nursery
86813 Central Road
Eugene, OR 97402
Telephone: (541) 935-3915
Website: www.northwestgardennursery.
    com

Piccadilly Farm
Sam and Carleen Jones
1971 Whippoorwill Road
Bishop, GA 30621
Telephone: (706) 769-6516

Pine Knot Farms Perennials
681 Rockchurch Road
Clarksville, VA 23927
Telephone: (434) 252-1990
Website: www.pineknotfarms.com
Email: pineknot@gloryroad.net

Plant Delights Nursery at Juniper Level
    Botanic Gardens
9241 Saul's Road
Raleigh, NC 27603
Telephone: (919) 772-4794
Website: www.plantdelights.com
Email: office@plantdelights.com

Royal Botanical Gardens
PO Box 399
Hamilton, ON, Canada L8N3H8
Telephone: (905) 527-1158
Website: www.rbg.ca

Scott Arboretum
Swarthmore College
500 College Avenue
Swarthmore, PA 19081
Telephone: (610) 328-8294
Website: www.scottarboretum.org

Sunshine Farm and Gardens
HC 67 Box 539 B
Renick, WV 24966
Telephone: (304) 497-2208
Website: www.sunfarm.com
Email: barry@sunfarm.com

Wave Hill
675 West 252nd Street
Bronx, NY 10471
Telephone (718) 549-3200
Website: www.wavehill.org

United Kingdom

Ashwood Nurseries
Greensforge, Kingswinford
West Midlands, DY6 0AE England
Telephone: 01384 401996
Fax: 01384 401108
Website: www.ashwood-nurseries.co.uk
Email: ashwoodnurs@hotmail.com

Blackthorn Nursery
Kilmeston, Alresford, Hampshire, SO24
    0NL
Telephone: 01962 771796
Fax: 01962 771071

Beth Chatto Gardens
Elmstead Market, Colchester, Essex
England CO7 7DB
Telephone: 01206 822007
Fax: 01206 825933

Crûg Farm Plants
Griffith's Crossing, Caernarfon
Gwynedd, Wales, LL55 1TU
Telephone: 01248 670232
Fax: 01248 670232
Website: www.crug-farm.co.uk
Email: bleddyn&sue@crug-farm.co.uk

Glebe Cottage Plants
Pixie Lane, Warkleigh, Umberleigh,
Devon, England EX37 9DH
Telephone: 01797 253107

Great Dixter
Northiam, Rye, East Sussex
England TN31 6PH
Telephone: 01797 253107
Website: www.greatdixter.co.uk
*Open year-round; closed Sundays November
to March*

Hadlow College
Hadlow, Tonbridge
Kent, England TN11 0AL
Telephone: 01732 853288

Harveys Garden Plants
Mulberry Cottage, Bradfield St. George,
Bury St. Edmunds
Suffolk, England IP30 0AY
Telephone: 01284 386777
Website: www.harveysgardenplants.
co.uk
Email:roger@www.harveysgardenplants.
co.uk
Contact for hellebore open days

The NCCPG (National Council for the
Conservation of Plants and Gardens)
c/o Jeremy Wood
Lower House, Whiteparish
Salisbury, England SP5 2SL

Phedar Research and Experimental
Nursery
Bunkers Hill
Romiley, Stockport
Cheshire, England SK6 3DS
Telephone: 0161 430 3772

Rarer Plants, Ashfield House
Austfield Lane, Monk Fryston
Leeds, England LS25 5EH
Telephone: 01977 682263

Royal Botanic Gardens, Kew
Richmond, Surrey, England TW9 3AB
Telephone: 020 8332 5000
Website: www.rbgkew.org.uk
Email: info@rbgkew.or.uk

Royal Horticultural Society Garden,
Harlow Carr
Crag Lane, Harrogate
North Yorkshire, England HG3 1QB
Telephone: 01423 565418
Website: www.rhs.org.uk/gardens/
harlowcarr
Contact for hellebore open days

Royal Horticultural Society Garden,
Wisley
Woking, Surrey, England GU23 6QB
Telephone: 01483 224234
Website: www.rhs.org.uk/gardens/wisley

Rushfields of Ledbury
Ross Road, Ledbury
Herefordshire, England HR8 2LP
Telephone: 01531 632004
Email: rush01531@aol.com

SOURCES

North America

Although in recent years hellebores have become more widely available in North America, it can still be difficult to track down really good forms. These nurseries can be relied upon to provide good quality plants.

Arrowhead Alpines
PO Box 857
Fowlerville, MI 48836
Telephone: (517) 223-3581
Fax: (517) 223-8750
Website: www.arrowheadalpines.com
Online catalog

Eco-Gardens
PO Box 1227
Decatur, GA 30031
Telephone: (404) 294 6468
Mail order

Gossler Farms
1200 Weaver Road
Springfield, OR 97478
Telephone: (541) 746-3922
Fax: (541) 744-7924
Website: www.gosslerfarms.com
Online catalog and mail order

Graham's Hellebores
   (Gloucestershire, U.K.)
Plants available in United States:
c/o Dixie Hougen
2101 Wittington Boulevard

Alexandria, VA 22308
Telephone: 011 44 1594 860544
Website: www.hellebores.hort.net
Email: gbirkin@hort.net
Online catalog

Heronswood Nursery
7530 NE 288th Street
Kingston, WA 98346-9502
Telephone: (360) 297 4172
Fax: (360) 297 8321
Website: www.heronswood.com
Email: heronswood@silverlink.com
*Contact for hellebore open days; online
   catalog and mail order*

Honeyhill Farms Nursery
5910 SW Hamilton Street
Portland, OR 97222
Telephone: (503) 292-1817
Email: honeyhill2@aol.com
Open by appointment

Northwest Garden Nursery
86813 Central Road
Eugene, OR 97402
Telephone: (541) 935-3915
Website: www.northwestgardennursery.
   com
Contact for hellebore open days

Piccadilly Farm
Sam and Carleen Jones
1971 Whippoorwill Road
Bishop, GA 30621
Telephone: (706) 769-6516
Contact for hellebore open days

Pine Knot Farms Perennials
681 Rockchurch Road
Clarksville, VA 23927
Telephone: (434) 252 1990
Fax: (434) 252 0768
Website: www.pineknotfarms.com
Email: pineknot@gloryroad.net
Online catalog and mail order

Plant Delights Nursery
9241 Saul's Road
Raleigh, NC 27603
Telephone: (919) 772 4794
Fax: (919) 662 0370
Website: www.plantdelights.com
Email: office@plantdelights.com
Online catalog and mail order

Russell Graham, Purveyor of Plants
4030 Eagle Crest Road NW
Salem, OR 97304
Telephone: (503) 362-1135
Email: grahams@open.org
Mail order

Sunshine Farm and Gardens
HC 67 Box 539 B
Renick, WV 24966
Telephone: (304) 497-2208
Fax: (304) 497-2698
Website: www.sunfarm.com
Email: barry@sunfarm.com
Limited mail order

Wayside Gardens
1 Garden Lane
Hodges, SC 29695
Website: www.waysidegardens.com
Email: info@waysidecs.com
Online catalog and mail order

United Kingdom

Good hellebores are much sought after around the country, and these nurseries specialize in the best hellebore species and varieties. Please check that they still have the plants you require before traveling and do not try to visit outside normal opening hours. Not all nurseries operate a mail-order service, and a few will export to other European countries, although there may be special charges. Few export to North America.

Ashwood Nurseries
Greensforge, Kingswinford
West Midlands, DY6 0AE England
Telephone: 01384 401996
Fax: 01384 401108
Website: www.ashwood-nurseries.co.uk
Email: ashwoodnurs@hotmail.com
Catalog

Blackthorn Nursery
Kilmeston, Alresford
Hampshire, England SO24 0NL
Telephone: 01962 771796
Fax: 01962 771071
No mail order

Beth Chatto Gardens
Elmstead Market, Colchester
Essex, England CO7 7DB
Telephone: 01206 822007
Fax: 01206 825933
Mail order

Crûg Farm Plants
Griffith's Crossing, Near Caernarfon
Gwynedd, Wales LL55 1TU
Telephone: 01248 670232
Fax: 01248 670232
Website: www.crug-farm.demon.co.uk
Email: bleddyn&sue@crug-farm.
   demon.co.uk
No mail order

Farmyard Nurseries
Llandysul, Dyfed, Wales SA44 4RL
Telephone: 01559 363389
Fax: 01559 362200
Website: www.farmyardnurseries.co.uk
Email: richard@farmyardnurseries.
   co.uk
Mail order

Fibrex Nurseries
Honeybourne Road, Pebworth,
   Stratford-on-Avon
Warwickshire, England CV37 8XT
Telephone: 01789 720788
Fax: 01789 721162
Website: www.fibrex.co.uk
Mail order

Glebe Cottage Plants
Pixie Lane, Warkleigh, Umberleigh
Devon, England EX37 9DH
Telephone: 01769 540554
Fax: 01769 540544
No mail order

Graham's Hellebores
Gloucestershire, U.K.
Plants available in the United States:
c/o Dixie Hougen
2101 Wittington Boulevard
Alexandria, VA 22308
Telephone: 011 44 1594 860544
Website: www.hellebores.hort.net
Email: gbirkin@hort.net

Harveys Garden Plants
Mulberry Cottage, Bradfield St. George,
   Bury St. Edmunds
Suffolk, England IP30 0AY
Telephone: 01284 386777
Fax: 01284 386777
Website: www.harveysgardenplants.
   co.uk
Email: roger@www.
   harveysgardenplants.co.uk
No mail order

Tim Murphy—Hellebore & Cyclamen
   Specialist
5 School Road, Broughton
Cambridgeshire, England PE28 3AT
Telephone: (0044) (0) 1487 822900.
Email: cilicium@aol.com
No mail order

Phedar Research and Experimental
   Nursery
Bunkers Hill
Romiley, Stockport
Cheshire, England SK6 3DS
Telephone: 0161 430 3772
Fax: 0161 430 3772
Mail order

Rarer Plants
Ashfield House
Austfield Lane, Monk Fryston
Leeds, England LS25 5EH
Telephone: 01977 682263
No mail order

Rushfields of Ledbury
Ross Road, Ledbury
Herefordshire, England HR8 2LP
Telephone: 01531 632004
Fax: 01531 6334544
Email: rush01531@aol.com
No mail order

EUROPE

Hans Kramer
De Hessenhof
Hessenweg 41
6718 TC Ede
Netherlands
Telephone: 0318-617334
Fax: 0318-612773
Email: Hessenhof@planet.nl
Catalog and hellebore open days

Gisela Schmiemann
Belvederestrasse 45 A
Cologne Mungersdorf
Germany D-50933
Seeds and the book Helen Ballard: The
    Hellebore Queen

Staudengärtnerei Alpine Raritäten
Jürgen Peters
Auf dem Flidd 20
D – 25436 Uetersen
Telephone: 49 (0) 41 22 / 33 12
Fax: 49 (0) 41 22 / 48 639
Email: info@alpine-peters.de
Catalog

Matthias Thomsen
Rheinpromenade 17
D – 70790 Rheinheim
Germany
Email: thomsen.matthias@web.de
Seeds of species and hybrids

Koen Van Poucke
Heistraat 106 – B-9100
Sint-Niklaas
Belgium
Telephone: (32)03/777 76 42
Fax: (32)03/766 16 98
Email: KvanPoucke@skynet.be
Catalog

JAPAN

Hanakibi Yumeori
Kaoru Honjo
266 Misono Shizunzi-cho
Hokkaido, Japan 056-0141
Telephone: 0146 46 2424
Fax: 0146 46 2424
Email: Flower@mx6.et.tiki.ne.jp

Isao Aisaka
1569-1, Maki-ko
Maki-machi
Nishikambara-gun
Niigata, 953-0041, Japan
Telephone: 81-256-72-6742
Fax: 81-256-72-0575
Website: www.kazenoko.org
Email: vent@kazenoko.org *or*
    kazenoko@lily.ocn.ne.jp

Ohgi Nursery
Toshiaki Ohgi
2-26-13 Nakano Kami-cyo Hachioji-shi
Tokyo, Japan 192-0041
Telephone and Fax: 81(0)426-27-2256
Email: info@ohgi-nursery.com

Takayuki Miura
Yumehanabito
9091-20 Motoshimada Shimada
Shizuoka, Japan 427-0057
Telephone: 0547-36-5312
Website: www3.tokai.or.jp/
    yumehanabito
Email: yumehanabito@sf.tokai.or.jp

Uichiro Noda
4-20-12 Imagawa
Suginamiko
Tokyo, Japan
Telephone: 03 - 3399 - 2008
Fax: 03 - 3399 - 1571
Website: www.nodaengei.com
Email: Hana@nodaengei.com

Yokoyama Nursery
Satoru Yokoyama
Naoki Yokoyama
4 1175, Nakakiyoto Kiyose-Shi
Tokyo, Japan
Telephone: 0424 91-6157
Fax: 0424 93- 2530

Australia

Ian Collier
PO Box 802
Civic Square
Australian Capital Territory
Australia 2608
Telephone: (02) 6249 6841
Fax: (02) 6248 5904

Elizabeth Town Hellebores
PO Box 28
Deloraine, 7304
Tasmania, Australia
Website: www.southcom.com.au/
    ~hortus/
Email: hortus@southcom.com.au

Hill View Rare Plants
Sue Wallbank and Marcus Harvey
400 Huon Road
South Hobart
Tasmania 7004, Australia
Telephone: (03) 6224 0770, (03) 6223
    1608
Email: hillview@tasmail.com

Barbara Jennings
11 Margaret Street
Sandy Bay, Hobart
Tasmania 7005, Australia
Telephone: 61 (0)3 6224 1434

Peter Leigh
Post Office Farm Nursery
PO Box 744
Woodend
Victoria 3442, Australia
Website: www.postofficefarmnursery.
    com.au
Email: peter@postofficefarmnursery.
    com.au

Sheringa Nursery
Danny Kaines
Greenhill Road
Carey Gully
South Australia 5144
Telephone: 61 8 8390 3153

Woodbridge Nursery
Daniel Magnus
PO Box 90
Woodbridge
Tasmania 7162, Australia
Telephone and fax: 61 3 62674437
Website: www.woodbridgenursery.com.
    au
Email: woodbridge@southcom.com.au

New Zealand

Hereweka Garden & Nursery
Peter Cooke
10 Hoopers Inlet Road
R D 2, Dunedin, New Zealand
Telephone: 03 4780880
Fax: 03 4780600
Email: drpetercooke@hotmail.com

Joy Plants
Terry and Lindsay Hatch
Jericho Road
RD 2 Pukekohe
New Zealand
Telephone: 64 9 2389129
Fax: 64 9 2389127
Website: www.joyplants.co.nz
Email: cwebb@joyplants.co.nz

Kate and Ken Telford
Clifton Homestead Nursery
R D 2 Clinton
South Otago, New Zealand
Telephone and fax: 0064 0345 7212
Website: www.hellebores.co.nz
Email: ken@hellebores.nz.co *or*
    info@hellebores.co.nz

Appendix A

HELLEBORES IN MEDICINE

All hellebores are toxic. Although they were called "herbs" in ancient literature, they are absolutely not to be used as such in modern society. The Cornell University Poison website tells us that the cardiac glycoside present in *Helleborus* is *helleborin*, a colorless, crystalline, water-insoluble, poisonous solid ($C_{28}H_{36}O_6$) obtained from the rhizome and root. *Hellebrigenin* (the aglycone or nonsugar compound that is produced from the reaction of a glycoside with water) of helleborin is more potent than the glycoside itself. Simply put, if you eat the plant's roots you could die; if you grind them and mix them with water you may die faster.

At least one hellebore was being used medicinally when the ancient Greeks and Romans were superpowers. Caius Plinius Secundus, known as Pliny the Elder, mentions using the black hellebore in his encyclopedic work *Historia Naturalis*. Although we do not know for sure which species of hellebore was called *melampode*, the black hellebore, Pliny tells of a cure for madness performed by Melampus, whom the nominal honors. Melampus, who practiced the unusual dual occupational combination of physician and shepherd, first observed the reaction of his goats after eating the plants. He purportedly cured the daughters of Proteus, the King of Argus, of derangement by dosing them with milk from goats that had eaten the herb. Madness was listed with palsy, dropsy, and what sounds like arthritis as diseases for which the herb was a useful remedy; melampode was also listed as a purgative. Pliny also described the ritual method of digging up the roots of the plant that involved first drawing a circle around the plant with a sword, then praying for permission to collect the roots. If the person who planned to collect the roots saw an eagle flying overhead, it would probably be better to gather hellebore roots another day, since the presence of the eagle forecasted the death of the collector within the year.

More uses were described in *De Materia Medica*, one of the world's first pharmacopoeiae, probably written between the years 64 and 77, by Pedianos Dioskourides, also known as Pedanius Dioscorides from Anazarbus, in the area now called Turkey. Dioscorides lists melampode as being useful for madness and melancholy, as a purge, as a method of aborting a fetus, as an expectorant, and for epilepsy.

Theophrastus Phillippus Aureolus Bombastus von Hohenheim, called Paracelsus, was born in Einsiedeln, Switzerland, in 1493, just after Columbus's voyage to North America. Paracelsus is credited by some as the person who introduced the black hellebore to European pharmacology, prescribing the correct dosage necessary to alleviate certain forms of arteriosclerosis.

In the perhaps more familiar *The Herball*, originally written by John Gerard in 1597, a description is given of a hellebore:

> It floureth about Christmas, if the winter be mild and warm . . . called Christ herbe. This plant hath thick and fat leaves of a deep green colour, the upper part whereof is somewhat bluntly nicked or toothed, having sundry diversions or cuts, in some leaves many, in others fewer, like unto a female Peony. It beareth rose-coloured flowers upon slender stems, growing immediately out of the ground, an handbreadth high, sometimes very white, and ofttimes mixed with a little shew of purple, which being faded, there succeed small husks full of black seeds; the roots are many; with long, black strings coming from one end.

In the 1814 *Culpeper's Complete Herbal*, Nicholas Culpeper describes the plant black hellebore, also called setter-wort, setter-grass, bear's-foot, Christmas-herb, and Christmas flowers. In discussing *H. niger*, he recalls the "sundry fair green leaves rising from the root" and mentions that "all the Winter—about Christmas-time, if the weather be any thing temperate, the flowers appear on foot stalks." He also mentions what is probably *H. foetidus* or *H. occidentalis*, "which grows up and down in the woods very like this, but only that the leaves are smaller and narrower, and perish in the Winter."

Eclecticism, a 19th-century medicinal cult that promoted the uses of herbal medicines, was popular for more than a century in North America. In 1866, a teaching manual by John M. Scudder became the basic text at Eclectic Medical Institute for the next 40 years. In his book *Specific Medicines*, Scudder writes of a tincture of *H. niger* prepared with alcohol that, though an "irritant poison," was used as "a stimulant to the spinal and sympathetic nervous systems." He also mentions, "I have used it with advantage in sterility of the female, and to increase virility in the male."

In 1888, the *American Journal of Pharmacology*, published by the Philadelphia College of Pharmacy, reported that "Helleborin, the glucoside of *Helleborus niger* and *Helleborus viride*, has been used as a substitute for digitalis."

King's American Dispensary in 1898 gives instructions for "Vinum Hellebori Compositum Compound Wine of Hellebore." The "wine" recipe calls for "black hellebore (in coarse powder), logwood chips or raspings, helonias root (in powder)," and sherry. This preparation, used as a "tonic or cathartic," exerted "a direct influence on the female reproductive organs. It has proved serviceable in menstrual derangements, as amenorrhoea, dysmenorrhoea, and some painful uterine affections."

Hellebore powder made from ground roots was also said to be an effective treatment for lice. In a 1899 publication entitled *The Uses of Elliman's Embrocation for Horses, Dogs, Birds, Cattle*, among the liniments and powders is a recipe for a dust to rid caged birds and fowl of lice. Under the warning that this preparation is rather troublesome to make, the directions advise the mixing of "Spirit of Tar" with hellebore powder and flowers of sulphur. The mixture was administered as follows:

"Holding the bird upside down by the feet the powder must be dusted into them two to three times at intervals of as many days."

The *Manual of Organic Materia Medica and Pharmacal Botany*, written in 1917 by Lucius E. Sayer, lists *H. niger* as well as *H. viridis*. It describes *H. niger* and its use as an agent which promotes menstrual discharge, an anthelmintic is a medication capable of causing the evacuation of internal parasites. Sayer says that Helle'borus viri'dis Linné is used as a diuretic, cathartic, and emmenagogue and should not be confounded with veratrum viride (also called green hellebore), a cardiac and nervous sedative.

Finley Ellingwood was a Chicago obstetrician and gynecologist who was associated with the Eclectics. In his 1919 *The American Materia Medica, Therapeutics and Pharmacognosy*, he lists *H. niger* and its preparation:

> Black Hellebore, when locally applied, causes irritation of mucous membranes and of the conjunctiva, inducing redness, swelling and increased secretion. A moderate dose taken internally produces no effect, but a considerable quantity causes loss of appetite, nausea, vomiting, pain and inflammation of the stomach and bowels. Medicinal doses strengthen the heart and increase the force of the pulse; while toxic doses cause paralysis with rapid pulse and sudden arrest of the heart. The effect on the nervous system is partial paralysis with tremors, followed by violent convulsions. The agent in its maximum dosage is a drastic hydragogue cathartic in its fresh active form. It is emetic also and emmenagogue. In overdoses it readily produces hyper-catharsis and hyper-emesis. It is a constituent of proprietary pills, but is not widely used in general medicine. In small doses it acts as a stimulant to the liver and to the secretory glands of the gastro-intestinal tract.

In her 1931 book *A Modern Herbal*, Maud Grieve offers doses of hellebore extract, powdered root, and a decoction. A book entitled *Useful Prescriptions*, compiled by Dr. Cloyce Wilson in 1935, also lists *H. niger* and prescribes it for "Flashes of heat, burning of surfaces, sensitiveness of perineal structures. Weak, rapid irregular heart action, low arterial tension. Jelly-like, mucoid bowel evacuations, dullness and stupor."

World War II brought with it a different outlook, and medicinal uses of herbal preparations began to fall into disrepute. Articles identifying poisonous herbs began to appear in print, listing *H. niger* and other herbal remedies as dangerous. Uses of medicaments created by pharmaceutical companies were thought to be safer and more effective than herbal remedies.

In the 1960s, medical publications began to print articles from researchers working with all forms of natural material. Recent research includes studies done with *H. purpurascens* as a cancer treatment, work done with powders made from *H. foetidus* being used to eat away necrotic tissue, and powders of *H. niger* used to shrink tumors.

The hellebore has been proposed as a potential medicament for the vacant stare and stupefaction associated with senile dementia. Another published study regards a highly purified *Helleborus* species extract that strongly potentiates the T-cell suppressive effect of cyclosporine which may hold promise for treating certain cancers.

In this time of easy access to information via the Internet, we find quite a number of lists from herbalists and botanical websites that offer preparations containing various hellebores as potential cures for any number of conditions. While it would be exceedingly unwise to foster false hope in patients with severe medical conditions, there is perhaps an element of encouragement in recent preparations either based on or made from a plant-based pharmacopoeia. Perhaps the wisdom of the ancients is indeed a sound perspective achieved by attention to environs, and modern herbalists may begin to make use of this philosophy to the benefit of all.

Appendix B

BLACK DEATH OF HELLEBORES

Etiology of "Black Death," a New Disease of *Helleborus* Species in North America

Dr. K. C. Eastwell, Washington State University, Prosser, WA 99350-9687; keastwell@wsu.edu

Dr. L. J. du Toit, Washington State University, Mt. Vernon, WA 98273-4768; dutoit@wsu.edu

Dr. K. S. Pike, Washington State University, Prosser, WA 99350-9687; kpike@wsu.edu

Summary

"Black death" is the common name for a disease that quickly degrades the marketability and appearance of several *Helleborus* spp. (family Ranunculaceae). The black lines and spotting induced by the disease led to the name "black death." This report summarizes the results of several years of research on this disease that has recently emerged and spread rapidly to many countries where hellebores are grown. The rapid necrosis of plant tissue associated with this disease devastates the esthetic beauty of these flowering evergreen plants, and destroys their commercial value in the nursery. Because hellebores are perennial and relatively slow growing plants, diseased plants can represent a considerable loss of investment to the nursery industry.

We have identified and characterized the pathogen associated with "black death" disease; the pathogen is a *Carlavirus* for which we have proposed the name *Helleborus net necrosis virus* (HeNNV). At least one aphid vector of the virus has been identified. *Helleborus* aphid (*Macrosiphum hellebori* Theobald & Walton) has been identified on hellebores in North America and has been demonstrated to serve as a vector of this disfiguring disease. Without proper control measures, *Helleborus* aphid populations may spread the disease rapidly to adjacent plantings, particularly in the dense plantings typically encountered in nursery settings. These data are key elements in developing plans to minimize the economic impact of "black death." As methods for the early detection of the virus and for controlling the *Helleborus* aphid are advanced, a program for controlling spread of "black death" is attainable. Nurseries will be able to contain the virus if it is already present in their facilities, and should be able to exclude the pathogen from other sources.

This report has not previously been published. It was prepared specifically for this book based on research funded by the USDA ARS Northwest Nursery Crops Research Center and the Perennial Plant Association, with in-kind support from various nurseries that produce and/or distribute hellebores.

The authors gratefully acknowledge financial and in-kind support for this project from the USDA ARS Northwest Nursery Crops Research Center, the Perennial Plant Association, various nurseries in the eastern and western U.S.A. and the Agricultural Research Center of Washington State University.

The relationship of *Carlaviruses* to diseases of Hellebores in the U.S.A.

Under horticultural conditions of the Pacific Northwest region of the U.S.A., initial symptoms of the disease called "black death" include dark line patterns on leaves, followed by black spotting of the stems. Black veinal necrosis results in severe leaf distortion, and discoloration of the sepals. These symptoms can develop very quickly, particularly as spring temperatures increase. Young leaves of severely affected plants may become necrotic shortly after emergence.

In spite of a reputation for being susceptible to relatively few diseases, a number of viruses have been reported in *Helleborus* spp.: *Chrysanthemum B carlavirus*, *Helenium S carlavirus*, *Helleborus mosaic carlavirus*, *Broad bean wilt 1 fabavirus*, and *Cucumber mosaic cucumovirus* (Murant & Roberts, 1977; Koenig, 1985; Kleinhempel, 1991; Waterworth, *personal communication*), and additional unidentified carlaviruses have been found in hellebores with "black death" symptoms (Koenig, 1985; Mansour et al., 1998). This has complicated the search for the identity of the etiological agent(s) of "black death." Samples of *H. ×hybridus* that expressed symptoms of "black death" were tested by serological methods (enzyme-linked immunosorbent assays, or ELISAs) for a number of viruses known to infect ornamental plants. The viruses included *Tobacco mosaic virus*, *Tobacco streak virus*, *Arabis mosaic virus*, *Cucumber mosaic virus*, *Tomato spotted wilt virus*, *Chrysanthemum B virus*, and *Broad bean wilt virus*. A small number of samples yielded a positive test result for *Cucumber mosaic virus* (CMV). However, these samples displayed rugosity and mottling that are characteristic of CMV infection of other hosts. In some cases, these symptoms were present in addition to "black death" symptoms. All other test results were negative. In addition to serological assays, group-specific reverse-transcribed polymerase chain reaction (RT-PCR) tests for Potyviruses and Carlaviruses were performed. Samples derived from plants with "black death" yielded a positive reaction in the *Carlavirus* group-specific test.

The DNA produced from "black death" samples during the course of the *Carlavirus* group-specific RT-PCR analysis was characterized. The sequence exhibited similarity to a number of carlavirus sequences. From this sequence, one pair of specific primers was designed and a robust assay based on RT-PCR was developed. Specimens of *Helleborus* spp. were obtained from the states of Washington, Oregon, Pennsylvania, and West Virginia. Over 70 plants with "black death" symptoms have been tested and all symptomatic plants react positively with the diagnostic RT-PCR assay indicating the reliability of this procedure for detecting the causal agent of "black death" disease.

The accumulated data, including that described below, demonstrate that a distinct *Carlavirus* is associated with "black death." We have completed characterization of the entire genome of this virus and demonstrated that it is different from any previously reported virus. We propose the name *Helleborus net necrosis virus* (HeNNV) for the agent associated with "black death" of hellebores.

Comparison of the *Carlavirus* found in the Pacific Northwest with virus(es) associated with diseases of hellebores in the eastern U.S.A., and with the "black death" disease reported in Europe/UK

The putative coat protein region of the HeNNV genome has been cloned and sequenced from diseased plants obtained from three independent nurseries in West Virginia and Washington. A collection of thirty *H. ×hybridus* from one nursery, eight *H. ×hybridus* from a second nursery, and eight *H. niger* from a third nursery exhibited a range in disease severity. The symptoms ranged from mottling with occasional black vein necrosis, to black line patterns on the leaves, to emerging shoots that were necrotic and grew to one-tenth normal size and then died, to normal appearing leaves that developed black necrotic lines parallel to the mid-rib. All plants reacted positively in the diagnostic RT-PCR test. Using the methods described above, the coat protein coding sequence was amplified and sequenced from a total of nine plants representing the range of symptoms from the three independent nurseries. Two distinct strains of the same carlavirus were identified. The putative coat protein contains 311 amino acids. The nucleotide sequences of the two isolates share 84% identity. However, when the predicted translation products were examined, they were 99% identical. Of the seven amino acid substitutions, five were conservative substitutions, and only two amino acid changes resulted in a different amino acid character (K→I and T→A). Strain variation did not correlate with the severity of the symptoms. Based on these observations, it is believed that the range of symptoms observed was the result of the host genetic background. *Helleborus ×hybridus* are predominantly propagated from seed, so each plant represents a different genetic background upon which the disease symptoms are displayed. This is likely a major factor contributing to symptom variation. The influence of environmental conditions on expression of symptoms remains to be investigated.

In the past, some plants affected with "black death" were found to be infected with *Chrysanthemum B virus* (CVB) (Waterworth, *personal communication*). However, sequence comparison of the coat protein of HeNNV revealed a virus that is significantly different from CVB. These viruses share only 41% identity and 60% similarity in the core region of the coat protein. As a point of reference, Carlaviruses are considered distinct species if they have less than 68% homology and are considered strains of the same virus if they have 75–90% homology (Brunt et al., 2000). By these criteria, it is evident that the virus associated with "black death" is not CVB.

Another *Carlavirus*, *Helleborus mosaic virus* (HeMV), has been reported in *H. niger* in Germany (Koenig, 1985; Mansour et al., 1998). However, HeNNV is readily distinguished from HeMV because HeMV infection of *H. niger* is symptomless whereas HeNNV causes veinal necrosis in *H. niger*. Moreover, HeMV is serologically related to CVB but HeNNV did not react with antisera prepared against CVB. Finally, there is no evidence of spread of HeMV in Germany while HeNNV has spread rapidly wherever it has been found. We compared the coat protein sequence of HeNNV with that of HeMV. At the nucleotide level, they share only 30% identity while at the amino acid level, they have 58% identity and 60% similarity. Based on biological and molecular data, HeNNV and HeMV are two distinct viruses.

Other viruses or infectious agents that may be associated with the diverse range of symptoms observed on the infected plants

Attempts to isolate pathogenic fungi or bacteria from "black death" diseased tissue have failed. The so-called fastidious bacteria including phytoplasmas and *Xylella fastidiosa* would not have been detected by standard methods. Therefore, established extraction and PCR procedures were used to test for *X. fastidiosa* and a broad spectrum of phytoplasmas. All of these tests were negative.

Analysis of double-stranded RNA (dsRNA) is a broad-spectrum test for the presence of most RNA-containing viruses. DsRNA was isolated from diseased plants and from healthy *Helleborus* spp. A major band of approximately 8.0 kilobase pairs (kbp) was isolated from diseased samples. This was consistent with infection by a *Carlavirus*. Occasionally, three minor bands of approximately 3.3, 3.0, and 2.4 kbp were observed. These three minor bands correspond to those anticipated from plants infected with CMV.

Diagnostic capabilities to test hellebores for "black death"

We have developed a prototype serological test for HeNNV. We have not been able to isolate this virus from symptomatic hellebore tissue, nor has the virus been transmitted to other plant hosts that are more amenable to laboratory studies (e.g., *Nicotiana* spp. or *Chenopodium* spp.). Therefore, we cloned and sequenced the genome of HeNNV, and identified the coat protein gene. The virus coat protein was synthesized in bacteria by subcloning the gene into a bacterial protein-expression system. Subsequently, polyclonal antibodies were produced in response to this bacterially synthesized protein. Similar strategies have been used successfully to develop serological assays for viruses that are recalcitrant to traditional isolation and purification methods (e.g., Theilmann et al., 2002). The enzyme-linked immunosorbent assay (ELISA) is commonly used for the detection of plant viruses and would be an appropriate technology for screening symptomatic and asymptomatic nursery stock to eliminate plants that are potentially contagious, regardless of whether they are expressing "black death" symptoms. Successful development of the prototype ELISA has verified that this concept is valid for detection of HeNNV. The serological test has detected the virus from all sources examined to date, and the test has been used at the request of several nurseries to screen new plants and existing plants in their breeding programs.

The availability of a serological test has also aided determining the distribution of virus within infected plants. The calyx and anthers have been demonstrated to be rich sources of the virus. This information enabled us to demonstrate, for the first time, mechanical transmission of HeNNV using extracts of sepals as inoculum, whereas leaf and stem extracts have not been used successfully as a source of virus for mechanical transmission.

The time of initial infection relative to the age of the plant plays a key role in symptomatology and disease detection. Since hellebores are evergreen perennials, the virus does not move efficiently into older foliage. Consequently, symptoms do not develop in the previously established foliage until much later in the disease cycle. The virus and attendant symptoms are evident in older foliage only after extended incubation periods. In order to detect the virus reliably, only the youngest leaves should be sampled for virus testing.

The role of aphids in the transmission of "black death"

Little is known about the aphid populations that colonize hellebores. Indeed, one of the attractive features of hellebores in the landscape is the relative freedom from insect and disease pests. However, during the course of our research, a population of *Helleborus* aphid (*Macrosiphum hellebori* Theobald & Walton) was found. Reference specimens have been submitted to the Museum of Natural History, Smithsonian Institutions (USNM). Since this is the first known occurrence of this insect in North America, no information is available on its biological properties within the North American context. However, the *Helleborus* aphid has been reported in New Zealand, the United Kingdom, and in Germany (Lowe, 1976; Badmin, 1994; Tomiuk & Woehrmann, 1984, respectively).

The vast majority of aphids collected from hellebores in the U.S.A. is the *Helleborus* aphid. These aphids appear to flourish on hellebores, and thus constitute potential vectors for the movement of Carlaviruses and the spread of "black death" disease. The association between a virus and its insect vector is often very specific; not all aphid species are able to transmit all viruses. Aphid transmission studies were carried out to investigate the role of aphids in transmission of HeNNV and development of "black death." In preliminary trials, hellebores aphid-transmission of HeNNV to larkspur (*Consolida ajacis*; family Ranunculaceae) was successful, but not to hellebores. However, prolonged exposure of the *Helleborus* aphid to diseased and virus-free plants for one month resulted in transmission of HeNNV to the healthy plant. The plants were then grown in a shade house until virus symptoms developed. As new shoots developed, they were assayed by ELISA for the presence of HeNNV. A prolonged assessment period of 3 to 18 months was necessary because of the long latent period reported (Rice & Strangman, 1993).

We have also identified and established colonies on hellebores of the crescent-marked lily aphid, *Aulacorthum circumflexum* (Buckton), and the violet aphid, *Myzus ornatus* (Laing). However, as of this writing, we have not successfully transmitted HeNNV with either of the latter two aphid species.

The discovery that the bracts and sepals of hellebores are sources of high virus titers, and the apparent affinity of aphids for this same tissue suggests that these structures associated with flowers produced annually from midwinter to early spring may be important in the aphid-mediated transmission of HeNNV.

Preliminary tests demonstrated that the *Helleborus* aphid has a very narrow range of host plants on which it will feed or colonize. A colony could not be sustained on wild mustard, potato, or columbine.

Disease management

Most Carlaviruses have a restricted natural host range and are transmitted by aphids non-persistently. As a consequence, the viruses can be transmitted by investigative probing by the aphid into mesophyll cells; feeding in the phloem is not required. A strategy to minimize aphid movement and transmission of viruses is a key element of an integrated disease control program.

The use of neonicotinyl insecticides is promising for the control of "black death" because, in other agroecosystems, these chemicals have exhibited anti-feeding behavior with respect to aphids. Inhibition of feeding and probing activity of aphids would effectively prevent the transmission of carlaviruses. The anti-feedant activity of such chemicals applied to hellebores needs to be investigated. Tests in greenhouse studies have indicated that the systemic insecticide imidacloprid (Merit) is effective in controlling aphids on infested hellebores. Merit is registered for use on landscape and nursery plants in some states and this option appears to be available for nursery production of hellebores. Field tests must be completed to confirm the utility of this chemical in controlling the *Helleborus* aphid in the nursery setting.

Pymetrozine (Fulfill) is an insecticide that is highly selective against plant-sucking insects, including aphids. This anti-feeding substance penetrates green leaves and is transported systemically within the plant. It has been demonstrated that a single application of pymetrozine can prevent transmission of the aphid-transmitted virus *Cauliflower mosaic virus* from infected turnip plants (Bedford et al., 1998). Buprofezin (Applaud) is a chitin synthesis inhibitor that selectively prevents maturation of many insects, including aphids. Both of these substances are bee-friendly and have reduced impact on beneficial insects that could aid in the sustained management of aphid populations. Thus, they could be significant components of the sustainable production of virus-free nursery plants. Research is needed to evaluate these products in hellebores production programs.

Since both HeNNV and the predominant aphid vector have narrow host ranges, there is little risk of influx of this disease from outside sources if appropriate management recommendations are implemented. Thus, control of aphid populations combined with readily available testing methods should put the control of "black death" within practical reach.

Although very little information can be found in the scientific literature regarding "black death," our experience with this disease, and an article in the popular press suggests that "black death" does not appear during the initial year of infection (Rice & Strangman, 1993). This period of latency provides an opportunity for the inadvertent distribution of infected plants before acute symptoms appear. In order to stop spread of this disease throughout the ornamental nursery industry, the ability to detect the causal agent of "black death" *before* symptoms appear is crucial. The availability of a robust RT-PCR assay, an ELISA system, and a sampling strategy that can detect both isolates of the *Carlavirus* may facilitate development of a certification program for the hellebore nursery industry.

Literature cited

Badmin J. 1994. Hoverfly predators of the hellebore aphid *Macrosiphum hellebori*. *Entomologist's Monthly Magazine* 1130:1564-1567.

Bedford I. D., Kelly A., Banks G. K., Fuog D., Markham P. G. 1998. The effect of pymetrozine, a feeding inhibitor of *Homoptera*, in preventing transmission of cauliflower mosaic caulimovirus by the aphid species *Myzuz persicae* (Sulzer). *Annals of Applied Biology* 132:453-462.

Brunt A. A,, Foster G. D., Morozov S.Y., Zavriev S. K. 2000. Genus *Carlavirus*. Pages 969–975 in: *Virus Taxonomy: Classification and Nomenclature of Viruses. 7th Report of the International Committee on Taxonomy of Viruses.* van Regenmortel MHV. (eds). Academic Press, San Diego.

Kleinhempel H. 1991. [The causal agent of the *Helleborus* ringspot disease.] *Archiv Fur Phytopathologie Und Pflanzenschutz*, Berlin 27:415.

Koenig R. 1985. Recently discovered virus or viruslike diseases of ornamentals and their epidemiological significance. *Acta Horticulturae* 164:21-31.

Lowe A. D. 1976. Occurrence of the aphid *Macrosiphum hellebori* in New Zealand. *New Zealand Journal of Zoology* 3:113-114.

Mansour A., Al-Musa A.,Vetten H. J., Lesemann D. E. 1998. Properties of a cowpea mild mottle virus (CPMMV) isolate from eggplant in Jordan and evidence for biological serological differences between CPMMV isolates from leguminous and solanaceous hosts. *Journal of Phytopathology*, Berlin 146:539-547.

Murant A., Roberts I. M. 1977. An isolate of broad bean wilt virus serotype II from *Helleborus vesicarius*. Page 83. In: *23rd Annual Report for the Scottish Horticulture Research Institute for 1976.*

Rice G., Strangman E. 1993. Pests and diseases. Page 17. In: *The Gardener's Guide to Growing Hellebores.* Timber Press, OR. 160 pp.

Theilmann J., Mozafari J., Reade R.,Wu Z., Xie W., Jesperson G., Bernardy M., Eastwell K. C., Rochon D. 2002. Partial nucleotide sequence and genome organization of a Canadian isolate of Little cherry virus and development of an enzyme-linked immunosorbent assay-based diagnostic test. *Phytopathology* 92:87-98.

Tomiuk J.,Woehrmann K. 1984. Enzyme polymorphism and taxonomy of aphid species. *Zeitschrift fuer Zoologische Systematik und Evolutionsforschung* 21:266-274.

Recently contributed scientific presentations and abstracts

Eastwell K. C., du Toit L. J., Druffel K., Pike K. S.,Walsh D.B. 2004. Etiology of 'black death' of *Helleborus* spp. Western Turf & Ornamental Disease Conference, 14 January 2004, Portland OR.

Eastwell K. C., Druffel K. L., du Toit L. J. 2004. Etiology of 'black death' of *Helleborus* spp. Abstract P40-13, 23rd Annual Meeting of the American Society for Virology, 10–14 July 2004, Montreal, Canada.

Appendix C

NUTRIENT STUDY

Nutrient and pH Management Programs for Nursery Production of *Helleborus* ×*hybridus*

Helen T. Kraus and Stuart L. Warren

NC State University, Dept. of Horticultural Science, Raleigh, NC 27695-7609

Nature of work

The use of herbaceous perennials in landscape plantings has increased tremendously over the last few years. As such the production of herbaceous perennial plants by nurseries has also increased including sales of perennials that fit specialty gardening niches such as butterfly and shade gardening. The genus *Helleborus* includes many exciting species and selections that offer winter to early spring flowers for southeastern United States shade gardens (Rice and Strangman, 1993). In the landscape, *Helleborus* ×*hybridus*, the lenten rose is quite easy to cultivate having few disease and insect problems and tolerating a wide range of soil. Such is not the case with nursery production of hellebores. In a container hellebores suffer from phytophthora, botrytis, nutrient deficiencies, and slow growth rates. Growers complain of apparently healthy one year old seedlings suddenly dying and those that do survive taking 3–5 years to flower so that they can be sold by flower color.

Developing a nursery production program for any plant must begin with addressing the basics of fertility; furthermore, when a plant is not performing well in an existing program, fertility and pH need to be reassessed and modified for the production of this plant. A review of the literature turned up a confusing picture of recommendations for nutrient solution applications for the production of herbaceous perennials ranging from 100 to 200 mg/liter N applied with every irrigation to between 100 and 150 mg/liter N applied once weekly (Armitage, 1993; Nau, 1996). Dubois et al. (2000) found that 150 mg/liter N applied three times a week

Reprinted with permission from Helen T. Kraus and Stuart L. Warren, Nutrient and pH Management Programs for Nursery Production of *Helleborus* ×*hybridus*. In *Southern Nursery Association Research Conference Proceedings*, vol. 42, 2002, or online at www.sna.org/research/02proceedings/section0102.html.

maximized growth of *Anemone ×hybrida*. No actual nursery production information for the lenten rose could be found.

Development of a fertility program that addresses both the nutritional and pH requirements of helleborus would be a good first step in resolving some of the production issues associated with the lenten rose. Therefore, an experiment was designed to evaluate N rates in combination with lime additions for their effects on root and shoot dry weight and root to shoot ratio of *Helleborus ×hybridus*.

The experiment was a 5×5 factorial in a split plot block design with N rates (10, 20, 40, 80, and 160 mg/liter) as the main plot and lime rate (0, 3, 6, 9, and 12 lbs. of dolomitic lime incorporated per cubic yard) as the subplot with four replications. One year old seedlings were potted into 4 quart containers with a pine bark substrate that was amended with the different lime rates. Nitrogen rates were applied every other day using pressure compensated spray stakes (Acu-Stick, Wade Mfg. Co., Fresno, CA) at a rate of 200 ml/min (0.3 in/min.). As the N rate was increased in the nutrient solution from 10 mg/liter N through 160 mg/liter N, the P and K rates were also be increased to maintain a 4:1:2 N:P:K ratio. Ammonium nitrate, potassium phosphate, and potassium sulfate supplied the N, P, and K and a modified Hoagland s solution supplied the micronutrients in the nutrient solutions. Since our irrigation water contained adequate Ca and Mg, no additional Ca or Mg were applied other than that available from the lime additions.

At project termination, shoot and root dry weights were determined and used for growth comparisons and calculations of root: shoot ratios (root dry weight ÷ shoot dry weight). Data were tested for differences using analysis of variance and regression analyses (SAS Inst., Inc., 1985) and were considered significant at $P < 0.05$.

Results and discussion

There was a significant interaction between N rate and lime rate for shoot dry weight while the N rate by lime rate interaction was nonsignificant for root dry weight and the root to shoot ratio (data not shown). Within each lime rate helleborus shoot dry weight increased linearly with increasing N rate. Lime rate alone affected root dry weight with the largest increase in root grow occurring between the 0 lime treatment (3.4 g) and the 3 lb/yd^3 (5.1 g). The 3, 6, 9, and 12 lb lime per cubic yard treatments averaged 5.0 g root dry weight. Root to shoot ratio was affected by the N rate only (data not shown). Low N rates (10 and 20 mg/liter N) resulted in greater root to shoot ratios (1.6 and 1.3, respectively). As N rate increased, the root to shoot ratio decreased (0.6 and 0.3 for 80 and 160 mg/liter N, respectively) as the plants directed energy to shoot growth with little increase in root growth.

Significance to industry

Helleborus is best grown with at least 3 lbs of dolomitic limestone amended per cubic yard of pine bark substrate and high rates of nutrition. Higher rates of lime appeared to neither increase nor reduce growth. Nitrogen rates of 160 mg/liter N with P and K balanced in a 4:1:2 N:P:K ratio applied with each irrigation resulted in greatest shoot growth; while N rate had no effect on root growth.

Literature cited

Armitage, A. M. 1993. *Specialty Cut Flowers*. Varsity Press/Timber Press, Portland, Oregon.

Dubois, J.-J. B., S. L. Warren, and F. A. Blazich. 2000. Nitrogen nutrition of containerized *Anemone ×hybrida*. *J. Environ. Hort.* 18(3): 145–148.

Nau, J. 1996. Ball perennial manual: Propagation and production. Ball Publishing, Batavia, Illinois.

Rice, G. and E. Strangman. 1993. *The Gardener's Guide to Growing Hellebores*. David & Charles/Timber Press, Portland, Oregon.

SAS Inst., Inc. 1985. SAS User's Guide: Statistics. Version 5 ed. SAS Inst., Inc., Cary, North Carolina.

HELLEBORES AS CUT FLOWERS

Hellebore Stems as Specialty Cut Flowers

F. L. Fanelli and J. M. Dole, Department of Horticultural Science, North Carolina State University, Raleigh, NC 27695-7609

Hellebores are a great late winter flowering perennial that signals spring is just around the corner. Individual flowers may be brought inside and floated in a bowl as cut stems are thought to not last as cut flowers. The other drawback of hellebores is that the numerous stamens drop after a few days causing an unacceptable mess to the floral industry. Two studies were conducted to determine if hellebores are a viable specialty cut flower and to determine the best means of treating the stems for optimum consumer vase life. The first study tested the application of commercial pretreatment (hydrator) and holding preservative solutions from two manufacturers. The second study compared the vase life of stems at different stages of maturity.

Materials and methods

Stems of *Helleborus* ×*hybridus* were harvested from a seedling bed in late March. The flower stems were cut as long as possible generally producing branched stems, and placed directly into tap water. The stems to be tested using the commercial products were sorted according to flower maturity and number of flowers/stems, recut to 13 inches and placed in the following treatments:

> Hydrator only
> Holding preservative only
> Hydrator followed by holding preservative
> Deionized water (control)

Stems were pretested with Chrysal Professional RAB or Floralife 100 hydrating solutions for the number of hours recommended by the manufacturer, 4 hours for Chrysal and 2 hours for Floralife. Stems were held in Chrysal Professional 2 or Floralife Professional holding preservative until the end of vase life. Solutions

---

Reprinted with permission from *The Cut Flower Quarterly*, vol. 17(1), pages 68, 70.

were mixed according to the manufacturer's guidelines. The stems were placed in individual jars at 68+4° F under approximately 200 ftc light for 12 hrs/day.

The flowers for the second study were divided into two groups: flowers with stamens and flowers in which the stamens had naturally dropped. Individual stems with one flower were recut to 12 inches and placed in Floralife Professional holding solution. No pretreatment was utilized. The stems were placed in the same environment as the first study.

Stems were monitored daily to determine the end of the consumer vase life which was designated as the day the typical consumer would dispose of the stem. The hellebore stems were terminated when the petal edges began browning or the stems lost turgidity.

Results

In the first study stems treated with the commercial holding preservative solutions without pretreatment (hydrator) solutions had an average consumer vase life of 17.5 days. The stems pretreated with the hydration solutions and held in the preservative solutions averaged 16.7 days. Both the stems pretreated with the hydration solutions and held in water and the controls (no pretreatment) had a consumer vase life of 10.5 days. There were no differences between the products from Chrysal compared to Floralife.

In the second study flower maturity had no effect as both stages had a consumer vase life of 10.5 days.

Conclusions

Helleborus ×hybridus harvested directly into buckets of water then held in commercial preservative had an average consumer vase life of 17.5 days. Flowers with stamens and flowers in which stamens had naturally dropped had equal vase life. Flowers in both studies continued to mature and form seed pods, which were also attractive.

Stems from the first study lasted 7 more days than those in the second study. This may be due to the fact that the stems in the first study had more than one flower while those in the second study had only one flower. The presence of additional flowers on branching stems may have caused the longer vase life.

Acknowledgments

We would like to thank the American Floral Endowment for providing the funding for this postharvest research. Dick and Judith Knott Tyler, of Pine Knot Farms, pineknot@gloryroad.net, provided the plant material generously allowing us to harvest from their seedling beds. Beth Harden, research technician, participated as a valuable partner in the harvesting and the postharvest efforts.

BIBLIOGRAPHY

Abercrombie, John, and Thomas Mawe. 1767. *Every Man His Own Gardener*. 18th ed. London: William Tegg, 1805.

Ahlburg, Marlene. 1993. *Hellebores: Christmas Rose, Lenten Rose*. London: B.T. Batsford, Ltd.

Armitage, Allan M., and Judy M. Laushman. 2003. *Specialty Cut Flowers: The Production of Annuals, Perennials, Bulbs, and Woody Plants for Fresh and Dried Cut Flowers*. 2nd ed. Portland, Oregon: Timber Press.

Bailey, Liberty H. 1891. *Cyclopedia of American Horticulture*. 5th ed. New York: Macmillan, 1906.

Berkeley, Edmund, and Dorothy S., eds. 1992. *The Correspondence of John Bartram*. Gainesville, Florida: University Press of Florida.

Betts, Edwin Morris, ed. 1944. *Thomas Jefferson's Garden Book: Collection of journals from 1766–1824*. Philadelphia: The American Philosophical Society.

Blanchan, Neltje. 1909. *The American Flower Garden*. New York: Doubleday Page & Company.

Bush-Brown, Louise and James. 1939. *America's Garden Book*. Revised ed. New York: Macmillan, 1996.

Clark, Harold. 1906. Bulbs and Perennials for November Planting. *The Garden Magazine* IV, no. 4.

Coats, Alice M. 1956. *Flowers and Their Histories*. New York: Pitman Publishing.

Culpeper, Nicholas. 1814. *Culpeper's Complete Herbal*. Richard Evans: London.

Cumming, R. W., and R. E. Lee. 1960. *Contemporary Perennials*. New York: Macmillan.

de Fossard, Ronald A. Notes on Tissue Culture. http://blogontheweb.com/tissue_culture/archive/2004/06/20/12059.aspx. Accessed May 2005.

de Tournefort, Joseph. 1717. *Relation d'un Voyage du Levant*. Paris: ImprimerieRoyale.

Donnelly, D. J., and W. E. Vidaver, 1988. *Glossary of Plant Tissue Culture*. Portland, Oregon: Timber Press.

Editor. 1912. This Month's Cover. *The Garden Magazine* XIV, no. 6: 282.

Ellingwood, Finley. 1919. *American Materia Medica, Therapeutics and Pharmacology*. Reprint. Sandy, Oregon: Eclectic Medical Publications, 1994

Ellwanger, George H. 1889. *The Garden's Story*. New York: Appleton.

Felter, Harvey Wickes, and John Uri Lloyd. 1898. *King's American Dispensatory*. 18th ed. Reprint. Sandy, Oregon: Eclectic Medical Publications, 1983.

Genders, Roy. 1983. *The Cottage Garden and the Old-Fashioned Flowers*. London: Pelham Books.

Gerard, John. 1633. *The Herball, or Generall Historie of Plantes*. Reprint. Revised and enlarged by Thomas Johnson, based on the original 1597 edition. Mineola, New York: Dover Publications, 1975.

Grieve, Mrs. M. 1931. *A Modern Herbal*. Reprint. New York: Dover, 1971.

Griswold, Mac, and Eleanor Weller. 1991. *The Golden Age of American Gardens: Proud Owners, Private Estates, 1890–1949*. New York: Harry Abrams.

Henderson, Peter. 1881. *Handbook of Plants and General Horticulture*. New York: Peter Henderson and Co.

Hill, Susan, and Susan Narizny. 2004. *The Plant Locator, Western Region*. Portland, Oregon: Timber Press.

Hudak, Joseph. 1976. *Gardening with Perennials Month by Month*. 2nd ed. Revised and expanded. Portland, Oregon: Timber Press, 2004.

Hunt, William Lanier. 1982. *Southern Gardens, Southern Gardening*. Durham, North Carolina: Duke University Press.

Keeler, Harriet. 1910. *Our Garden Flowers: A popular study of their native lands, their life histories, and their structural affiliations*. New York: Charles Scribner's Sons.

Kyte, Lydiane. 1998. Plant Tissue Culture Presentation. http://www.accessexcellence.org/LC/ST/st2bgplant.html. Accessed May 2005.

Kyte, Lydiane, and John Kleyn. 1996. *Plants from Test Tubes: An Introduction to Micropropagation*. 3rd ed. Portland, Oregon: Timber Press.

Lawrence, Elizabeth. 1942. *A Southern Garden*. Reprint. Chapel Hill, North Carolina: University of North Carolina Press, 1984.

———. 1961. *Gardens in Winter*. Reprint. Baton Rouge, Louisiana: Claitors Publishing Division, 1973.

Linnaeus, Carolus. 1753. *Species Plantarum*. Stockholm: Laurentii Salvii.

Loudon, Jane. 1843. *Gardening for Ladies: A Companion to the Flower Garden*. London: John Murray.

Loudon, John C. 1838. *An Encyclopedia of Gardening*. London: Longman, Rees, Orme, Brown, Green, and Longman.

Luedy, Arthur E. and Mildred V. 1948. *The Christmas Rose*. Bedford, Ohio: Self Published.

Manning, J. Woodward. 1931. *The Plant Buyers Index*. Reading, Massachusetts: J. W. & E. G. Manning.

Mathew, Brian. 1989. *Hellebores*. Woking, Surrey, England: The Alpine Garden Society.

———. 1994. The spotted hellebore: *Helleborus orientalis* subsp. *guttatus*. *The New Plantsman* 1: 181–183.

McLewin, Will, and Brian Mathew. 1995. Hellebores: the first of a series of articles discussing the genus *Helleborus. The New Plantsman* 2: 112–122.

———. 1995. Hellebores. *Hardy Plant* 17, no. 2: 14–22.

———. 1995. In Brief: *Helleborus croaticus. Hardy Plant* 17, no. 1: 54–55.

———. 1996. *H. atrorubens*; the problem of speciation in acaulescent hellebores. *Hardy Plant* 18, no. 2: 47–54

———. 1996. Hellebores: 2. *Helleborus dumetorum. The New Plantsman* 3: 50-60.

———. 1996. Hellebores: 3. *Helleborus atrorubens. The New Plantsman* 3: 170–177.

———. 1997. Growth Idiosyncracies of Hellebores. *Hardy Plant* 19, no. 2: 57–59.

———. 1997. Hellebores: 4. *Helleborus multifidus* subsp. *hercegovinus. The New Plantsman* 4: 44–50.

———. 1997. Hellebores: 5. *Helleborus purpurascens. The New Plantsman* 4: 175–178.

———. 1998. Hellebores: 6. *Helleborus orientalis* and *Helleborus* ×*hybridus. The New Plantsman* 5: 117–124.

———. 1999. Hellebores: 7. *Helleborus vesicarius* and *Helleborus thibetanus. The New Plantsman* 6: 139–146.

———. 1999. *Fundamental Taxonomic Problems in and Arising from the Genus Helleborus*. S. Andrews, A. C. Leslie, and C. Alexander, eds. Taxonomy of Cultivated Plants Third International Symposium: Royal Botanic Gardens, Kew.

———. 2000. Hellebores: 8. *Helleborus argutifolius, Helleborus lividus* and *Helleborus* ×*sternii. The New Plantsman* 7: 95–102.

———. 2002. *Helleborus viridis. The Plantsman* 1: 150–153.

———. 2002. *Hellebore Notes*. Stockport, Cheshire: Phedar Research and Experimental Nursery. 1–44.

McLewin, Will, Brian Mathew, and Matthias Thomsen. n.d. *Helleborus bocconei* and the Hellebores of Italy. Unpublished manuscript.

M'Mahon, Bernard. 1806. *The American Gardener's Calendar*. Philadelphia: B. Graves.

Nicholson, George, ed. 1889. *The Illustrated Dictionary of Gardening: A Practical and Scientific Encyclopaedia of Horticulture for Gardentes and Botanists*. New York: The American Agriculturists.

Olmsted, Frederick Law, Frederick Coville, and Harlan Kelsey. 1924. *Standardized Plant Names*. Salem, Massachusetts: American Joint Committee on Horticultural Nomenclature.

Parsons, Samuel. 1891. *Landscape Gardening*. New York: G. P. Putnam's Sons.

Rand, Edward S. 1876. *Popular Flowers and How to Cultivate Them*. New York: Hurd and Houghton.

Renfroe, Michael H. Cloning Plants by Tissue Culture. Department of Biology, James Madison University, Harrisonburg, Virginina. http://www.jmu.edu/biology/biofac/facfro/cloning/cloning.html. Accessed May 2005.

Rice, Graham. 2002. *Hellebores*. (RHS Wisley Handbooks). London: Cassell Illustrated.

Rice, Graham, and Elizabeth Strangman. 1993. *The Gardener's Guide to Growing Hellebores*. Portland, Oregon: Timber Press.

Robinson, William. 1913. *The English Flower Garden*. London: John Murray.

Royal Horticultural Society. 2004. *Plant Finder: 2004–2005*. London: The Royal Horticultural Society.

Salminen, Outi. 2001. *Helleborus niger*—Christmas Rose. Cornell University Toxic Plant pages. www.ansci.cornell.edu/plants/christmasrose/. Accessed May 2005.

Schiffner, Viktor. 1890. *Monographia Hellebororum* in *Nova Acta der Kaiserlich Leopoldinisch-Carolinische, Deutsche Akademie der Naturforscher* 56, 1:1–199.

Schmiemann, Gisela, and Josh Westrich, eds. 1997. *Helen Ballard: The Hellebore Queen*. Cologne, Germany: Edition Art and Nature.

Schuler, Stanley. 1972. *The Winter Garden*. New York. Macmillan.

Scudder, John Milton. 1870. *Specific Medication and Specific Medicines*. Cincinnati, Ohio: Wilstach, Baldwin & Co., Printers.

Sedgwick, Mabel Cabot. 1907. *The Garden Month by Month*. New York: Garden City.

Steele, Fletcher. 1925. *Design in the Little Garden*. Boston: Atlantic Monthly Press.

Swem, E. G. 1957. *Brothers of the Spade: Correspondence of Peter Collinson, of London, and of John Custis, of Williamsburg, Virginia, 1734–1746*. Barre, Massachusetts: Barre Gazette.

Taylor, Albert Davis, and Gordon B. Cooper. 1921. *The Complete Garden*. New York: Garden City.

Taylor, Norman. 1957. *Taylor's Garden Guide*. 5th ed. Princeton, New Jersey: D. Van Nostrand Co. Inc.

Thomas, Rolla. 1906. *The Eclectic Practice of Medicine*. Cincinnati, Ohio: The Scudder Brothers Co.

University of Liverpool. Plant Tissue Culture Case Study 3. Demonstration of tissue culture for teaching. http://www.liv.ac.uk/~sd21/tisscult/case_study_3.htm. Accessed May 2005.

van Trier, Harrie and Hanneke van Dijk. 2005. *Helleborus: Winterroos*. An Theunynck, Stichting Kunstboek, Belgium.

Walker, Rick. Tissue culture in the home kitchen: It's not as hard as you might think! http://www.omnisterra.com/botany/cp/slides/tc/tc.htm. Accessed May 2005.

White, Katharine S., and E. B. 1979. *Onward and Upward in the Garden*. Reprint. Boston: Beacon Press, 2002.

Wilder, Louise Beebe. 1916. *My Garden*. New York: Doubleday.

———. 1937. *The Garden in Color*. New York: Macmillan.

Wilson, Cloyce. 1935. *Useful Prescriptions*. Cincinnatti, Ohio: Lloyd Brothers.

Wilson, Helen Van Pelt. 1945. *Perennials Preferred*. New York: M. Barrow Company.

———. 1978. *Color for Your Winter Yard and Garden*. New York: Schribner.

Wister, John. 1930. *Bulbs for American Gardens*. Boston: Stratford.

———. 1938. *Four Seasons in Your Garden*. Philadelphia: J. B. Lippincott.

———. 1947. *The Woman's Home Companion*. New York: Collier and Son.

Wright, Richardson. 1924. *The Practical Book of Outdoor Flowers*. Philadelphia: J. B. Lippincott.

INDEX

Page numbers in italic indicate illustrations.

Helleborus macranthus. See *H. niger* subsp. *macranthus*

Helleborus mosaic carlavirus (HeMV), 269, 270

Helleborus multifidus, 59, 80–87, 118, 133
  subsp. *bocconei,* 59, 78, *82,* 82–83, 84, *84,* 115, 119
  dividing, 199
  subsp. *hercegovinus,* 56, 61, 82, *85,* 85, 154, 155, 238
  subsp. *istriacus,* 82, 85, *86*
  subsp. *multifidus, 81,* 83, *83,* 110, 118, 119

Helleborus nemoralis. See *H. foetidus*

Helleborus net necrosis virus (HeNNV), 268, 270

Helleborus niger, 17, 21, 22, *26,* 26, 27, 30, 32, 38, 40, 41, 43, *44,* 45, 46, 48, 49, 50, 52, 53, 54, 56, *58,* 87–91, *88, 89,* 97, 116, 118, 121, 128, 129, 131, 133, 161
  var. *altifolius,* 47, 48
  Ashwood Form, 90
  black spot, *178,* 180
  'Blackthorn', 90, 215
  'Brockhurst', 30
  Crûg Hybrid, 90
  dividing, 199–200
  'Double Fantasy', 90
  'Harvington Hybrids', 90
  'Louis Cobbett', 90, 215
  subsp. *macranthus,* 87, 90, 91–92
  subsp. *macranthus* (Freyn) 'Schiffner', 92
  'Madame Fourcade', 90
  'Marion', 90
  'Maximus', 90
  'Nell Lewis', 36, 89, 90
  subsp. *niger,* 91
  'Potter's Wheel', 31, *32,* 91, 131, 141
  'Praecox', 47, 91
  propagating, 134–135
  'Saint Brigid', 91

seed characteristics, 188, 190, 193
'Sunrise', 91
'Sunset', 91
var. *typicus.* See *H. niger* subsp. *niger*
'White Magic', 90, 91, 159
in the wild, 119
'Wilder', 89

Helleborus ×*nigercors,* 30, 121–124, *122, 123*
  'Alabaster', 31, 123
  'Blackthorn', 123
  dividing, 200
  in the garden, 238
  'Green Corsican', 123
  'Honeyhill Joy', 123, *124,* 124
  'Micha White Beauty', 123
  propagating, 134–135
  seed characteristics, 188
  'Silver Moon', 123
  'Valentine Green', 123
  'Vulcan Beauty', 123
  Wall, 121
  'White Beauty', 123

Helleborus ×*nigristern,* 129

Helleborus occidentalis, 26, 27, 39, 41, 43, 45, 53, 92–95, *93, 94,* 118
  'Reuter', 94

Helleborus odorus, 43, 56, *57,* 70, 72, 92, *95,* 95–97, *96,* 118
  var. *istriacus.* See *H. multifidus* subsp. *istriacus*
  subsp. *multifidus.* See *H. multifidus* subsp. *multifidus*

Helleborus officinalis. See *H. orientalis* subsp. *orientalis*

Helleborus olympicus. See *H. orientalis* subsp. *orientalis*

Helleborus orientalis, 17, 22, 27, 28–29, 31, 32, 43, 47, 48, 53, 54, 56, 72, 97–101, 118, 137–138, 146
  subsp. *abchasicus,* 28, 29, 40, 46, 64, 100, 118

Montrose, 242–243
Moore, Sir Frederick, 29
Moore, Thomas, 30
Murphy, Tim, 60, 116
Muscari, 87
    botryoides, 72
Myddleton House, 76

National Botanic Gardens, 29
Natural Selection Nursery, 76
The New Plantsman, 35, 62, 87, 138
New York Botanical Garden, 43
New Zealand Gardens Online, 159
Nichols, Beverley, 226
Nicolay, Kevin, 220–221
Nihon Kurisumasu Roozu Kyookai, 158
Northwest Garden Nursery, 77, 153–
    154, 198, 222–223, 237–239
Nottle, Trevor, 37
Nunn, Liz and Hugh, 90
nursery listings, American, from 1800 to
    1950, 42
nutrient balance, optimal, 275–276

O'Byrne, Ernie and Marietta, 147, 153–
    154, 198, *237*, 237–239
Oehme, Van Sweden & Associates, 54
Ogisui, Mikinori, 35
The Ohio State University, 46
Old Country, 31, 55, 142, 145
Onward and Upward in the Garden
    (White), 52
orientalis hybrids. See *Helleborus*
    ×hybridus
Ornamental Plan Conservation
    Association of Australia, 158
Osler, Mirabel, 160
Otto Fröbel and Company, 28
Our Garden Flowers (Keeler), 45

Paeonia
    caucasica, 100
    mascula subsp. *aretiana*, 100
    rockii, 60

Pagles, Ernst, 149
Paracelsus, 264
parent, seed and pollen, 121
Pearce, Jill, 225
Perennial Plant Association, 54, 269
Perennials Preferred (Wilson), 53, 249,
    250
pH requirements of hellebores, 275–
    276
Phedar Research and Experimental
    Nursery, 21, 33, 55, 56, 60, 77,
    144, 153
Phytophthora, 182, 184
Piccadilly Farm, 56, 151–152
Pike, Dr. K. S., 268
Pine Knot Farms, 36, 77, 79, 90, 127,
    133, 152–153, 279
The Plant Buyer's Index (Manning), 48
Plant Delights Nursery, 40, 77, 156, 158
Plant Finder (RHS), 47
The Plant Locator (Hill and Narizny), 47
The Plantsman, 113, 116. See also *The
    New Plantsman*
Plantsman Nursery, 31, 156
pollen parent, 121
pollination, 19, 209–214, 222–223
Pomona Nursery, 50
Post Office Farm Nursery, 158
Potentilla, 110
Practical Floriculture (Henderson), 41
Prestwould, 38
Price, Charles, 55, 152, 220–221
Primula vulgaris, 84, 92, 96
    subsp. *sibthorpii*, 100
Prince Nursery, 39
Prunus, 110
Puget Garden Resources, 157
Pulmonaria saccharata, 66, 92, 96
Purdy, Carl, 150
pymetrozine (Fulfill), 273
Pythium, 182, 184

Quercus, 104